Praise For Sports Memorabilia For Dummies

"As a sports fan and a sports journalist, I'm grateful for Pete Williams's sustained work to expose a sports-related, greed-driven industry that, in large part, is designed to make suckers of fans."
> — Phil Mushnick, sports columnist, *New York Post/ TV Guide*

"The perfect 'All-in-one' resource for the novice collector. Pete brings a unique passion and knowledge to sports collecting."
> — Kit Young, veteran San Diego Sports Memorabilia Guru

"Tremendous skinny on exposing con artists and frauds. The 'Ten Commandments' inspired me to dig out my old bobbin' head doll collection."
> — Scott E. Ferrall, *CBS Radio NY*

"Before you spend another dollar on sports memorabilia, read this book! If you want smart, solid advice on how to buy sports collectibles and how to avoid getting ripped off, *Sports Memorabilia For Dummies* is for you."
> — Jeffrey Pollack, founder, *The Sports Business Daily*

"Pete Williams provides a long-awaited user's guide to this hobby-turned-business, helping collectors young and old navigate through the pastime's pitfalls and predators. Whether you collect anything, from cards to autographs to uniforms, from baseball or other sports, this breezy book teaches you how to collect, how to invest, and most importantly, how to enjoy yourself."
> — Alan Schwarz, columnist, *Baseball America*

"If only this book had been written 20 years ago, I would never have thrown-out my baseball card collection when I went off to college. Pete Williams provides a concise, realistic, thorough, and thoroughly entertaining guidebook for sports collectors. The only thing missing is a Sharpie pen for autographs — and after reading this book I want Williams's. His autograph, not his Sharpie."
> — Larry Stone, baseball writer, *The Seattle Times*

"Pete Williams's clean writing and common-sense suggestions make me want to buy a lock of his hair."
> — Steve Marantz, senior writer, *The Sporting News*

"Pete Williams has been providing invaluable insights on sports memorabilia for years. From the casual sports fan to the professional collector, *Sports Memorabilia For Dummies* is the ultimate guide to the fascinating world of sports collectibles."
— Ron Barr, National Sports Talk Show Host

"My favorite kind of book, informative and entertaining. A great read for a collectible dummy like me."
— Tim Kurkjian, *ESPN magazine*

"Think you know all about sports memorabilia? Hah! Read this eye-opening book, then ask yourself the same question. Pete Williams reminds us and captures what saving collectibles was all about and, sadly, where it's headed. No matter where you stand, this is the book that clears the air."
— Pedro Gomez, *The Arizona Republic*

"The world of sports memorabilia is as confusing as it is exciting. Pete Williams, a bright and rising light on the sportswriting scene, breaks down sports memorabilia as it actually is, not as it often appears to be. I found the chapter on unusual and oddball sports collectibles particularly enlightening."
— Pat Caputo, Oakland (Mich.) Press/WDFN Radio

"*Sports Memorabilia For Dummies* makes the world of tattered cards and faded autographs come into focus. It is a must-read for the collector, whether the motive is fun or profit."
— Dave Johnson, *WTOP Radio, Washington D.C*

"As not only a baseball writer but also an avid collector, I feel I know the business pretty well. But Pete Williams has given me an even better insight into it all and will save me a few dollars along the way. In fact, I think more than a few dollars."
— I.J. Rosenberg, national baseball writer for the *Atlanta Journal-Constitution* and radio talk show host

"Any fan will enjoy *Sports Memorabilia For Dummies,* even people who bought sets of baseball cards because they liked the stale gum. This book takes you on a tour of the greatest sports moments and the quirkiest trivia. In the end, you should know how to hold onto sports memories will all your heart — but only a modest portion of your bank account."
— Gwen Knapp, *San Francisco Examiner* columnist

References for the Rest of Us!™

BESTSELLING BOOK SERIES FROM IDG

Do you find that traditional reference books are overloaded with technical details and advice you'll never use? Do you postpone important life decisions because you just don't want to deal with them? Then our *...For Dummies*® business and general reference book series is for you.

...For Dummies business and general reference books are written for those frustrated and hard-working souls who know they aren't dumb, but find that the myriad of personal and business issues and the accompanying horror stories make them feel helpless. *...For Dummies* books use a lighthearted approach, a down-to-earth style, and even cartoons and humorous icons to diffuse fears and build confidence. Lighthearted but not lightweight, these books are perfect survival guides to solve your everyday personal and business problems.

> *"More than a publishing phenomenon, 'Dummies' is a sign of the times."*
>
> — The New York Times

> *"A world of detailed and authoritative information is packed into them..."*
>
> — U.S. News and World Report

> *"...you won't go wrong buying them."*
>
> — Walter Mossberg, Wall Street Journal, on IDG Books' ...For Dummies books

Already, millions of satisfied readers agree. They have made *...For Dummies* the #1 introductory level computer book series and a best-selling business book series. They have written asking for more. So, if you're looking for the best and easiest way to learn about business and other general reference topics, look to *...For Dummies* to give you a helping hand.

8/98i

SPORTS MEMORABILIA FOR DUMMIES®

SPORTS MEMORABILIA FOR DUMMIES®

by Pete Williams

Foreword by Gary Carter

IDG Books Worldwide, Inc.
An International Data Group Company

Foster City, CA ♦ Chicago, IL ♦ Indianapolis, IN ♦ New York, NY

Sports Memorabilia For Dummies®

Published by

IDG Books Worldwide, Inc.

An International Data Group Company

919 E. Hillsdale Blvd.

Suite 400

Foster City, CA 94404

www.idgbooks.com (IDG Books Worldwide Web site)

www.dummies.com (Dummies Press Web site)

Library of Congress Catalog Card No.: 98-87105

ISBN: 0-7645-5115-9

Printed in the United States of America

10 9 8 7 6 5 4 3 2 1

1O/RQ/QZ/ZY/IN

Distributed in the United States by IDG Books Worldwide, Inc.

Distributed by Macmillan Canada for Canada; by Transworld Publishers Limited in the United Kingdom; by IDG Norge Books for Norway; by IDG Sweden Books for Sweden; by Woodslane Pty. Ltd. for Australia; by Woodslane (NZ) Ltd. for New Zealand; by Addison Wesley Longman Singapore Pte Ltd. for Singapore, Malaysia, Thailand, Indonesia and Korea; by Norma Comunicaciones S.A. for Colombia; by Intersoft for South Africa; by International Thomson Publishing for Germany, Austria and Switzerland; by Toppan Company Ltd. for Japan; by Distribuidora Cuspide for Argentina; by Livraria Cultura for Brazil; by Ediciencia S.A. for Ecuador; by Ediciones ZETA S.C.R. Ltda. for Peru; by WS Computer Publishing Corporation, Inc., for the Philippines; by Unalis Corporation for Taiwan; by Contemporanea de Ediciones for Venezuela; by Computer Book & Magazine Store for Puerto Rico; by Express Computer Distributors for the Caribbean and West Indies. Authorized Sales Agent: Anthony Rudkin Associates for the Middle East and North Africa.

For general information on IDG Books Worldwide's books in the U.S., please call our Consumer Customer Service department at 800-762-2974. For reseller information, including discounts and premium sales, please call our Reseller Customer Service department at 800-434-3422.

For information on where to purchase IDG Books Worldwide's books outside the U.S., please contact our International Sales department at 650-655-3200 or fax 650-655-3297.

For information on foreign language translations, please contact our Foreign & Subsidiary Rights department at 650-655-3021 or fax 650-655-3281.

For sales inquiries and special prices for bulk quantities, please contact our Sales department at 650-655-3200 or write to the address above.

For information on using IDG Books Worldwide's books in the classroom or for ordering examination copies, please contact our Educational Sales department at 800-434-2086 or fax 317-596-5499.

For press review copies, author interviews, or other publicity information, please contact our Public Relations department at 650-655-3000 or fax 650-655-3299.

For authorization to photocopy items for corporate, personal, or educational use, please contact Copyright Clearance Center, 222 Rosewood Drive, Danvers, MA 01923, or fax 978-750-4470.

 is a trademark under exclusive license to IDG Books Worldwide, Inc., from International Data Group, Inc.

About the Author

Pete Williams is a writer and columnist for *USA Today's Baseball Weekly,* a major league baseball analyst for the Fox News Channel, and a contributing columnist for *Street & Smith's Sports Business Journal.* One of the media's top experts on the sports memorabilia field, Williams authored a "Collectibles Beat" column in *Baseball Weekly* from 1992 to 1994 that led to the publication of his first book, *Card Sharks: How Upper Deck Turned a Child's Hobby Into a High-Stakes, Billion-Dollar Business* (Macmillan, 1995). The book, which chronicled the explosive growth of the sports collectibles business and a card reprinting operation at the largest trading card manufacturer, was a finalist for the CASEY Award, given to the top baseball book of the year. From 1993 to 1995, he authored *Sports Card Trader Magazine's* annual list of the "Twenty-Five Most Powerful People in the Sports Card Industry."

Williams's articles have appeared in numerous publications, including *The Washington Post, USA Today, The Philadelphia Daily News,* and *The Charlotte Observer.* He has appeared as a baseball and sports memorabilia commentator on CNN, CNBC, MSNBC and The Bloomberg News and is a frequent guest on national radio programs, including ESPN Radio, CBS Sportsline, The Sportsfan Radio Network, and Westwood One's Ferrall on the Bench show. A native of Alexandria, Virginia, and a graduate of the University of Virginia, Williams and his wife, Suzy, live in St. Petersburg, Florida, where he can be heard regularly on WZTM Sports Radio 820 AM.

ABOUT IDG BOOKS WORLDWIDE

Welcome to the world of IDG Books Worldwide.

IDG Books Worldwide, Inc., is a subsidiary of International Data Group, the world's largest publisher of computer-related information and the leading global provider of information services on information technology. IDG was founded more than 25 years ago and now employs more than 8,500 people worldwide. IDG publishes more than 275 computer publications in over 75 countries (see listing below). More than 90 million people read one or more IDG publications each month.

Launched in 1990, IDG Books Worldwide is today the #1 publisher of best-selling computer books in the United States. We are proud to have received eight awards from the Computer Press Association in recognition of editorial excellence and three from *Computer Currents'* First Annual Readers' Choice Awards. Our best-selling ...For Dummies® series has more than 50 million copies in print with translations in 38 languages. IDG Books Worldwide, through a joint venture with IDG's Hi-Tech Beijing, became the first U.S. publisher to publish a computer book in the People's Republic of China. In record time, IDG Books Worldwide has become the first choice for millions of readers around the world who want to learn how to better manage their businesses.

Our mission is simple: Every one of our books is designed to bring extra value and skill-building instructions to the reader. Our books are written by experts who understand and care about our readers. The knowledge base of our editorial staff comes from years of experience in publishing, education, and journalism — experience we use to produce books for the '90s. In short, we care about books, so we attract the best people. We devote special attention to details such as audience, interior design, use of icons, and illustrations. And because we use an efficient process of authoring, editing, and desktop publishing our books electronically, we can spend more time ensuring superior content and spend less time on the technicalities of making books.

You can count on our commitment to deliver high-quality books at competitive prices on topics you want to read about. At IDG Books Worldwide, we continue in the IDG tradition of delivering quality for more than 25 years. You'll find no better book on a subject than one from IDG Books Worldwide.

IDG BOOKS WORLDWIDE

John Kilcullen
CEO
IDG Books Worldwide, Inc.

Steven Berkowitz
President and Publisher
IDG Books Worldwide, Inc.

*Eighth Annual
Computer Press
Awards ≥ 1992*

*Ninth Annual
Computer Press
Awards ≥ 1993*

*Tenth Annual
Computer Press
Awards ≥ 1994*

*Eleventh Annual
Computer Press
Awards ≥ 1995*

IDG Books Worldwide, Inc., is a subsidiary of International Data Group, the world's largest publisher of computer-related information and the leading global provider of information services on information technology. International Data Group publishes over 275 computer publications in over 75 countries. More than 90 million people read one or more International Data Group publications each month. International Data Group's publications include: **ARGENTINA:** Buyer's Guide, Computerworld Argentina, PC World Argentina; **AUSTRALIA:** Australian Macworld, Australian PC World, Australian Reseller News, Computerworld, IT Casebook, Network World, Publish, Webmaster; **AUSTRIA:** Computerwelt Osterreich, Networks Austria, PC Tip Austria; **BANGLADESH:** PC World Bangladesh; **BELARUS:** PC World Belarus; **BELGIUM:** Data News; **BRAZIL:** Annuário de Informática, Computerworld, Connections, Macworld, PC Player, PC World, Publish, Reseller News, Supergamepower; **BULGARIA:** Computerworld Bulgaria, Network World Bulgaria, PC & MacWorld Bulgaria; **CANADA:** CIO Canada, Client/Server World, ComputerWorld Canada, InfoWorld Canada, NetworkWorld Canada, WebWorld; **CHILE:** Computerworld Chile, PC World Chile; **COLOMBIA:** Computerworld Colombia, PC World Colombia; **COSTA RICA:** PC World Centro America; **THE CZECH AND SLOVAK REPUBLICS:** Computerworld Czechoslovakia, Macworld Czech Republic, PC World Czechoslovakia; **DENMARK:** Communications World Danmark, Computerworld Danmark, Macworld Danmark, PC World Danmark, Techworld Denmark; **DOMINICAN REPUBLIC:** PC World Republica Dominicana; **ECUADOR:** PC World Ecuador; **EGYPT:** Computerworld Middle East, PC World Middle East; **EL SALVADOR:** PC World Centro America; **FINLAND:** MikroPC, Tietoverkko, Tietoviikko; **FRANCE:** Distributique, Hebdo, Info PC, Le Monde Informatique, Macworld, Reseaux & Telecoms, WebMaster France; **GERMANY:** Computer Partner, Computerwoche, Computerwoche Extra, Computerwoche FOCUS, Global Online, Macwelt, PC Welt; **GREECE:** Amiga Computing, GamePro Greece, Multimedia World; **GUATEMALA:** PC World Centro America; **HONDURAS:** PC World Centro America; **HONG KONG:** Computerworld Hong Kong, PC World Hong Kong, Publish in Asia; **HUNGARY:** ABCD CD-ROM, Computerworld Szamitastechnika, Internetto online Magazine, PC World Hungary, PC-X Magazin Hungary; **ICELAND:** Tolvuheimur PC World Island; **INDIA:** Information Communications World, Information Systems Computerworld, PC World India, Publish in Asia; **INDONESIA:** InfoKomputer PC World, Komputek Computerworld, Publish in Asia; **IRELAND:** ComputerScope, PC Live!; **ISRAEL:** Macworld Israel, People & Computers/Computerworld; **ITALY:** Computerworld Italia, Macworld Italia, Networking Italia, PC World Italia; **JAPAN:** DTP World, Macworld Japan, Nikkei Personal Computing, OS/2 World Japan, SunWorld Japan, Windows NT World, Windows World Japan; **KENYA:** PC World East African; **KOREA:** Hi-Tech Information, Macworld Korea, PC World Korea; **MACEDONIA:** PC World Macedonia; **MALAYSIA:** Computerworld Malaysia, PC World Malaysia, Publish in Asia; **MALTA:** PC World Malta; **MEXICO:** Computerworld Mexico, PC World Mexico; **MYANMAR:** PC World Myanmar; **NETHERLANDS:** Computer! Totaal, LAN Internetworking Magazine, LAN World Buyers Guide, Macworld Netherlands, Net, WebWereld; **NEW ZEALAND:** Absolute Beginners Guide and Plain & Simple Series, Computer Buyer, Computer Industry Directory, Computerworld New Zealand, MTB, Network World, PC World New Zealand; **NICARAGUA:** PC World Centro America; **NORWAY:** Computerworld Norge, CW Rapport, Datamagasinet, Financial Rapport, Kursguide Norge, Macworld Norge, Multimediaworld Norge, PC World Ekspress Norge, PC World Nettverk, PC World Norge, PC World ProduktGuide Norge; **PAKISTAN:** Computerworld Pakistan; **PANAMA:** PC World Panama; **PEOPLE'S REPUBLIC OF CHINA:** China Computer Users, China Computerworld, China InfoWorld, China Telecom World Weekly, Computer & Communication, Electronic Design China, Electronics Today, Electronics Weekly, Game Software, PC World China, Popular Computer Week, Software Weekly, Software World, Telecom World; **PERU:** Computerworld Peru, PC World Profesional Peru, PC World SoHo Peru; **PHILIPPINES:** Click!, Cerebro/PC World, Computerworld/Correio Informático, Dealer World Portugal, Mac*In/PC*In Portugal, Multimedia World; **PUERTO RICO:** PC World Puerto Rico; **ROMANIA:** Computerworld Romania, PC World Romania, Telecom Romania; **RUSSIA:** Computerworld Russia, Mir PK, Publish, Seti; **SINGAPORE:** Computerworld Singapore, PC World Singapore, Publish in Asia; **SLOVENIA:** Monitor; **SOUTH AFRICA:** Computing SA, Network World SA, Software World SA; **SPAIN:** Communicaciones World España, Computerworld España, Dealer World España, Macworld España, PC World España; **SRI LANKA:** Infolink PC World; **SWEDEN:** CAP&Design, Computer Sweden, Corporate Computing Sweden, Internetworld Sweden, it.branschen, Macworld Sweden, MaxiData Sweden, MikroDatorn, Natverk & Kommunikation, PC World Sweden, PCaktiv, Windows World Sweden; **SWITZERLAND:** Computerworld Schweiz, Macworld Schweiz, PCtip; **TAIWAN:** Computerworld Taiwan, Macworld Taiwan, NEW ViSiON/Publish, PC World Taiwan, Windows World Taiwan; **THAILAND:** Publish in Asia, Thai Computerworld; **TURKEY:** Computerworld Turkiye, Macworld Turkiye, Network World Turkiye, PC World Turkiye; **UKRAINE:** Computerworld Kiev, Multimedia World Ukraine, PC World Ukraine; **UNITED KINGDOM:** Acorn User UK, Amiga Action UK, Amiga Computing UK, Apple Talk UK, Computing, Macworld, Parents and Computers UK, PC Advisor, PC Home, PSX Pro, The WEB; **UNITED STATES:** Cable in the Classroom, CIO Magazine, Computerworld, DOS World, Federal Computer Week, GamePro Magazine, InfoWorld, I-Way, Macworld, Network World, PC Games, PC World, Publish, Video Event, THE WEB Magazine, and WebMaster; online webzines: JavaWorld, NetscapeWorld, and SunWorld Online; **URUGUAY:** InfoWorld Uruguay; **VENEZUELA:** Computerworld Venezuela, PC World Venezuela; and **VIETNAM:** PC World Vietnam.   5/7/98

Dedication

To Suzy, my favorite collector.

Author's Acknowledgments

Collecting information for a book is a lot like collecting sports memorabilia. There's a lot of good stuff out there, but you need some assistance finding it. Fortunately, I have a valuable collection of friends and sources more than willing to help.

Phil Wood, in addition to being the technical editor of this book and a longtime radio colleague, patiently answered my frequent queries about collecting minutiae. Laurie Goldberg of Pinnacle Brands and Marty Appel of Topps, two of the hobby's best public relations people, dug up answers to the most trivial of questions. Thanks also to Rich Klein of Beckett Publications, Bob Ivanjack of Kit Young Cards, Don Harrison of The Tenth Inning, and press pin guru Dan Lovegrove of Recollectics.

Thanks, too, to Michael Heffner for allowing me to use photos from Leland's beautiful auction catalogs. I'm also grateful for my good friend Tom DiPace, one of the best photographers in sports, for tearing up his office and shooting many of the items you see in this book. Tom, I wish all of our collaborations went this smoothly.

Stacy Collins of IDG Books heartily endorsed the idea of a sports memorabilia book from the start. I'd also like to thank the Indianapolis-based editorial team: Bill Helling, Tina Sims, and Kathleen Dobie. In a world of commons, you are all valuable stars.

Publisher's Acknowledgments

We're proud of this book; please register your comments through our IDG Books Worldwide Online Registration Form located at http://my2cents.dummies.com.

Some of the people who helped bring this book to market include the following:

Acquisitions, Development, and Editorial

Project Editor: Bill Helling

Acquisitions Editor: Stacy S. Collins

Copy Editors: Tina Sims, Kathleen Dobie

Technical Editor: Phil Wood

Editorial Manager: Kelly Ewing

Editorial Assistant: Paul E. Kuzmic

Production

Associate Project Coordinator: Tom Missler

Layout and Graphics: Lou Boudreau, Linda M. Boyer, J. Tyler Connor, Angela F. Hunckler, Todd Klemme, Brent Savage, Janet Seib, Deirdre Smith

Proofreaders: Christine Berman, Kelli Botta, Michelle Croninger, Henry Lazarek, Rebecca Senninger

Indexer: Nancy Anderman Guenther

General and Administrative

IDG Books Worldwide, Inc.: John Kilcullen, CEO; Steven Berkowitz, President and Publisher

IDG Books Technology Publishing: Brenda McLaughlin, Senior Vice President and Group Publisher

Dummies Technology Press and Dummies Editorial: Diane Graves Steele, Vice President and Associate Publisher; Mary Bednarek, Director of Acquisitions and Product Development; Kristin A. Cocks, Editorial Director

Dummies Trade Press: Kathleen A. Welton, Vice President and Publisher; Kevin Thornton, Acquisitions Manager

IDG Books Production for Dummies Press: Michael R. Britton, Vice President of Production and Creative Services; Beth Jenkins Roberts, Production Director; Cindy L. Phipps, Manager of Project Coordination, Production Proofreading, and Indexing; Kathie S. Schutte, Supervisor of Page Layout; Shelley Lea, Supervisor of Graphics and Design; Debbie J. Gates, Production Systems Specialist; Robert Springer, Supervisor of Proofreading; Debbie Stailey, Special Projects Coordinator; Tony Augsburger, Supervisor of Reprints and Bluelines

Dummies Packaging and Book Design: Robin Seaman, Creative Director; Jocelyn Kelaita, Product Packaging Coordinator; Kavish + Kavish, Cover Design

◆

The publisher would like to give special thanks to Patrick J. McGovern, without whom this book would not have been possible.

◆

Contents at a Glance

Cartoons at a Glance

By Rich Tennant

The 5th Wave By Rich Tennant

"I can understand collecting autographed bowling balls, and I can understand wanting to own a houseboat. By why, in heavens name, you decided to combine the two, I'll never understand!"

page 9

"I don't care who autographed that thing, you still can't bring it on the bus."

page 173

"What do you mean, everyone on the bus has to sign the speeding ticket?"

page 135

"Sure it's mint. Taste it."

page 237

"It's a more expensive photo of Honus Wagner because it's signed by both Honus aaand Xena who's shaking his hand."

page 213

"I think it's going a bit far to call what the team's Bulldog mascot did to your shoe, an 'autograph'."

page 293

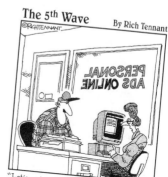

"Let's make sure I have your ad right. It reads, 'Single male, Very Good condition, handled, not abused; slightly rounded corners, some gloss lost from surfaces but no scuffing, seeks same in female companion'."

page 261

Fax: 978-546-7747 • E-mail: the5wave@tiac.net

Table of Contents

Part II: Acquisitions: From Shows to Shops to TV 135

Foreword

As a kid, I always enjoyed collecting baseball cards and dreamed of the day when I would make the Major Leagues and see my own face on a trading card. I was fortunate to have that dream come true. I now have a complete run of baseball cards dating from 1953 through the end of my career in 1993. For me, the sets represent the fun of collecting all those years. Looking at those cards now is like flipping through a photo album. It brings back memories of the guys I played with and against for 19 years.

Of course, you don't have to have played professional sports to enjoy collecting cards, autographs, and memorabilia. As you build your collection, you'll look back on favorite teams, players, and moments in sports. You'll find, as I did growing up, that you'll enjoy sports even more by collecting.

Back when I started collecting, there was not nearly the amount of memorabilia out there that you see today. There was just one card company, Topps, and most collectors focused their efforts on baseball. Today, more than a dozen companies produce cards and memorabilia related to baseball, football, basketball, hockey, golf, and NASCAR. Collecting has changed dramatically, even since I retired from baseball after the 1992 season.

It's also become a big business. The ball that my former New York Mets teammate Mookie Wilson hit through the legs of Bill Buckner in Game Six of the 1986 World Series sold at auction for $93,500! Fortunately, however, most sports memorabilia is more affordable. A lot of people get hung up on the business side of collecting and spend a lot of time worrying about what things are worth. To me, that takes the enjoyment out of it. Just collect what you like and have fun.

If you're just getting into collecting, it might seem a little confusing. But my friend Pete Williams has simplified the process for you. Regardless of what sport you're interested in and whether you want to collect cards, autographs, or memorabilia, he'll show you how. I'm sure you'll find that this book will be the perfect starting point for whatever collection you hope to put together. Good luck and happy collecting!

— Gary Carter, eleven-time National League All-Star and current Montreal Expos broadcaster

Introduction

Welcome to *Sports Memorabilia For Dummies.* Consider this book the first piece of your sports-related collection. Unlike many recently produced sports collectibles, however, it is not part of a limited edition; if sports fans keep buying the book, the publisher will keep printing more copies. And unlike some sports memorabilia, the book will not increase in value — unless you acquire the author's signature, for a nominal fee, of course. However, this book will keep you from wasting money on a lot of worthless junk. More importantly, it will help you enjoy the sports collecting hobby and enhance your sports viewing. All this, plus it comes with a slab of pink bubble gum in the back cover — just kidding.

This book promotes the idea that collecting sports memorabilia is a wonderful way to enhance your enjoyment of sports — if you know what you are doing. But if you believe that collecting sports memorabilia is the key to untold riches, then you are sadly mistaken. You are better off taking your money to Las Vegas than investing it in sports collectibles.

However, you still want to get good value for your sports collectible dollar. You need to know which items have genuine collector worth and which items are the sports equivalent of fool's gold. You may never sell your collection, but if you do, you may not get what you paid for it. So you probably want to know whether you have something of value in case you do ever need to sell.

For all those reasons, this book will come in handy. It won't turn you into a price-quoting, letter-of-authenticity-writing card shark, but it does show you how to enjoy a fabulous hobby without losing a fortune.

Of course, if you don't like *Sports Memorabilia For Dummies,* you always can trade it to a friend for one of those books with a title such as *How to Make Millions with Just a Few Packs of Baseball Cards!* Heck, maybe your buddy will throw in a rookie card of Rafael Belliard. Or maybe an old pink slab of gum.

About This Book

A few years ago, I appeared on a television special that a producer entitled "Sports Collectibles: The Investment of the '90s." During my sound byte, I stressed that sports collectibles were a terrible investment. Undeterred, the producer sunk a sizable chunk of change into sports cards and memorabilia. This event occurred right before the stock market began its record-setting rise that had yet to stop as this book went to press. I've often wondered if that producer still considers sports collectibles "the investment of the '90s."

Amazingly, people still ask me on a regular basis what cards and memorabilia make good investments. They've heard tales of people making huge profits in the sports memorabilia hobby/business (I use these words interchangeably because sports collecting is both) and wonder how they can do the same.

Resisting the urge to suggest professional help, I point out that those lucky people — those few lucky people — either cashed in stashes of collectibles accumulated before the sports collecting boom hit in the late 1970s or they were speculators who rolled the dice in the 1980s on a new-card market that now is all but dead.

My point is this: Unless you find an authentic, game-worn Babe Ruth jersey in your grandmother's attic, or at least some baseball cards from the 1950s in pristine condition, you've missed most of the sports collectibles investment heyday. But don't be depressed. At least you had to read only two pages to find out this information.

If the news that the sports collectibles market has peaked is a revelation to you, don't feel bad. The folks who manufacture, market, and broker sports collectibles have spent a lot of money to maintain the public perception that a huge investment market still exists. Sadly, even the trade press has fueled this thinking, dependent as it is on industry advertising.

This book tries to dispel some of those investment myths surrounding sports collectibles, making it an unusual and valuable resource. It tempers any lingering thoughts you have about making big money in sports collectibles. (If you want to invest in sports, buy stock in the Boston Celtics, Cleveland Indians, or Florida Panthers.) This book does not necessarily show you the money, but it can show you how to enjoy the sports collecting hobby.

If you want to start a collection as a natural extension of your love of sports, then congratulations. You've picked a wonderful time. Now that the investors have abandoned sports collectibles, more merchandise is available for the rest of us. And the prices are coming down to where they belong.

Who knows? Maybe they'll start putting gum back in the packs.

Why You Need This Book

At one time, Topps was the only card manufacturer. Back then, few collectors wanted cards of anyone not in a baseball uniform. No one forged an autograph. No one tried to pass off a phony jersey as genuine. And price guides hadn't been invented. About the only knowledge a collector needed was how much a pack of Topps cards cost and when the five-and-dime was getting its next "series" of cards.

Times have changed. These days, five companies produce baseball cards alone, each with multiple brands and dozens of card lines and subsets. Football, basketball, and hockey cards once were virtually nonexistent, but they now account for half the market. The FBI claims that 70 percent of sports autographs for sale, at least those of major stars, are forgeries. Even the players have trouble telling the difference between uniforms they actually wore and clever fakes. And packs of new cards start in the $2 range.

Where does a new sports collector begin? And how does a novice separate the hype and the scams from the memorabilia with genuine collector interest? This book can give you the answers. I can help guide you through the topic because I have been a collector for 20 years — an eternity in this young hobby — and have investigated and reported on this business for the last 7 years.

When I joined *USA Today Baseball Weekly* in 1991, I began covering the sports collecting business as a beat, examining it objectively. That work made me a something of a pariah among sports collectibles insiders, an old-boy network accustomed to nothing but puff coverage in the press.

But I looked at both sides of the industry: the booming, investment-fueled side and the darker, unethical side fraught with unscrupulous behavior. As I became an expert on this growing business, I realized that I had to let consumers know *everything* behind this so-called "investment of the '90s."

Covering this hobby is a full-time job. Even avid collectors have a tough time keeping up with all the changes and trends. For a novice, staying on top of the latest collecting news can be overwhelming. This book makes that task easier.

How to Use This Book

You don't have to read this book from cover to cover. You can pick your spots. Simply glance through the Table of Contents to find a chapter that interests you. Maybe you're only interested in collecting cards, not autographs and uniforms. Or maybe you've collected for a few years but still don't understand how price guides operate. This book can provide even the most advanced collectors with some new information.

But you can read this book in its entirety if you want. Many elements of sports collecting overlap. Perhaps you want to know whether you should have a valuable baseball card autographed (generally, no). Or maybe you're trying to find out what type of pens to use for autographs on various items (ballpoint pens for balls, Sharpie pens for photos). Novice collectors may want to read the glossary first.

Feel free to mark up your book (ballpoint or Sharpie). It's not going up in value — even with the author's autograph.

How This Book Is Organized

This book is organized so that you can walk through the process of becoming a sports memorabilia collector. Newcomers may need many questions answered as they embark on building a collection. I have organized this book so that you can take that journey one step at a time and can jump to any other section for a quick reference, especially as you focus your collecting goals.

Part I: Getting Started — What to Collect?

The answer to the question of what sports memorabilia to collect seems so simple. Why, you say, I collect what I like, thank you very much. Okay, but hold onto your wallet for just a moment. The mistake many new collectors make is not in choosing what to collect, but what *not* to collect. After a few months of acquiring every trading card, autograph, and sports trinket they can find, their house is full of clutter and they have no idea what they have. Maybe they like the look of a pair of Shaquille O'Neal game-used sneakers atop their entertainment center. Interior decorating taste aside, those boots may seem out of place next to a few boxes of hockey cards, a binder full of random autographs, and a six-pack of Cal Ripken commemorative Coca-Cola bottles. Many newcomers experience sensory overload, thinking "There's no way I can collect it all!" So they throw up their hands and give up. In this section, I help you focus your collecting goals to match your interests and your checkbook. I explain the nuances of sports cards, autographs, game-worn gear, and "oddball" collectibles and describe the difference between manufactured and true collectibles. Collecting sports memorabilia is a never-ending learning process, and you can start right here.

Part II: Acquisitions: From Shows to Shops to TV

Think twice when you hear that familiar television pitch, "We're just giving this stuff away!" Before you whip out your American Express card and start dialing television shopping channels to pay $39.95 for a strip of rubber from one of Jeff Gordon's tires, read this part. I explain the production and distribution of sports memorabilia and why prices vary wildly between sports collectibles shops, retail outlets, and home shopping television. First, however, I perform the impossible: I show you how to find a reliable, trustworthy sports memorabilia dealer — yes, such a person does exist — and tell you how to find rare, priceless collectibles at estate sales and yard sales and in your great-aunt's attic. I guide you through your first sports card show and help you find what you're looking for, without spending much time or money. You can visit a sports card shop and attend a major memorabilia auction, all without leaving these pages. Finally I ask you to turn on your television. (Parents of younger readers, trust me here.) While carefully balancing this book on your lap, you flip to a sports memorabilia shopping program so that I can help you separate the legitimate collectibles (yes, there are a few) from stuff people shouldn't even be giving away.

Part III: Pricing and Selling: Is This Stuff Worth Anything?

In this part, you find out why sports memorabilia is a terrible investment. I show you how the market boomed in the 1980s and how some quick-acting entrepreneurs made a killing. I explain why the sports memorabilia market will never, ever be as profitable again. I illustrate how sports leagues, card manufacturers, and hobby trade publications wrongly promote the investment potential of sports collectibles. I show the factors involved in valuing memorabilia and discuss why many collectors misinterpret price guides. I help you differentiate between "real" collectibles and those that are manufactured with scarcity and marketability in mind. And, for those of you who already have collectibles to sell, I suggest where and how to unload them for the most cash.

Part IV: Frauds, Scams, and Other Dangers

Perhaps you purchased this book because you've already been burned by purchasing one of the many counterfeits, forgeries, and bogus items floating around the hobby. If so, I can help you make sure that you're never cheated again. The rest of you also should listen up, because the sports memorabilia business is a magnet for con artists and the ethically challenged. In this part, I show you how unscrupulous card dealers trim and alter cards to improve their appearance. You discover the reasons that many autographs are either fake, ghostsigned, or the product of autopens and stamps. Most importantly, you find out how some companies carefully — and, unfortunately, legally — get away with marketing autographed replica jerseys as game-worn merchandise. You see why those ads for "$89 worth of out-of-print baseball cards for only $10," while technically true, are nothing but an invitation to throw your money away.

Part V: How to Become Your Own Best Expert

If you want to collect sports memorabilia, you already consider yourself an expert on sports, right? But don't assume that your knowledge also automatically makes you an authority on sports *memorabilia.* The same people who search far and wide through team yearbooks, media guides, or, perhaps, the *Baseball Encyclopedia* to settle a $5 barstool bet will conduct absolutely no research before dropping hundreds or thousands of dollars on a sports item. Here, I show you how to become a tough, educated sports memorabilia customer. You discover how and why to question authenticity. You come to appreciate the value of research and how to remove much of the doubt behind an item. You get an idea about what to believe and what not to believe from the hobby media and how to become a bargain shopper.

Part VI: The Part of Tens

Look in Part VI for the best — and worst — of the sports memorabilia hobby, arranged in nifty little lists. If you care to know how much a lock of Mickey Mantle's hair sold for in an auction, you may find this part interesting. If not, please read it anyway because I spent entirely too much time compiling this trivia for you to blow it off.

Part VII: Appendixes

Sports memorabilia collectors have a language all their own, one that seems to change constantly. If you can't tell the difference between a 1950s gray flannel Tigers road jersey and a Tiger Woods gold foil hologram, you probably want to refer to this part. Appendix A lists all of the terms that you need to add to your vocabulary. Appendix B lists team addresses. In Appendix C, you can find a listing of Hall of Fame members. And Appendix D has contact information for some of the more popular sports collectibles companies and organizations.

Icons Used in This Book

I guide you through this maze of sports memorabilia wit and wisdom with some handy road signs. Look out for these friendly icons; they point you toward valuable advice and hazards to watch out for.

You won't lose your life savings if you fail to read the information next to this icon. But if you skip this information, don't say I didn't warn you.

This icon alerts you about juicy information that makes you a more informed sports collector.

Don't forget to remember these important points. (You may want to at least dog-ear the pages with this icon so that you can look them up in the future.)

This icon identifies terms that you'll run across in the sports memorabilia field. If you use these terms, those hairy, 300-pound, gold-chain-wearing sports memorabilia dealers will cower in your presence.

This icon points out occasions in sports memorabilia collecting where you risk being taken — or at least being sold a worthless memorabilia item. You want to remember these alerts.

Part I

Getting Started — What to Collect?

The 5th Wave — By Rich Tennant

"I can understand collecting autographed bowling balls, and I can understand wanting to own a houseboat. By why, in heavens name, you decided to combine the two, I'll never understand!"

In this part . . .

This part explains the sports memorabilia hobby and how it became a passion for thousands of sports fans and a big business for others. For collectors, even those with no interest in profiting from sports collectibles, the "big business" part is too important to ignore. Although I do not encourage collecting for profit — indeed, I can think of only a few worse areas to invest your money — I recognize that sports memorabilia is as much an industry as a pastime. So I'm keeping your bottom line in mind when I give advice here and throughout the book.

I show you how to collect sports memorabilia. Perhaps more importantly, I show you how not to collect. I discuss the three primary areas of sports collectibles — trading cards, autographs, and uniforms — along with figurines, advertising pieces, and other "oddball" items. I take you on a whirlwind tour of this crazy hobby, from the baseball tobacco cards of the early years to the gold-foil stamped, holographic, die-cut, limited edition versions of today.

Whatever your collecting goals, this part can point you in the right direction. If you want to go hog-wild into the new card market, this part shows you how. If you want to narrow your focus to, say, cards and memorabilia relating to Biff Pocoroba's days with the Atlanta Braves, the first chapter explains what to look for. If you're new to sports memorabilia, the first chapter answers the question that you've been afraid to ask in your neighborhood card shop: "How do I get started in this, anyway?"

Chapter 1

What Is Sports Memorabilia?

*R*emember the last time you returned home from a sporting event? Chances are, you left a huge paper trail. You probably tossed the ticket stub in a desk drawer. You placed a pocket schedule on the refrigerator. You added a game program or team yearbook to a pile in the closet. You hung a team photo, pennant, or Styrofoam knickknack that was a promotional giveaway in the family room. Congratulations, you're already a sports memorabilia collector.

Most of us accumulate things without realizing it, so starting a formal sports memorabilia collection is a small step to take, a logical outgrowth of following sports and attending games. For many, that process never goes any further than the piles of ticket stubs or magazines hoarded until spring cleaning comes around. But some sports fans wish to take their collecting a step further, to assemble a display that pays tribute to a favorite sport, team, or player.

Maybe you're a member of both groups. Perhaps you're a parent whose mother tossed out your collection of 1950s baseball cards that would have given your family financial independence for five generations. Back then, only two companies made baseball cards: Topps and Bowman. Now your kid can choose between dozens of manufacturers and hundreds of card sets and subsets. And you thought that computer stuff was confusing.

This chapter simplifies the collecting process for you. If you haven't followed sports collecting in 20 years, you're probably wondering how this went from a kiddie hobby, where packs of cards sold for a nickel, to a big business, where a pack of cards costs more than a pack of cigarettes. This chapter fills in the gaps.

Why Is There a Boom in Sports Collecting?

Consider the sports landscape of 1976. The average Major League Baseball salary was $52,300. There were only 24 teams. The struggling National Basketball Association was years away from the debuts of Magic Johnson, Larry Bird, and Michael Jordan. The National Hockey League had only a limited audience in the U.S. There was no ESPN, Fox, TNT, CNN/SI, *USA Today, Baseball Weekly,* or sports talk radio.

And a pack of baseball cards made by Topps, the only manufacturer, cost 15 cents. Topps made one set of 660 cards, which generally hit supermarkets and convenience stores in early March.

Now compare the current situation. In 1997, the average baseball salary was $1.3 million. Sports had become a huge business, and so, too, had sports memorabilia. Topps was one of many card manufacturers that together produced 260 sets or subsets of baseball cards alone. A pack of cards cost at least 99 cents, although most cost between $2 and $4. Like everything else in life, you seem to get less for your buck, 10 cards instead of the 15-card packs of 20 years ago.

The baseball card explosion

But why the boom in collecting? During the economic glory days of the early '80s, Baby Boomers had discretionary income to invest. Some of these people noticed that the cards from their '50s childhood had soared in value, at least according to the few mimeographed price guides that existed at the time. In 1980, at an auction near Philadelphia, three 1952 Mickey Mantle cards sold for $3,000 apiece. Suddenly, everyone was searching attics and basements for long-lost collections.

Meanwhile, collectors took an interest in newer cards, swiping up the first *rookie cards* of baseball's youngest stars, figuring they would appreciate in value over time like Mantle's did. The Rickey Henderson card appeared in 1980. Then came Fernando Valenzuela in 1981 and Cal Ripken the following year. Rookies seemed to come in bunches in the succeeding years, with Wade Boggs, Tony Gwynn, and Ryne Sandberg in 1983 and Don Mattingly and Darryl Strawberry in 1984. Collectors looked at each issue of new cards like a public stock offering, buying cards for pennies in the hopes that they would soar in value. Financial magazines began touting the blue-chip potential of baseball cards. In 1988, *Money* magazine published a study by two Marquette University professors that showed that baseball cards, from 1980 to 1987, outperformed stocks, bonds, and Treasury bills.

Before you cash in your stock portfolios and head to your local baseball card shop, remember the familiar fine-print warning that past performance is not indicative of future returns and that people can and do lose money. I explain later in this chapter why making an analogy between baseball cards and the stock market is inaccurate. For now, just remember that in 1984, some collector in Seattle probably said, "Hmmmm. I could invest in this local software company or in Alvin Davis rookie cards. I gotta go with the cards. Alvin is going to lead my Mariners to the World Series and be in the Hall of Fame some day. Who's going to care about this Microsoft 20 years from now?"

The rise of dealers and price guides

During the early '80s, a formal "secondary" market emerged for sports cards. Card "dealers," some of whom had been purchasing collections since the mid-70s, began gathering at card shows to buy, sell, and trade cards. Price guides emerged, most notably *Beckett Baseball Card Monthly,* published by a collector and dealer from Dallas named James Beckett, who held a doctorate in statistics. By 1984, every card — past and present — had a price.

No longer was Topps the only card manufacturer. Since buying out its only competitor, Bowman, in 1956, Topps had a monopoly on the baseball card market. Fleer, which had produced a set of "Baseball Greats" cards, depicting former players, from 1960 to 1962, had filed an antitrust suit against Topps. In 1980, a judge ruled in favor of Fleer, opening the market for Fleer and a third company, Donruss, for 1981. The National Football League, National Basketball Association, and National Hockey League, long dormant in the card industry, capitalized on the growing interest in collectibles, over the next decade issuing licenses to companies such as Score, Upper Deck, Pacific, Pro Set, Action Packed, Wild Card, and SkyBox.

Beyond the card market

While the card market boomed, other collectors looked for memorabilia that had been worn or touched by an athlete. Autograph collecting soared in popularity, to the point where athletes and former athletes could make steady incomes from appearing at card shows to sign autographs. By the mid-'80s, any ball, uniform, or piece of equipment used in a sports event had collectible value. The sports collectibles hobby had become big business.

The meaning of memorabilia

The word *memorabilia* means different things to different collectors. Most use it broadly, as I do in this book, to refer to the entire realm of sports collectibles. But others use it to refer only to the non-card element of collecting or even the non-card, non-autograph segment. You may hear someone refer to "cards, autographs, and memorabilia." All definitions are acceptable.

You may also hear the words *hobby* and *industry* used interchangeably. Sports memorabilia is both, of course, although some collectors prefer to use *hobby*. They use it in snobby, reverential terms, as if they were among the few involved before everyone jumped on the bandwagon and it became a major industry. They say things like "The hobby has been hurt by all the people who got into it just for the money." Yes, you will hear these collectors refer to "the hobby," as if there were no other pastimes besides sports collecting. Sadly, for some of these poor souls, there isn't.

The Collector Mentality

Before the sports collecting boom, what is now considered memorabilia had more practical purposes. Kids gambled their baseball cards by flipping them against walls. They placed them on their bicycle spokes to emulate the sounds of a motorcycle. If they obtained a foul ball from a player at the stadium, they'd probably use it at the sandlot. A broken bat could be taped and used. Few fans thought of displaying these items in a trophy case.

Somewhere, however, things got a little out of whack, although it's hard to pinpoint when. It definitely came some point after those guys paid $3,000 for the Mickey Mantle cards in 1980. Maybe it came in 1989, when Pete Rose appeared on a television program selling autographed balls, bats, and jerseys the night he was banned from the game itself. Maybe it came in 1992, when a promoter advertised a final autograph signing with Hall of Famer Billy Herman, who had terminal cancer and died before some of the flyers were received in the mail. Maybe it's come since Mantle's death from liver cancer in 1995, as some collectors have ordered organ donor cards featuring Mantle's likeness for the sole purpose of reselling them. Or maybe it came in 1996, when a Baltimore businessman paid a $500,000 annuity to the fan who caught the 500th home run ball hit by the Orioles' Eddie Murray.

If you follow sports, you know how significant Hall of Fame status is for an athlete. For collectors, memorabilia relating to Hall of Famers is treasured, particularly that of baseball players who reach their Hall of Fame in Cooperstown, New York. It represents the ultimate career accomplishment and sparks a slew of instant collectibles and an increased interest in existing memorabilia. Anywhere you see the abbreviation HOF, you'll know that it's referring to Hall of Fame.

The sports collector mentality test

The growth of the sports memorabilia business seems to have inspired the collector mentality in everyone, even the athletes themselves. Sporting events routinely are stopped to remove a ball or puck for even the most modest milestones. Baseball players who hit historic home runs face tough negotiations with fans who catch the balls. And when a bat boy returns to the dugout with a broken bat, he's inevitably approached by a dozen fans with outstretched hands.

Think you may have the sports collector mentality? Here's a test:

Have you ever done any of the following?

1. Saved a box of Wheaties, either opened or unopened, featuring an athlete on the cover?
2. Paid more than regular price for a bottle or can of Coca-Cola because it had a sports-related logo?
3. Attended an auto show or store opening because an athlete was on hand signing autographs?
4. Saved your daily newspaper following a significant sports event?
5. Maintained a box of ticket stubs or game programs?
6. Kept a pocket game schedule years after the season ended?
7. Asked a store manager for a sports-related cardboard display?
8. Argued with a family member over the amount of space dedicated to your sports collection?
9. Attended a game only to get a free souvenir?
10. Purchased a collecting-oriented book?

If you answered yes to four or more questions, congratulations. You have the sports collector mentality.

Why Baseball Collectibles Are More Popular Than Other Sports Collectibles

If you're thinking that I'm placing a heavy emphasis thus far on baseball over the other sports, it's because I am. Even though Major League Baseball has lost a lot of its fan base in recent years, particularly among the younger generation, it continues to be the most popular category among sports collectors.

History

Much of the reason for baseball's popularity is historical. Baseball has the longest tradition as a high-profile sports league, with a long line of heroes from Babe Ruth to Joe DiMaggio to Jackie Robinson to Ted Williams to Mickey Mantle to Nolan Ryan to Cal Ripken. It was, until recently, considered "America's pastime." And although more Americans watch football on television and basketball players such as Michael Jordan, Grant Hill, and Shaquille O'Neal are bigger celebrities than any of their baseball counterparts, more fans attend baseball games than any other sport. Although its market share has declined, baseball is woven deeper into the fabric of the country than other sports and, not surprisingly, is the subject of more memorabilia.

Statistics

Statistics also account for baseball's favored status among collectors. Although baseball is a team sport, it's really about individual achievement. Football, basketball, and hockey have few milestones that rival the magical figures of 300 wins, a .300 or .400 batting average, 61 home runs, or 3,000 hits. The numbers provide a context for debate over which player is the best and, inevitably, who does or does not belong in the Hall of Fame. For many years, before *USA Today* and the Internet, baseball cards were a primary source of statistical information for many fans. Over the years, they became collectibles.

Tradition

Another reason for baseball memorabilia's popularity is tradition. Football, basketball, and hockey cards were produced only in modest amounts until the mid-1980s because card manufacturers saw little potential market. The origins of autograph collecting began with Mike "King" Kelly, a late nineteenth-century baseball player, believed to be one of the first celebrities to sign autographs. More baseball memorabilia also is available because baseball players compete in more games and thus are available for auto-graphs more often. Plus, they have more disposable equipment — bats, hats, balls, batting gloves, and so on — that collectors want. Baseball is also the only one of the four major league sports that lets fans keep any errant equipment, unless you count the occasional, potentially lethal hockey puck that flies into the stands.

What Should I Collect?

This advice may sound obvious, but collect what you like. Too many new collectors get hung up on value and worry about what things will be worth a month, a year, or 10 years from now. If you've gotten into sports memora-bilia collecting for investment purposes, look elsewhere. This hobby is a terrible place to invest your money.

Remember, with so much sports memorabilia out there, collecting it all is impossible. You may want to collect all the cards of a certain player, team, sport, or manufacturer. Believe it or not, just limiting yourself to certain players — such as Michael Jordan or Cal Ripken — is a huge challenge. Some collectors began collecting each year's set of Topps baseball cards years ago, when that was the only baseball card set available. These days, Topps produces numerous sets, but collecting the standard edition still is enough for some collectors.

Others focus their collection on a type of memorabilia. Some people collect only game-used bats or uniforms. Some fans like seats from stadiums. Other collectors focus on programs, newspapers, pennants, Starting Lineup figurines, or ticket stubs.

Here's just a sampling of popular themes among sports collectors:

- ✔ Baseballs, footballs, or basketballs single-signed by members of each Hall of Fame.
- ✔ Memorabilia belonging to World Series or Super Bowl MVPs
- ✔ Autographed Wheaties boxes
- ✔ Seats, fixtures, signs, AstroTurf, or any other item from a ballpark or stadium
- ✔ Press pins from baseball All-Star games, the World Series, or the Super Bowl.
- ✔ Sports books signed by the author

✔ World Series or Super Bowl programs

✔ Olympic pins

✔ Golf flags signed by Professional Golfers' Association members

✔ Memorabilia from baseball's old Negro Leagues

✔ Memorabilia from defunct leagues, such as football's United States Football League (USFL) or basketball's American Basketball Association

Whatever you decide, it should be enough of a challenge and should be a collection that you can expand as time goes by. But having a theme is important, not only so that you have a flashy display to show your friends but also to preserve your own sanity and checkbook. Even Barry Halper, the New Jersey megacollector who has more famous baseball memorabilia than the Baseball Hall of Fame, had to draw the line somewhere.

Although making money in sports memorabilia is difficult, you'll have a much easier time selling your collection if it has a theme. The collection will sell much faster, and for more money, at auction or to a dealer, if it's all related. If you have a collection of baseballs single-signed from Hall of Famers, they'll be much easier to unload than the same signatures on odds and ends.

What Should I Not Collect?

Don't buy something because you're told that it has great investment potential. Unless it fits into the theme of your collection, it's only going to take up space in your home and cost money that, at the very least, you can use to buy something on your want list.

Don't buy something unless you have a keen sense of its value. Not everything has a price guide — although it may seem that way with sports memorabilia — but you can bet that a pocket of collectors has set a market for it. If you're already following my advice to have a theme, you won't buy anything that doesn't fit into your collection. But you may stumble upon something that fits the theme of your collection that you've never seen before. Maybe you have a Michael Jordan collection. One day, you see a North Carolina phone book from the early 1980s with Jordan on the cover in his Carolina blue uniform. If it's priced under $20, you probably won't go wrong. But if it's $100, you should walk away until you find out what it's worth. You won't find it in a price guide, but you can bet that plenty of Jordan collectors do know its value.

Chapter 2

Sports Cards (Whatever Happened to the Gum?)

*P*arents are always asking me which brand of sports cards to purchase for their kids. Unfortunately, there's no easy answer. These days, roughly a dozen manufacturers produce hundreds of sets and subsets year-round. Whether you're shopping at your local sports card shop, drugstore, shoppers club, or sporting goods store, you can easily be overwhelmed by the sheer volume of cards.

If you grew up collecting Topps and/or Bowman, you may feel like Rip Van Winkle as you shop for cards today. Names such as Fleer, Donruss, Pinnacle, Upper Deck, and Pacific probably mean nothing to you. You're probably confused when you open a pack and find different variations. Some cards are printed with fancy foil stamping and or with a different design. Others are "die cut" or feature special holographic art. Even though you recognize the players, you're probably not quite sure what you got.

In this chapter, I guide you through the maze of the new card market. But first, a little historical perspective. Even if you don't plan on collecting anything but new sports cards, you'll want to understand the evolution of sports cards and how technology has changed the product, particularly over the last decade.

I explain the relationship between the sports leagues, their players associations, and the card manufacturers — and how they produce and market cards in order to take the most money out of your pocket. I describe the gimmicks and other chicanery that some card companies occasionally employ and help you make your own decisions about what to buy.

Tobacco Cards and Other Pictures of Dead Guys

Imagine the uproar that would occur today if one of the major tobacco manufacturers announced a promotion in which anyone purchasing a pack of cigarettes received a popular toy. Everyone would see it as a blatant attempt to introduce young people to smoking. And yet, that's about how baseball cards were invented around the turn of the century.

In the 1880s, a tobacco baron by the name of James Buchanan "Buck" Duke discovered that some packs of his company's cigarettes were getting crushed in shipping. A shrewd marketer who was the first to mass-produce cigarettes and the first to include graphics on advertising and packaging, Duke corrected the problem by including cardboard inserts that served not only as ways to stiffen the packs but also as premiums to boost sales. Duke was not the first to produce *baseball* cards — his tobacco packs featured cards of actors and actresses — but his idea inspired competitors to place baseball cards in their products. Figure 2-1 shows a T205 tobacco card of Hall of Fame pitcher Christy Mathewson, produced between 1910 and 1912.

Figure 2-1: An early tobacco card of Hall of Famer Christy Mathewson.

Photo by Tom DiPace

Sales soared, either because nonsmokers had to pick up the habit — as the companies hoped — or find a smoker willing to part with the cards. Duke has faded into relative obscurity since his death, although he's largely responsible for cigarettes, baseball cards, and Duke University. Depending on your point of view, he was either one of America's finest businessmen or a very evil man.

Baseball cards appeared regularly in tobacco products from 1886 until the early 1920s when, ironically, R.J. Reynolds officials unveiled a campaign that stressed, essentially, that its Camel cigarettes were of such high quality that they did not need to include premiums. Its competitors soon followed suit. Tobacco cards that have survived through the years are among the most treasured baseball collectibles. Today, a set of 522 T206 cards, produced by American Tobacco from 1909 to 1911 during the heyday of tobacco cards, is worth more than $50,000. That's not including the two rarest cards in the set, Hall of Famers Eddie Plank and Honus Wagner. Some collectors also include a rare variation of the Joe Doyle card, bringing the total to 523 cards.

You'll probably never deal with a T206 Honus Wagner firsthand, unless you have a deep wallet or hit the lottery by discovering one in an old home or estate sale. But you can acquire tobacco cards of lesser or common players for the relatively low price of $20 to $50 apiece, depending on condition.

Referring to some pro athletes as *common* may seem insulting, because they beat staggering odds to reach the top of their profession. But when valuing sports memorabilia, players are classified as *stars* and *commons.* Players that fall between the two categories sometimes are placed in a third category, *minor stars.* Expect to pay a heavy premium for stars and a modest premium for minor stars.

Early Post-Tobacco Cards

After the demise of tobacco cards, no one rushed to fill the void. Several companies, most notably the American Caramel Company, produced cards during the 1920s, but no one did so regularly until the Goudey Gum Company in 1933.

Between 1933 and 1941, Goudey issued six major baseball card sets, along with several minor ones. Its 1933 set remains one of the most popular. With numerous future Hall of Famers such as Babe Ruth, Lou Gehrig, Rogers Hornsby, Bill Dickey, Jimmie Foxx, Joe Cronin, and Mel Ott, it's now valued between $20,000 and $40,000. Another gum company, Gum, Inc., produced sets of "Play Ball" cards between 1939 and 1941.

You probably won't see pre–World War II cards unless you go looking for them. Only larger dealers tend to buy and sell these pricier cards. Should these pique your interest, publications such as *Sports Collectors Digest* and *Tuff Stuff,* which I discuss in Chapter 15, feature advertisements from dealers brokering these cards.

The Honus Bonus

You may hear collectors refer to Honus Wagner in reverential tones, and not just because he was perhaps the greatest shortstop ever. His T206 card is the Holy Grail of sports collectibles, with a history open to debate. As the legend goes, the Pittsburgh Pirates star objected to being included in the set, either because he disliked tobacco or, at the very least, the terms of his compensation. The card was pulled, but not before a few dozen slipped into circulation. The card's rarity went unnoticed until 1939, when a collector named Jefferson Burdick had difficulty locating one to photograph for his American Card Catalog. The card gradually increased in value, selling for a relatively modest $1,500 as recently as 1972. The card garnered national attention in 1991 when hockey star Wayne Gretzky and Bruce McNall, then the owner of the Los Angeles Kings, paid $451,000 at a Sotheby's auction for a Wagner in pristine condition. When McNall filed for bankruptcy in 1994, Gretzky bought out his partner and sold the card to Treat Entertainment. In 1996, the company made the card the focal point of a Wal-Mart sweepstakes. The winner consigned it to Christie's Auctions, where it sold for $640,500, a record for a sports collectible. Take a look at the highest prices paid for a T206 Honus Wagner card:

1930–1950: $50

1950–1970: $150

1972: $1,500

1979: $10,000

1981: $25,000

1987: $110,000

1991: $451,000

1996: $640,500

WAGNER, PITTSBURG

Bowman, Topps, gray cardboard, wax packs, and stale gum

Baseball card production shut down during World War II. When the war ended, the Bowman Gum Company (formerly Gum, Inc.) began the modern era of baseball cards with a 48-card set of black-and-white cards. The company produced cards through 1955, when it was purchased by Topps.

In the 1950s, many collectors chose sides when it came to Bowman and Topps. Just as New York baseball fans rooted passionately for one of their three baseball teams and against the other two, collectors usually were loyal to one brand. But even though Topps ultimately drove Bowman out of business, cards produced by both companies remain popular today. If you're looking to assemble a collection of '50s cards, you can't go wrong with either brand. (See Figure 2-2 for a sample of these early cards.)

Figure 2-2: The 1952 Bowman card of Joe Adcock and the 1956 Topps card of Hoyt Wilhelm.

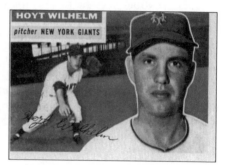

From the late 1950s through the late 1980s, cards were remarkably consistent. In 1957, Topps reduced the size of its cards from $2^5/_8$ x $3^3/_4$ inches to $2^1/_2$ x $3^1/_2$ inches. The company used a gray cardstock the thickness of cereal boxes. The cards were dominated by portraits and posed photos and featured few action shots. Most cards came in slick "wax" packs that easily unwrapped from the back, with the flaps folding outward. With no competition, Topps had no reason to upgrade its product, and Topps didn't manufacture slicker looking cards until printing technologies improved and Upper Deck arrived in 1989.

Topps got into the baseball card business to promote its popular Bazooka bubble gum. Ironically, the company stopped placing gum in packs in the early '90s in response to collectors' complaints that the powdery, pink slabs stained the backs of cards or left a layer of gloss on the fronts, depending on where in the pack the gum was inserted. Collectors had never complained about these problems before, but as card collecting became an investment-driven industry in the '80s, Topps was forced to comply. So if you purchase cards made before 1992, be on the lookout for gum stains.

Hobby people still refer to unopened packs as "wax" packs, even though every card manufacturer now uses some sort of foil packaging. As sports cards became big business, some unscrupulous entrepreneurs found that they could carefully open wax packs, remove the star cards, replace them with lesser players, and reseal the packs for sale. Millions of unopened packs have been saved through the years, and there's a huge market for them because they can contain valuable cards in pristine condition. Always look at cards packed in wax with a suspicious eye. Many dealers market them as "guaranteed unopened." Insist on such a guarantee, especially when purchasing older cards.

Other early sports cards

Card manufacturers didn't totally ignore football, basketball, and hockey cards until the 1970s. But they did focus their attention on their baseball cards, mainly because the sport was far more popular and because other athletes could not compare in the minds of sports collectors. Nothing against Sammy Baugh, Bill Russell, and Gordie Howe, but none of them inspired the passion of a Mickey Mantle or Willie Mays — at least among collectors.

But if you're looking to collect old cards from the other three sports, you're in luck. They're often available at a fraction of the cost of baseball cards from the same era. Leaf, Topps, Bowman, and Fleer produced football cards at various points after 1948. Hockey cards go back to the late '30s, with companies such as O-Pee-Chee and Parkhurst responsible for many of the early editions. These names may sound familiar because their brand names were later used by Topps and Upper Deck, respectively.

Basketball cards, like the sport itself, took a little longer to develop a following. A 1948 Bowman set and a 1957–58 Topps edition and a 1961–62 Fleer were produced, but none of them is readily available. The next major set, however, is interesting for several reasons. Like the players themselves, the 1969–70 set is oversized and features many of the game's early greats at reasonable prices. Basketball cards generally were poor sellers, so much so that Topps stopped producing them after the 1981–82 season and did not resume production until 1992.

Although football, basketball, and hockey fans are just as passionate about their sports as baseball fans, there are far more baseball memorabilia collectors. Even as the other sports have boomed, baseball remains the memorabilia king.

Trading, Flipping, and Bicycle Spokes

If you're under 25, you probably have no idea what the preceding heading means. Why would anyone trade or flip a baseball card, let alone put it in a bicycle spoke? Kids in the 1950s and 1960s did not view baseball cards as investment commodities to be kept in pristine condition. Cards were playthings to be gambled away in flipping contests in which the winner took the cards that were matched, turned over, or knocked down appropriately. Kids kept their cards in back pockets and wallets or placed them in bicycle spokes to generate the sound of a motorcycle.

Until the 1980s, when sports card shops became fixtures at shopping malls, kids had only two ways to complete a set of cards. You either kept buying more packs and accumulating more duplicates and triplicates, or you traded with buddies. Kids got to act like general managers, debating the merits of players. One kid might offer Frank Robinson for Willie Mays. The other would counter with Mays for Robinson and Phil Niekro. As the trade progressed, the collectors might examine the statistics on the back of the cards. Cards actually were referred to as trading cards, which now sounds as outdated as calling your stereo a "hi-fi."

In the early '80s, as cards evolved from playthings to collectibles to even investments, the games stopped. Collectors no longer needed to trade, because they could purchase individual cards from dealers and card stores. Cards went directly from the pack to a plastic sheet or holder. If trades were made, they were based on values in a price guide, not statistics on the field. Perhaps not coincidentally, the growth of fantasy sports leagues in which fans draft and trade players occurred just as the popularity of actually trading the cards ended.

A lot of cards that you see made before 1980 are in terrible condition for one reason: They were treated more as toys than collectibles. Even if you're following my advice and ignoring the notion of sports memorabilia as an investment, you still want to keep your cards or your kid's cards in top-notch condition. I talk more about this later in this chapter, but remember that the three most important things to pay attention to when assembling a sports memorabilia collection are condition, condition, and condition.

The Modern Card Manufacturers

Today's card collector has many more choices than his 1950s counterparts, who had only Topps and Bowman. You may be terribly confused when you enter a card shop or a retail outlet that sells cards and see a bewildering number of manufacturers, brands, and card lines. Fortunately, you're a lot better off than you would have been ten years ago. The downsizing of the industry has claimed numerous casualties, and even the survivors have consolidated. Still, a lot of cards are out there, and you may find it helpful to know which companies are part of one another.

The card line that you collect is not that important. If you're focusing your efforts on an individual player, you probably want to acquire all of his cards produced across the board. But this section helps clear up some of the confusion.

Topps

If you ever collected cards in the past, you probably bought a few packs of Topps. Founded in Brooklyn, New York, in 1938 by brothers Abram, Ira, Philip, and Joseph Shorin, the company focused on candy and bubble gum until it produced its first baseball cards in 1951. Ironically, the company had its origins in the tobacco business. In 1890, Morris Shorin, their father, created the American Leaf Tobacco Co. Although the company was merely a wholesaler of tobacco, some of the product that passed through its channels inevitably was packaged with some of the first baseball cards.

Because of its long tradition, you probably won't mistake Topps for another company. It had a virtual monopoly on the sports card market from 1957 to 1980 and fought hard to maintain its position as the only card manufacturer. In 1980, it lost a court battle that paved the way for other card producers.

Topps is perhaps most famous for its 1952 baseball card set. Although it produced a pair of 52-card sets in 1951, the 1952 line was its first full-length set and the first card line to incorporate color team logos. The set, which measured $2^5/8$ x $3^3/4$ inches, became the prototype for future Topps editions, employing color pictures, statistics, and personal information. It included perhaps the most-sought-after post-war card, the Mickey Mantle rookie (see Figure 2-3). The card has sold for as much as $42,000 at auction but is generally valued around $30,000. Bowman produced Mantle's first card, in 1951, but collectors view the 1952 Topps as the true rookie.

Until 1974, Topps released its cards by series. The first 100 or so cards came out at the beginning of the year, followed by the next 100 a few months later. Because the first few series tended to rest on the shelves for a while, some stores slashed orders for the latter series, which makes the high-numbered cards a little more rare.

Many card collectors and dealers try to draw a line of demarcation to determine when cards went from being genuine collectibles to overproduced, overhyped bogus investments. Many point to 1974, the last year that Topps released cards by series. Although cards from 1975 to 1979 have retained some value, little collectible market exists for sports cards produced after 1979.

Figure 2-3:
The Mickey
Mantle
rookie card.

These days, Topps is just one of the pack, fighting for a share of a shrinking market. It has produced cards of all four major sports since 1992. Like everyone else, Topps cranks out dozens of sets and subsets year-round. In the early '90s, it developed lines called Stadium Club and Finest that employed the latest advances in photography and printing. After buying out Bowman in 1956, it resurrected the name in 1989, producing a Bowman brand of baseball cards. Topps has been the most consistent manufacturer of hockey and football cards since the late '50s, although it is now essentially out of the hockey business. After a decade away from the National Basketball Association, Topps reacquired a license to produce basketball cards for the 1992 season (see Figure 2-4).

Topps is the only major card manufacturer that is a publicly traded company, listed on the NASDAQ stock exchange as TOPP. In recent years, however, Topps stock has been just as poor an investment as sports cards, which speaks volumes about the state of the card business. Although Wall Street investors enjoyed one of the best bull markets in history from 1995 to 1997, Topps stock has plummeted, from $11 in 1993 to $2 in early 1998. That's not a reflection on the company so much as on the sports memorabilia market. If nothing else, collectors who invest in Topps receive a glossy, somewhat collectible annual report each spring. In recent years, its grim letter from the president serves as another reminder not to collect sports cards for investment purposes.

Figure 2-4:
A 1977 Topps O.J. Simpson football card and a 1979–80 Topps Moses Malone basketball card.

Fleer

Just as James Buchanan Duke's contributions to the tobacco industry and sports card market have gone largely unnoticed, a former Fleer employee has never received his due for inventing a product used by almost everyone born in the twentieth century.

In 1928, a 23-year-old Fleer employee named Walter Diemer invented the first bubble gum that did not stick to the chewer's face. When Diemer made the gum, the only available food coloring was pink, and even today pink is the most prevalent color of bubble gum. Fleer's success with products such as Dubble Bubble gum fueled the company's initial growth.

Fleer struggled for years to get into the baseball card market. It produced four sets before 1981, including a set of cards featuring Ted Williams in 1959 and sets of all-time greats in 1960 and 1961. (See Figure 2-5.) In 1963, Fleer released a set of current players. This set angered Topps, which contended that its exclusive rights to market cards with confectionary items had been violated — even though the Fleer cards came with cookies so low in sugar content that they tasted like dog biscuits. After winning its lengthy court battle with Topps in 1980, Fleer produced its first baseball card line in 1981 (a sample is shown in Figure 2-6). In 1990, it returned to the football card market for the first time since the 1960s. In 1992, it began producing hockey cards, joining Topps and Upper Deck as the only card manufacturers licensed to produce cards of all four sports leagues.

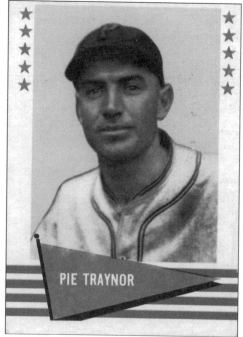

Figure 2-5:
One of the all-time greats, 1961 Fleer Pie Traynor card.

Figure 2-6:
A 1981 Fleer card of Kirk Gibson.

Fleer, like Topps, significantly upgraded its cards after Upper Deck came along in 1989. In 1991, it released a premium edition called Ultra. Two years later, it created a super premium edition called Flair.

An easy way to make a distinction between the various card sets is to divide them into three categories: *base brand, premium,* and *super premium*. Each manufacturer has its regular base brand that sells for between 99 cents and $1.50 a pack. The premium and super premium cards feature advanced printing, superior cardstock, and more gimmicks. They naturally cost more. I get into more specifics and the reasons behind these marketing strategies later in this chapter.

Fleer is perhaps best known as the company that kept basketball cards alive in the late 1980s. In 1986, it picked up the rights to produce NBA cards from the Star Company and issued a set that included the rookie cards of Michael Jordan, Patrick Ewing, and Karl Malone. It now ranks, along with the Star Co. issues, as perhaps the most valuable sports card set of any produced in the 1980s.

The Star Co. produced some of the most beautiful cards ever, although its products depicting Hooters waitresses and Hawaiian Tropic girls were considered novelties rather than collectibles. It's hard to believe now, given the NBA's global marketing reach, that Star was the only manufacturer of basketball cards from 1983 to 1986. The cards were issued by team but were numbered as one set, so they can be put together to form a complete set. Because Star produced some of the first Michael Jordan cards, they've become very popular among collectors.

Fleer was a publicly held company like Topps until it was purchased by the Marvel Entertainment Group in 1992. Marvel later purchased SkyBox, which is licensed to produce football and basketball cards. Marvel's card wing often is referred to as Fleer/SkyBox, which is located in Mount Laurel, New Jersey.

Fleer has made some terrific sports cards through the years. Its late-1980s basketball cards are highly sought after. But because it produced most of its sports cards after 1980 and therefore was not around before the preinvestment era, many collectors dismiss the company as irrelevant. I advise you not to *invest* in sports cards, however, so nothing's wrong with collecting Fleer.

Upper Deck

In 1989, a group of entrepreneurs revolutionized the sports card market by making a better baseball card. The company took its name from an Upper Deck card shop in Anaheim, California, whose owner joined forces with two printing executives and several investors to make an attractive, counterfeit-proof baseball card that quickly became the hobby favorite. Two years later, the company was licensed to make cards for all four major sports and enjoyed a handsome $67.5 million profit on $263.2 million in sales. It was a great American success story. Heck, someone could even write a book about it. (Excuse me for the shameless plug.)

The founders of Upper Deck realized that Topps had made little improvement in its cards over the years, despite innovations in the printing business. The cards made by Fleer and Donruss, which came along in 1981, were of even lesser quality for much of the decade, produced on thin cardstock and easily counterfeited. To solve the problem, Upper Deck placed irremovable holograms on each card, employing the same technology used for credit cards. They used a high-quality white cardstock, with pictures on both the front and back of the cards, and enlisted some of the best photographers in the country to provide the shots. For the inaugural edition, a young employee had the foresight to make Ken Griffey Jr. the No. 1 card in the set. At the time of production, during the winter of 1988–89, there was no guarantee that the young outfielder would even make the Seattle Mariners roster in 1989. But "Junior" had a tremendous spring training, made the team, and helped make the initial Upper Deck card set the hottest new release in history.

By 1991, Upper Deck had moved its headquarters from Yorba Linda, California, south to Carlsbad. It was largely responsible for turning the sports collecting hobby into an investment-driven business. In its early years, whenever Upper Deck released a new product, the value of both unopened packs and individual cards soared. Dealers lucky enough to be on the company's distribution list made a fortune. No one, it seemed, could get enough Upper Deck.

Upper Deck has come up with many of the innovations and gimmicks that have driven the card business in the 1990s. But, like Fleer, it's ignored by many collectors because it doesn't have a history dating before the investment era of cards. Its card lines still hit the market amid much hoopla at prices that inevitably soar before settling down. Consider, for instance, that in 1991 alone Upper Deck produced 4 *billion* baseball cards, including a Michael Jordan card produced after Jordan took batting practice with the Chicago White Sox one afternoon, long before he briefly gave up basketball to pursue baseball. With that kind of production, you're not exactly acquiring an unusual collection. And if you still aren't sold on the notion that baseball cards are a terrible investment, consider that collectors in 1991 either bought the Upper Deck set whole for between $30 and $40 or assembled it by buying packs for even more money. Today that set is worth a whopping ten bucks!

This kind of depreciation hardly makes Upper Deck unique. I can provide you with similar examples for any of the major card manufacturers. Nothing is wrong with collecting new cards, and Upper Deck produces some of the finest ones. After all, today's collector still can enjoy the age-old tradition of opening packs and finding hidden treasures. But don't get caught up in the hype surrounding the release of new card lines. You'll inevitably overpay for packs that will quickly lose interest among collectors as soon as the next product line comes out.

Pinnacle/Leaf/Donruss/Action Packed

No company is more representative of the downsizing and consolidation of the sports card market than Pinnacle Brands. This company, headquartered in Grand Prairie, Texas, began in the 1970s as a printing company called Optigraphics. In 1983, it issued multiple-image discs for 7-Eleven stores. You could tilt the discs, which were about the size of half-dollar coins, to reveal different views. The Magic Motion process was later used in cards called Sportsflics, produced from 1986 to 1990 and brought back again in 1994.

In 1988, the company, which was then known as Score, began producing standard baseball cards and acquired rights to produce football (1989), hockey (1989), and NASCAR (1994) cards. In 1991, the company unveiled its Pinnacle line. The success of the brand, along with a change in the company's ownership in 1993, prompted another name change, to Pinnacle Brands. The company still does not have a license to produce NBA cards, although it does manufacture cards for the new Women's National Basketball Association league.

Since 1993, Pinnacle has added more brands. In 1995, it purchased Action Packed, an Illinois company that had used a patented embossing technology on its football and hockey cards. The following year, it purchased Leaf/Donruss, which had changed hands several times in its 15-year existence.

Donruss, named after founders Don and Russ Wiener, was the first company to obtain a baseball card license when the Topps monopoly was broken. It was largely responsible for the hobby's rookie obsession in the 1980s, launching a Rated Rookie subset as part of its 1984 card line. It also inspired competitors, particularly Upper Deck, to take anticounterfeit measures after the 1984 Donruss rookie card of Don Mattingly was widely counterfeited.

Don't try to collect everything. Keeping track of the dozens of card sets is difficult, and no one makes this more confusing than Pinnacle Brands. The company produces countless sets and subsets between its Pinnacle, Score, Leaf, Donruss, and Action Packed lines. In recent years, it's taken the lead in technological advances; its cards have more bells and whistles than any other company's. But unless you want to lose your sanity and a good chunk of cash, focus your Pinnacle efforts on one or two brands.

Pacific

Founded in Phoenix in 1968 as Cramer Sports Promotions, the company now known as Pacific Trading Cards has worked its way into the ranks of major manufacturers, producing popular football, baseball, and hockey cards.

Pacific, now based in Lynnwood, Washington, always has maintained a low profile in the industry. For a long time, it didn't have a choice. The company began by manufacturing minor league baseball card sets and non-sports cards for television shows such as *Andy Griffith* and *I Love Lucy*. In 1990, the National Football League awarded Pacific a license to produce football cards, but at the time, the NFL seemed to be giving out licenses to anyone with a printing press.

If you like the thrill of opening packs, buy some unopened boxes of football cards from the late 1980s and early 1990s. They were cranked out in wretched excess by a dozen or so companies who seemed determined to produce a hundred packs for every American. You still can find unopened "wax" boxes of football cards from this era at card shows and some toy stores for $5 a box — less than 15 cents a pack! Now, these cards are worthless as collectibles, but they're worth $5 just for the entertainment value of opening the packs and reminiscing about former players.

Pacific inched its way into the baseball card market, first acquiring a license to produce baseball cards in Spanish in 1993 and then to produce cards printed in both English and Spanish and finally just English. For a while, Pacific seemed to be struggling to get into price guides, which kept some collectors from taking the company seriously. But every guide now includes the cards, and Pacific is considered among the industry's big five manufacturers, along with Topps, Fleer/SkyBox, Upper Deck, and Pinnacle Brands.

Are your kids taking Spanish in school? Or are you trying to pick it up yourself? Reading the backs of Pacific's bilingual baseball cards can help, although you'll want to learn basic Spanish first. Knowing how to say "He hit 38 home runs last season" only comes in so handy.

The other guys

If you understand the Big Five, you're well on your way to making sense of the sports card business. But don't forget these other card companies, past and present:

> ✔ **Best:** When many baseball players see their faces on cards for the first time, they can thank this suburban Atlanta company. By signing players to contracts long before they reach the majors, Best can produce cards of minor leaguers without a license to produce major league cards. Collectors who still follow the rookiemania craze often look to Best for a player's first card.

✔ **Collector's Edge, Playoff, Pro Set, and Wild Card:** These are a few of the many companies that have been licensed to produce football cards over the last decade. Pro Set and Wildcard went out of business in the early '90s. The Denver-based Collector's Edge and Playoff Corp., headquartered in Grand Prairie, Texas, continue to make football cards.

✔ **Hoops:** Hoops is also known as NBA Hoops, the official basketball card of the NBA. Once a division of SkyBox, it's now one of the brands produced by Fleer/SkyBox.

✔ **The Score Board/Classic:** The Score Board is better known for its memorabilia, but it has produced sports cards in its own name and its Classic subsidiary throughout the '90s. When it struggled to obtain licensing from the major sports leagues, it signed top draft picks from all major sports, including Shaquille O'Neal in 1992, and produced "exclusive" sets long before the major companies came out with their own. The company is now licensed to produce football cards and continues to produce cards of up-and-coming stars. As this book went to press, The Score Board was operating under Chapter 11 bankruptcy protection, casting its future in doubt.

✔ **Mike Schechter and Associates:** MSA is more a licensing agent than a card manufacturer. For years, the Major League Baseball Players Association farmed out much of its licensing to MSA, based in Tampa, Florida. Hundreds of smaller and one-time-only card sets were produced through MSA, usually for insertion in food products (as shown in Figure 2-7). MSA produced dozens of sets, for companies including Meadow Gold, Fantastic Sam's, Chef Boyardee, Post Cereal, and M&M's, before its relationship with the MLBPA ended in the mid-1990s. Because Major League Baseball did not sign off on most of these sets, many of the cards picture players with their hat and uniform logos airbrushed out. If you see the familiar MSA logo on the back of the card, you'll know that it originated in the offices of Mike Schechter and Associates.

✔ **The Ted Williams Card Company:** Founded by a group of ex-Upper Deck executives and some of the baseball Hall of Famer's marketing people, TWCC manufactured a baseball and football card set in 1993–94. The cards featured all-time greats and were beautifully printed. But the market for nostalgia was not big enough, ironic considering that's what the hobby is supposed to be about, and the company went out of business.

The Licensing of Sports Cards

With so many companies producing so many card sets, you may think that anyone with a printing press and some quality photos can crank out their own cards. How can any of this possibly be collectible if an unlimited quantity of it is available?

Figure 2-7:
Nolan Ryan
on a round
card from
Mike
Schechter
and
Associates.

That's a very good question. Actually, not just anyone can produce cards. Prospective manufacturers must obtain permission from each sports league and its players association. The associations license the rights to the players' images, while the leagues control the rights to the team logos and uniforms. Thus, if you obtain only the rights to the players' images, you can't picture them in uniform, which sort of defeats the purpose of printing sports cards. These restrictions didn't stop some companies from producing one-of-a-kind sets in the '70s that were inserted into food products. Many of these sets featured photos with players clearly in uniform but with the logos airbrushed out. The cards looked ugly at best and ridiculous at worst.

The leagues and the associations walk a fine line. Because they each take between 6 percent and 15 percent of gross sales, they make a ton of money from the sale of sports cards. But sports cards must be perceived as collectibles. To do that, the number of cards printed and the number of sets produced must be at least somewhat limited. (It sure doesn't seem that way, now, does it?)

So many different card sets and manufacturers are out there, not because there's a demand for them, but because the sports leagues, players associations, and card companies want collectors to spend the maximum amount on new cards. Any collectible market is determined by supply and demand; the demand must be at least slightly greater than supply. But not much of a market for sports cards produced after 1980 will ever exist because supply has far, far exceeded demand.

Maybe you're a sports fan who is appalled at how much money pro athletes make and how expensive tickets have become. Think about that the next time you drop $5 on some super premium brand of sports cards. Because of licensing agreements, about 65 cents goes to the players, and 40 cents goes into the owners' coffers.

Remember the ugly baseball strike of 1994–95? If you bought cards in the early '90s, you helped finance it. For years, the Players Association distributed its earnings from baseball card sales annually to players, minus the costs of running its New York headquarters. But as the labor war heated up, the union held back $175 million as a potential strike fund. In 1991, during the heyday of sports card sales, the union collected more than $80 million — or $80,000 per player! During the strike, when players did not receive their salaries, the union distributed checks drawn from the strike war chest. So if you bought baseball cards during this period, you can take part of the blame for prolonging the shutdown of the sport that caused you to collect in the first place.

For several reasons, don't spend too much time or money on new sports cards. You're overpaying for cards with a lot of bells and whistles rather than any true collectible value. Plus, you're further lining the pockets of some very rich people. Thankfully, most card companies still produce at least one brand of cards that sells for around $1 a pack. Buy these, and you'll still enjoy the thrill of opening a pack, assembling a collection, and following your favorite sport.

Rookie Cards

During the early 1980s, a phenomenon known as *rookiemania* swept through the card collecting hobby. As collectors — and a growing number of investors — watched the price of Mickey Mantle's 1952 Topps rookie card skyrocket, they figured they could capitalize on the burgeoning card market by successfully picking the stars of tomorrow.

When investing in rookie cards, don't believe the hype. From the beginning, the logic behind rookiemania was wrong. Yes, Mickey Mantle's rookie card increased in value, but only after many years had passed. What made it relatively rare was that it was produced in 1952, long before people looked at trading cards as investments. No one ever thought they would be worth anything. Topps, in fact, destroyed millions of leftover cards — including its inaugural 1952 Topps edition — when it dumped its excess inventory into the Atlantic Ocean in 1960. Many cards that were saved were in terrible condition. During the '80s, however, more companies were producing more cards. People scooped them up like penny stocks and kept them in pristine condition. Companies never destroyed excess inventory; they sold the remainders to repackagers or shopping networks that could unload it on television. Given these factors, no one should be surprised that post-1980 cards are worth little.

As an example, consider the 1980 Topps rookie card of Rickey Henderson (shown in Figure 2-8.) As recently as 1987, it was valued at $100. In the following years, he broke Lou Brock's all-time stolen base record, was named the American League's Most Valuable Player, and played on two World Series championship teams. Considered the greatest leadoff hitter ever, he'll make the Hall of Fame as soon as he's eligible. And yet, today, his rookie card is worth about $30. Part of the decline can be attributed to his hot-dog personality. He also turned off a lot of fans when, upon breaking Brock's record, he announced, "Today, I am the greatest." Still, that behavior makes him no less of a player. So much for the investment potential of rookie cards.

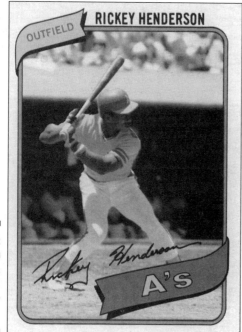

Figure 2-8:
The 1980
Topps
rookie card
of Rickey
Henderson.

With few exceptions, such as the basketball cards produced by Star and Fleer in the mid-1980s, cards produced after 1980 have been so mass-produced and overcollected that they have little collectible value.

Error Cards and Variations

Another '80s collecting fad was the *error card.* Whenever a card manufacturer made a mistake, either through a misspelling or printing blunder, collectors got excited. Although mistakes and variations dated to the tobacco card era, the investment furor of the '80s created another submarket. Usually, the manufacturer corrected the error at some point during the press run. The correction limited the number of error cards, creating another rush; collector/investors figured that each variation was rarer than a standard card because it was produced in lesser quantities.

Each version of the card, the error and the correction, is known as a *variation.* For instance, in 1979, Topps initially produced cards of Texas Rangers second baseman Bump Wills with "Blue Jays" appearing below his name. (See Figure 2-9.) Topps corrected the card to read "Rangers," and both variations, for a while at least, were worth more than if the Wills card had been produced correctly.

Figure 2-9:
This error card from Topps features Bump Wills with the Toronto Blue Jays.

The Billy Ripken error card

Sometimes errors are controversial. In 1989, Billy Ripken, then a second baseman for the Baltimore Orioles, posed for his Fleer card with a bat over his shoulder. When the card was printed, the expletive ———Face was clearly visible on the knob of his bat.

Fleer officials were mortified and immediately altered the photo on subsequent press runs. The card quickly began selling at shows for $125, but today can be had for about $3.

In 1981, Donruss and Fleer had to rush their products to press because the court decision breaking Topps's monopoly came just months before the start of baseball card production. Not surprisingly, dozens of errors were made. Fleer started its press run with the card of Yankees third baseman Graig Nettles spelled "Craig" Nettles. At one point, the "Craig" Nettles card was worth $30. Today, collectors have so little interest in error cards that they're rarely printed in price guides. Even the "Craig" Nettles card is listed at only $5. The 1981 Donruss and Fleer sets sell for $20 apiece, about what they went for in 1981. This is yet another example of the terrible investment potential of sports cards.

Another common error is the *reverse negative,* in which the negative is accidentally flipped before the photo is printed. In 1989, for its inaugural set, Upper Deck accidentally printed a reverse negative of Atlanta Braves outfielder Dale Murphy, then one of the game's biggest stars. Because Murphy posed holding a bat against his chest, covering much of the Braves logo across his jersey, no one at Upper Deck noticed. But collectors did, and the company felt compelled to correct the error. An Upper Deck vice president told several hobby publications that he thought that 20,000 or so Murphy reverse negatives had been printed before the error was discovered. Of course, no one knew how many cards were produced, but 20,000 sounded like a small quantity to collectors, and the error card rose to $60.

These days, the card is worth $10. Part of the drop can be attributed to the decline of Murphy, whose Hall-of-Fame-caliber career was cut short by injury. But the passing fad of error cards probably plays a bigger role in the decreased value.

Don't get hung up on error cards and variations. If you're collecting an older set, feel free to pick up both variations of a card if they're inexpensive. But don't worry if you pick up the lesser-valued one. After all, why should something be a collectible just because the manufacturer screwed up? Believe it or not, some memorabilia producers still misspell Cal Ripken as Cal "Ripkin." If you collect Ripken memorabilia, do you want such an eyesore in your collection? If it's a cool piece, maybe. But not just because it's an error.

The Willy Wonka-ization of card collecting

If you're familiar with the movie *Willy Wonka and the Chocolate Factory,* the idea of insert cards might ring a bell for you. The Upper Deck vice president who came up with the idea of insert cards was inspired by the movie. This movie was the story of the eccentric candy manufacturer named Willy Wonka, who offered a tour of his magical chocolate factory to five lucky children who found "golden tickets" inserted in Wonka chocolate bars. The contest set off a mad scramble for the golden tickets, with kids discarding the chocolate in a desperate search for tickets. Ironically, as insert cards became more popular during the mid '90s, many collectors tossed aside the non-insert cards, keeping only the inserts.

Insert Cards and Other Gimmicks

In the early '90s, as the card market began to soften, the manufacturers scrambled to come up with ways to keep sales from sliding. No longer could they rely on rookiemania, and the investment mentality of many collectors to fuel sales. And although manufacturers continued to make innovations in printing technologies, consumers were unimpressed.

Enter the *insert* or *chase card,* which actually had its origin in 1990. That year, an Upper Deck vice president came up with a brilliant marketing scheme. Upper Deck included valuable "insert" cards in its packs chronicling the career of former slugger Reggie Jackson, who personally autographed 2,500 of them.

The inserts were a huge success, and the other card companies followed suit, including numerous subsets in all of its products. Some cards were autographed, but most were simply printed differently, with fancy gold foil stamping or other distinguishing features. These days, a typical card set contains so many insert sets that sometimes you don't know what you've received, even after you open the pack. Kids often open a pack, keep the insert cards, and toss the "regular" cards in the trash. The hotter the insert card, the pricier the pack.

The logic behind the promotion of inserts is simple. Card companies realized that they could not get collectors to buy more of their cards, so they created more products. No longer are cards released once or twice a year; they come out constantly. Each new card line has about a two-month shelf life before collectors move on to the next issue.

Of course, you should not feel obligated to buy any of this stuff.

Like error cards and variations, don't get hung up on insert and chase cards. Instead of having any true collectible value, they're just another attempt by card companies to manufacture rarity. After all, why should a card printed in the 1990s be worth hundreds of dollars just because a card company produced only a few of them? Who are card companies to dictate rarity and collectibility? If you get a rare card in a pack, you may be better off selling it, although finding anyone who actually buys these things is difficult. It's one of many examples of how, despite what the price guides say, cards are only worth what someone is willing to pay for them. In the case of these insert and gimmick cards, that's not much.

What would happen if a card company produced just one of a certain card? Following the warped logic of insert cards, would that not be the most valuable card of all time? Fleer seems to be testing that theory. In 1997, it unveiled a Flair Showcase Legacy Collection subset as part of its Flair Showcase Row 2 line of cards. Only three of each card were produced. Taking this a step further in 1998, the company included a One of One Masterpiece card of each player in its Ultra Platinum Medallion subset. Early in the year, Beckett Baseball Card Monthly reported that a California dealer paid $6,000 to a collector for a One of One of Los Angeles Dodgers pitcher Hideo Nomo.

Just because someone paid $6,000 for a card, does that mean it's worth $6,000? Of course not. For that price, you could purchase the complete 1957 Topps baseball card set. Granted, it may not be as rare, but the set is definitely more collectible and will hold its value long after people forget about the One of One Masterpiece collection.

Holograms, Gold Foil, and $18 Packs

Today's sports cards look far different than the predictable gray cardboard editions that Topps cranked out for a generation. The holograms and gold foil stamping that seemed so revolutionary when Upper Deck introduced them in 1989 now are standard features. For much of the '90s, card companies have tried to one-up each other by applying the latest printing technologies to sports cards. Imagine if the U.S. Treasury department spent as much effort on printing money; counterfeit bills would never be made again!

You'll also find that the Willy Wonka mentality is alive and well. (See the sidebar "The Willy Wonka-ization of card collecting," earlier in this chapter.) But although Upper Deck popularized the use of insert cards, card manufacturers now include *redemption certificates* that are the card industry equivalent of Wonka's golden tickets. Promotions have included certificates redeemable for autographed balls and photos, rare sports cards from the past, and chances to meet sports celebrities. Upper Deck has a popular campaign called "You Crash the Game" that allows winning collectors to appear on future cards.

Redefining memorabilia

As the memorabilia market shifted in the mid-'90s from cards to memorabilia, everyone seemed to want items with a more personal tie to the athletes. So companies started carving up uniform jerseys, footballs, and tires from NASCAR automobiles and attaching tiny pieces of cloth, leather, or rubber on the cards themselves.

In recent years, collectors have made a more formal distinction between cards, autographs,

and memorabilia. Although *memorabilia* still refers to everything within the realm of sports collectibles, it often is used to refer specifically to equipment that was used anywhere in sports, such as a baseball or football. Hockey sticks, golf putters, and hoods from NASCAR automobiles also fall into this category. The use of the word memorabilia is a matter of personal preference.

You can easily get caught up in some of these promotions. After all, in many cases, they offer fabulous prizes. But don't buy the cards just for a shot at the prizes. The odds are steep, and if you really want the prize, chances are that it's something readily available in the market, albeit for a price. Because card companies pay dearly to obtain items such as Mickey Mantle rookie cards for these promotions, they pass the costs along to you. So unless you're collecting the cards, you're overpaying essentially for a lottery ticket. Thankfully, laws require card companies to print on the packs the chances of winning. So at least you know how slim your chances are.

Of course, you could make a pretty good argument that cards are overpriced whether they include insert cards or not. When Upper Deck debuted its first baseball cards in 1989, at 89 cents a pack, other card manufacturers could not contain their laughter. Why, that was nearly twice the going rate for a pack of cards! Who in their right mind would possibly pay that? As it turned out, plenty of collectors were willing to pay for quality, and the other card manufacturers scurried to come up with their own premium brands. Topps created Stadium Club. Fleer unveiled Ultra, and Donruss printed a line under the name of its parent company, Leaf.

In the never-ending game of one-upmanship, the creation of premium lines still was not enough. Today, most card lines can be classified as *super premium, premium,* and *base* brands. The prices for a super premium pack of cards such as Topps Finest ($13 for a pack of just *six* cards) are staggering. A pack of Donruss Signature Certified cards — a five-card pack that includes one autographed card — sells for $18! Compared to these, the premium lines look reasonably priced. A pack of Donruss Elite, Topps Stadium Club, Pinnacle Certified, Fleer Ultra, or Upper Deck SP will cost you between $3 and $5 a pack.

Thankfully, collectors still can choose between several base brands such as Upper Deck's Collectors Choice, Pacific's Crown Collection, and sets simply classified as Topps, Fleer, and Donruss, priced at between $1.25 and $2.50 a pack. In an encouraging sign of the times, Topps's base brand — at $1.75 a pack — remains one of the industry's top sellers. Perhaps collectors are buying them to experience the nostalgic feeling of when a pack of cards cost less than a gallon of milk.

You can easily lose a sense of perspective when buying new sports cards. Pack prices have risen so quickly that many collectors believe that these new cards must be valuable because they cost so much. In reality, little secondary market exists for new cards. Try selling that freshly-minted Kobe Bryant rookie card to a dealer. You'll be peddling it for a long time. Nothing's wrong with buying new cards. But don't pay a premium for some extra features that don't increase a card's true collectible value.

Promo Cards

Another gimmick that card companies have used to hype new products is the release of promotional or *promo* cards. Often handed out at major card conventions or in conjunction with an All-Star Game or Super Bowl, these cards are distinctively marked and sometimes numbered. Unless you attend the giveaway or know someone who did, you have no shot at getting these cards. If you've ever attended the All-Star FanFest at the Major League Baseball All-Star Game or the NFL Experience at the Super Bowl, you've probably seen a long line of collectors at each card manufacturer's booth. Amazingly, thousands of people get in these lines and wait patiently for hours — even though they have no idea what they're getting!

A second line of promo cards is produced for dealers and the hobby media (Figure 2-10 shows an example). Card manufacturers send them to dealers as a preview of upcoming sets to help them determine their orders. The cards also serve as a thank-you to loyal dealer customers, who can sell the promos for steep prices, sometimes as much as $100. For the media, the cards serve as art for stories previewing the upcoming card lines. The media, like the dealers, are not above selling the cards themselves.

Like much of the modern card business, the promo market is a misleading market. Yes, many of these cards are rare, with limited production size and release. Yes, many of them are beautiful, because they're serving as advertising. And they're usually restricted to star players. After all, if you're promoting your product, are you going to choose Ken Griffey Jr. or Jack Howell? No commons (non-stars) are included in promo cards.

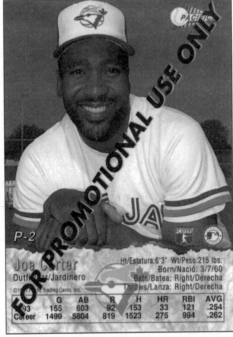

Figure 2-10:
A 1994
Pacific
promo card
of Joe
Carter of
the Toronto
Blue Jays.

Having said that, nobody actually wants to *buy* promo cards. Fans who stood in line to obtain them naturally want to sell them. But most dealers have received their own quantity of promo cards. And the dirty little secret about promo cards is that more of them are always available. Card manufacturers hold some promo cards back for privileged clients and dealers. Others just seem to slip through the cracks.

Promo cards are a waste of time. Unless you know that a promo card is being produced of a player you specifically collect, it's not worth the aggravation. Even if a promo card does feature your guy, you're better off just waiting for the actual card line to come out.

Storage Conditions

Because you're dealing with cardboard, follow that advice to "store in a cool, dry place," especially when housing unopened packs of cards that still contain gum that, when heated, can stain the cards. Unfortunately, you'll have to refrain from using such natural storage areas as hot attics and damp basements. Carve out some space in a closet, even if it means displacing some clothes.

When trying to keep cards in pristine condition, immobilization is the key. If the cards don't move, they won't be subject to wear and tear.

The sports card box

Tossing your cards in a shoe box is still acceptable, although many collectors prefer a corrugated cardboard shoe box made specifically for sports cards. This box has a divider down the middle, and the cards are placed upright, as opposed to on their sides.

A far more convenient storage option, although not practical for viewing, is the 800-count storage box so familiar at card shows and shops. These boxes, made popular in the '80s when Topps routinely produced 792-card sets, snugly hold sets. Some collectors like to insert a small piece of cotton or tissue paper at the ends of the box to protect the end cards from dinging and to prevent any movement. A little movement is fine; in fact, if the cards are too tight, you may find it difficult to remove them without damaging at least a few. The 800-count box is perfect for smaller sets as long as you use more cotton or tissue paper to minimize movement. These days, however, you can find a perfectly sized box for nearly any number of cards.

Never wrap rubber bands around cards. They will leave indentation marks and ruin the condition of the cards.

Plastic containers

You can place cards in individual holders. Some are made of a soft, sandwich-bag-like plastic. Others are produced as hard plastic covers. Among these, three different varieties are available: slip covers, screw-downs, and snap-its. The slip covers are open at the top, which presents a problem only if the cards are tossed around; they may slip out. The screw-downs are preferable for cards worth hundreds of dollars, but they're a bit of a hassle when you want to sell because dealers inevitably want to take the cards out of the holder. A good compromise may be the snap-it holders that you can open and close with the help of a coin.

For smaller sets, some collectors prefer clear plastic containers that hold anywhere from 10 to 200 cards. They're similar to the boxes that you might use to store fishing tackle or sewing supplies, only they're sized for cards. Keep movement to a minimum, just as you do with the 800-count box.

Card albums

Card collecting is not that different from accumulating family photos. Gary Carter, the former Montreal Expos and New York Mets catcher and avid collector, says he started collecting cards as a way of putting together a photo album of the guys he played with and against. Many collectors like to display their cards in albums of plastic sheets. If you opt for this route, be sure to buy sheets without PVC, or polyvinylchloride; this plastic has a tendency to melt when exposed to heat for even a short period. Insist on top-loading sheets because cards slide out of sheets with side pockets. And store binders the same way that you store books — upright on bookshelves.

Chapter 3

Excuse Me, Sir, May I Pay for Your Autograph?

· ·

· ·

Collecting autographs used to be so easy. A kid went to the ballpark armed with a ballpoint pen and a ball. If he was really industrious, he took along a scrapbook or a stack of baseball cards. Players routinely signed before and after games. Hall of Famers such as Ted Williams and Willie Mays would sign through the mail if you sent a self-addressed, stamped envelope. Few kids pursued autographs for resale purposes.

These days, kids go the ballpark armed with binders full of photos and cards and Sharpie markers. Some resell the autographs to dealers or card shop owners. Forgeries have become so rampant that the FBI has estimated that 70 percent of star athlete autographs are counterfeits. Not surprisingly, many athletes have become jaded, refusing to sign at the ballpark or in public at all. When they do, they receive five- and six-figure salaries to sign at card shows for just three hours of work. In fairness, though, many athletes have raised thousands for charitable causes by appearing at card shows and requiring a donation to sign through the mail.

Still, between the rampant forgeries and the unseemly sight of youngsters standing in line at card shows to pay big money to multimillionaire athletes, autograph collecting is the most controversial aspect of the sports memorabilia hobby. Players used to be flattered when someone asked for their autograph. Today, they make sure that if someone's going to sell it, they get their proper cut.

But who can blame them? Just as every sports card value is chronicled in hobby publications, each autograph has a market price. After all, if you had something that cost you nothing but nonetheless was worth $10 or $20, would you give it away just because someone asked for it? Of course not.

You can still assemble a decent autograph collection without spending a lot of cash — if you're willing to take the time and be a little industrious. It helps if you're under 12 years old and have a cute face and impeccable manners, but even adults can be successful autograph collectors.

In this chapter, I explain how to put together a solid sports autograph collection for a modest price. I help you make sense of the secondary market and show why you should avoid secondhand autographs if you can. I recommend the types of pens to use for different objects and warn you about the cards that should not be autographed. Most importantly, I explain how to avoid forgeries and remove at least some of the doubt regarding an autograph's authenticity.

What's the Big Deal about Autographs Anyway?

Asking why autographs are so sought after is a good question. Who decided that famous people should be approached for their signature on scraps of paper, photos, and even body parts? Autograph seeking is not a natural thing to do. Surely, children would never think to ask for autographs unless their parents suggested it or they saw their friends doing it first.

Most people have no idea why or when the autograph phenomenon began. But George Washington didn't sign autographs after he became the first president of the U.S. Collectors weren't running around trying to get the signatures of everyone who signed the Declaration of Independence or the U.S. Constitution. No one approached triumphant Civil War generals for their signatures. The autograph phenomenon did not occur until the public became more interested in professional sports.

Babe Ruth signed autographs frequently during the 1920s and 1930s, but he wasn't the first to be hit up for autographs. Before Ruth came the Boston Beaneaters' Mike Kelly, an immensely popular player of the 1880s. Each day, as "King" Kelly walked from his home to the ballpark, an entourage of adoring fans accompanied him. Fans, particularly young children, approached him with pencils in hand, asking, "Kel, could I have your autograph?" The fans kept his signature as a memento of their chance encounter with "The King."

Like James Buchanan "Buck" Duke, the founding father of baseball cards (who is discussed in Chapter 2), King Kelly has faded into relative obscurity, even though he is a member of Baseball's Hall of Fame and his life was exhaustively chronicled as part of the PBS "Baseball" series produced by Ken Burns several years ago. Today, one of those scraps of paper signed by Kelly is worth $2,000, and balls are valued at $5,000. Those prices aren't a bad buy for the signature of a man who was the Babe Ruth of his time, a guy who's largely responsible for this crazy autograph business.

Like the followers of King Kelly, today's collectors acquire autographs for sentimental reasons. Unlike sports cards, autographs represent a fleeting encounter with a professional athlete. Although the signed item likely did not spend time in the sport itself, it nonetheless has an indirect tie to the game because of the signature.

How to Obtain Autographs

In most parts of the country, you have in-person access to professional athletes. Expansion in the National Football League, National Basketball Association, National Hockey League, and Major League Baseball has brought sports to every major U.S. city. If you live in a slightly smaller town, such as Richmond, Virginia; Las Vegas, Nevada; Albuquerque, New Mexico; or Durham, North Carolina, you can catch top minor league baseball stars before they make it to the majors. The Professional Golfers' Association Tour and the NASCAR circuit stop at many communities far from big cities. Plus, many baseball and football teams train in small towns such as Port Charlotte, Florida, and Anderson, Indiana, where players are easily approachable for autographs.

Many collectors make the mistake of limiting their autograph pursuits to the stadiums and sports arenas where athletes compete. In reality, players often are more accessible away from the ballpark. That is, after all, where they work, and many athletes dislike any distractions as they prepare for battle. Other athletes take the opposite view, looking at autograph signing as part of their job. And because they're at work, they'd prefer to take care of it at the office and be left alone in their private life. With so many personal preferences, fans can't always know who will sign and under what circumstances.

Recognizing players out of uniform

The best way to increase your autograph chances is to recognize players out of uniform. Spotting actors and actresses in public is easy because usually you only see them in street clothes in movies and on television. Not so with athletes. Football players and NASCAR drivers wear helmets when they compete. Even baseball players can look dramatically different when they're not wearing caps. Athletes with less-than-perfect eyesight might wear glasses everywhere but on the playing field, where they opt for contact lenses. Remember, even though sports has become so popular, few athletes have risen to the celebrity level of actors. After all, many more Americans go to the movies and watch TV than follow sports. True, Michael Jordan and Troy Aikman can't walk through a mall any easier than Tom Cruise or Julia Roberts can. But even big-name players such as Atlanta Braves pitcher Greg Maddux and Herman Moore of the Detroit Lions routinely go unnoticed in busy public places.

Because of the events of recent years, many professional athletes put their guard up when they're away from the ballpark. Who can blame them? Remember the woman in Toronto who was arrested for stalking baseball star Roberto Alomar? Or the man who stabbed Monica Seles while she was resting during a tennis match? Many athletes, because of their fame and wealth, are afraid of public interaction in today's era of frivolous lawsuits and random violence.

Increasing your chance of a random encounter

You can take advantage of random encounters with athletes. You can improve your chances of running into athletes by finding out which hotels they stay at; the bars, restaurants, malls, and golf courses they frequent; and the times they arrive at and leave the ballpark. Admittedly, a fine line exists between autograph hunting and stalking, but if you conduct yourself in a friendly and courteous manner, you should have no trouble obtaining autographs.

Etiquette

Fortunately, most sports figures recognize that signing autographs is an unwritten part of their job. The fans pay their salaries, and most players realize that a good public image can lead to additional income through endorsement opportunities. Still, they are under no obligation to sign for anyone, and even the most agreeable signers grow weary of being approached every time they step out in public.

Take some time to talk

The next time you run into an athlete in a public setting, don't ask for an autograph at first. Instead, ask for some advice on how to improve your game. This tip applies particularly to kids. You may get a few minutes of priceless instruction or, at the very least, have an interesting conversation. The key is to treat the sports celebrity the same way you would treat any stranger: with respect but as an equal. Believe it or not, athletes grow tired of being fawned over and treated like commodities capable of producing marketable autographs. By taking this approach, you may end up having an encounter far more memorable than you would if you had just immediately asked for a signature. You still can ask for an autograph; the player may even volunteer. This strategy only works if just you, or you and a small group of like-minded friends, stumble upon a player. When athletes see a group of pen-wielding fans, their mission becomes to sign as quickly as possible, with little time allowed for conversation.

Be polite

The most important rule of autograph collecting is to be polite. Everyone likes to hear "please" and "thank you." If you must jockey for position among a crowd of fellow fans, make sure that you give the athlete some space. Most importantly, have your signing implement and item ready to go. If you have a photo or sports card, try placing it on a clipboard; you'll get a better signature. Have the cap off the pen and point it toward you and away from the athlete; players don't like having their clothes stained with ink.

Don't ask for too much

Don't be greedy. If a player is generous enough to give you a free autograph, don't take advantage of the situation by presenting more items to be signed. After you get your signature, move on and give someone else a chance.

Don't approach the same athlete day after day. Players have an uncanny ability to recognize faces, so don't be surprised if they notice when you turn your hat around backwards or switch shirts and come back. You'd be surprised by how much players remember, even from day to day and city to city. In 1997, I saw Tony Gwynn of the San Diego Padres look at a collector at the All-Star Game in Cleveland and mention that he had just signed something for him the week before in Los Angeles. The collector was stunned that Gwynn remembered. Gwynn, to his credit, rolled his eyes and signed again. "I haven't hit .300 all these years by not paying attention to things," he said.

If you get shut out, don't take it personally. Athletes could spend their entire days signing. They have to draw the line somewhere. If they start signing for 5 people, they're usually surrounded by 50 people within seconds. They can't possibly sign for everyone.

Many autograph seekers forget common courtesy and decorum when dealing with professional athletes. Remember, for all of the wealth and fame bestowed upon them by the paying public, sports stars still deserve the same privacy and respect afforded anyone else. If you have any doubt that you're approaching an athlete at an inappropriate time, you probably are.

At the Stadium

Obtaining autographs at major sports facilities is difficult. Glass separates fans from hockey players, who are otherwise the most accessible signers. NBA players appear on court only during the game and for pregame warm-ups. NFL players spend the pregame period whipping themselves into a frenzy. Even baseball players, once the most willing game-day signers, have become less accessible at the ballpark. Higher ticket prices for prime seating account for some of the limited access to athletes. No longer do ushers allow children to linger before games in the front rows, where they may annoy high-paying customers.

So should you forget about obtaining autographs at the ballpark? Hardly. In some respects, stadiums offer more signing opportunities than ever before. Smart teams have realized that the recent player strikes and work stop-pages, along with the ever-increasing player salaries, have further distanced the fans from the players; they, therefore, may schedule free pregame autograph sessions. Some teams, like the Philadelphia Phillies, even require their players to participate in annual signings where the modest autograph fees go to charity.

Outside the stadium

The playing field itself is not the only opportunity for autographs. Many of the surrounding areas are a haven for savvy autograph seekers. Get to know the players' parking lot and the drop-off site for the visiting team's bus. Position yourself inconspicuously enough so that you won't attract attention from stadium officials, but casually enough to draw the attention of players passing through.

After a game

Sometimes, the best opportunities for autographs come after the game. Some players routinely sign on the way to the parking lot, the bus, or the hotel. In 1995, when Cal Ripken was on the verge of breaking Lou Gehrig's record for consecutive games played, he often stood along the railing behind home plate and signed for hours. That's a bit unusual, because his presence meant that a few security people had to hang around. But some players linger for lengthy periods in the parking lot, where fans can slip items through the fence. For these players, this time period represents a chance to wind down before heading for home.

Naturally, baseball players will be more accessible at the ballpark because they play more games — 162, as opposed to 82 in the NBA or 16 in the NFL.

Don't be offended if a player blows you off after a game. He may have his family with him or be on his way home for a family commitment. And, naturally, players who performed well generally are more amenable to signing than those who did not. Although playing professional sports is the best job in the world, it's still a job. Like everyone else, athletes like to go home as soon as possible when the work is done.

Training Camp

The preseason is a great time to be an autograph seeker. Players are more relaxed. They haven't yet gotten into the grind of playing every day and dealing with constant requests from fans and the media. For veterans, training camp can be a vacation of sorts, a way to kill time between golf outings. Everyone is in a good frame of mind.

And why not? Baseball players train in beautiful Arizona and Florida. Football camps, although grueling, often are held on picturesque college campuses. Basketball and hockey camps take place in less-exotic locales, but they're generally off the beaten path, which favors the aggressive autograph seeker.

Many of the spring baseball facilities built over the last decade are not as fan-accessible as their predecessors. But they have more fields, which means that you may be the only autograph seeker at a back field where some of a team's young minor leaguer prospects are playing. In Peoria, Arizona, just north of Phoenix, the San Diego Padres and Seattle Mariners share a spectacular site that includes about two dozen fields. Because of fenced walkways, players can move between diamonds without having to cut through fans. But if you position yourself along a fence, particularly in the early morning when workouts begin, you may encounter the likes of Alex Rodriguez or Tony Gwynn.

If you ever get a chance, go to baseball spring training in Arizona and Florida. Even if you don't get a single autograph, you'll enjoy the low-key atmosphere, the smaller ballparks, and, of course, the fabulous 70-degree, early March afternoons.

Hotel Lobbies and Other Opportunities

Hotel lobbies can be a great place to get autographs. Of course, a little common courtesy goes a long way here, as it does everywhere else. Teams make little effort to keep their lodging on the road a secret; it's available in many media guides, which usually are sold at the ballpark.

Don't trespass

Many hotels have strict policies against autograph seekers lingering in the lobby, on guest floors, and even around the property, in some cases. These rules should be duly respected. Sports teams, with their large traveling parties and deep travel budgets, represent significant business for hotels, which ensure privacy and safety as part of their contract with the team. Hotels are not afraid to press trespassing charges against autograph hounds who threaten their business.

Many hotels have outdoor areas unofficially designated as autograph areas because collectors have congregated there for years. In some cities, these areas are located near the taxi stand or the team bus departure spot.

Learn the players' schedules

Be sure to learn a player's schedule before committing to a long wait at a hotel. Baseball players often leave for the ballpark as much as five hours before game time. Team buses generally depart around two and a half hours before, but many players find their own rides. NBA and NHL players generally don't leave as early. Schedules often vary by team and by city.

If you are allowed to congregate in the lobby of a hotel, don't be conspicuous. Dress nicely and act like you belong. But don't ride the elevators or walk the floors of the building unless you're a guest. Don't try to be sneaky either, because players know all the tricks. These days, even benchwarmers register under assumed names — not just to avoid autograph hounds but also the sports radio stations that call at all hours. Don't try to ambush a player by leaving photos or cards in an envelope at the front desk. Most importantly, don't attempt to find out a player's room number or, worse, follow him back to his room. Acting like a stalker will yield nothing but negative results.

Professional athletes are both celebrities and seasoned travelers. As a result, they're particularly suspicious of strangers on the road. If you must pursue them at hotels, try to do so from designated areas. Another strategy is to offer assistance if the athlete looks lost. Several visiting baseball players routinely agree to have autograph collectors accompany them on the New York subway for safety purposes and to make sure that they don't get lost. Some veteran autograph seekers offer rides to players who miss the team bus and need a lift to the ballpark. The best strategy is to always act polite and friendly.

Visit restaurants and malls

Another way to obtain autographs from players visiting your city is to check out restaurants and malls near the team hotel. Many players will spend the late morning and early afternoon before a game walking a mall or having a lengthy lunch. Use common sense here and try not to come across as a stalker.

Try to avoid asking for a signature while a player is eating, no matter how tempted you are to do so. The biggest complaint that I hear from athletes regarding autograph seekers is that they interrupt a meal, a personal time often spent with friends and family. Remember, players like to go incognito to restaurants and bars. Once one person asks for an autograph, the athlete may as well leave unless he wants to spend the rest of the visit signing.

Take the late evening off from autograph seeking. When players return to their hotels late at night, the last thing they want to do is deal with collectors. Because it's dark, their natural paranoia kicks up a notch. Plus, some players like to unwind with a few drinks. The more they have, the worse their signature becomes.

Autograph Seeking by Mail

As recently as the mid-1980s, you could put together a pretty good collection of autographs through the mail. Many players routinely signed autograph requests through the mail. But like so much of sports collecting, that habit changed as the hobby evolved into big business. In fairness to the athletes, many received far too much mail to possibly answer. It quickly became obvious that many collectors were making multiple submissions in order to sell the extras.

However, you still may be able to obtain autographs through the mail. It's still the best way to reach current players, so I've included a list of team addresses for all four major sports leagues in Appendix B. *The Baseball Address List,* by Jack Smalling, is a popular annual book that is very valuable for locating ex-baseball players. Active big leaguers, along with their counterparts from the other three leagues, are most reachable where they spend the most time — at the stadium or practice facility.

How to make your request

You're more likely to receive an autograph response in the mail if you keep your request simple. Include a short, handwritten note of no more than one page. Try to come up with something more creative than "I really would like your autograph, please." If the player finds your letter interesting, he may jot down a short note himself that will become a special, personalized part of your collection. Include no more than two cards or photos; if sending two items to be autographed, make them different so that you don't look as if you're going to sell or trade the extra one. Most importantly, always include a self-addressed, stamped envelope (SASE). Not even the nicest players are going to spot you the postage.

Mail autograph requests are a mixed bag. Over the years, players have used rubber stamps and *autopens* (mechanical devices that reproduce signatures), paid locker-room attendants to ghostsign their mail, forwarded it to their fan clubs, or simply thrown their fan mail in the trash. Generally speaking, the bigger the star, the less likely your chance of receiving a response. Lesser players get less mail and not only are more likely to return it but will do so more quickly. Because you never know whether your request will be returned, never include valuable cards and photos that you do not want to lose.

Don't be surprised if you get your autograph request returned with a card requesting a donation. Some players raise money for charity by asking fans to make a small contribution in return for an autograph. This request is certainly reasonable and, although it's not free, at least you feel better than you would if you paid a player directly for his signature at a card show.

Using common courtesy

Use the same courtesy with mail autograph requests that you use in person. "Please" and "thank you" go a long way, along with some encouraging words about the player's career. If you're from the player's hometown or alma mater or have a mutual acquaintance, be sure to mention it. If you get a nice response, send a postcard with a thank-you note. If you're computer literate, include your e-mail address. Who knows? Perhaps you'll start corresponding with a favorite player.

The Autograph Show

One of the more controversial aspects of sports collecting is the autograph show. Actually, promoters do not hold autograph shows so much as they bring autograph guests to card shows, which I discuss in more detail in Chapter 7. Here's how an autograph show works. A promoter agrees to pay a player an appearance fee, generally for a two- or three-hour block of time or for a specific number of signatures. The promoter figures that the player will sign a certain number of autographs during that period, so he divides the fee by that number to determine the price per signature. The promoter then sells that many tickets at that price — or slightly above. Most promoters just want to break even on the deal. They hope that the increased traffic at the show will bring in additional income at the gate and make for a quality show that dealers — who pay table fees — and collectors will want to return to in the future.

Suppose that a player agrees to appear at a show for three hours on a Saturday afternoon for $20,000. (We should all be so lucky!) The dealer figures that the player can sign 700 signatures, roughly $28.57 an autograph. So the dealer charges $30 for each autograph ticket and hopes to sell most of the tickets. Many times, the promoter and the athlete will reach an agreement on a number of signatures rather than an element of time. This way, the promoter is not hustling people through the line and can let them pose for photos or ask a few questions. This approach usually is more effective than trying to crank out 700 signatures in three hours, which, at 15 seconds an autograph, leaves precious little time for interaction.

Why you pay

But wait, you say. Thirty bucks for an autograph is outrageous! Who do these guys think they are demanding $20,000 for three hours of work. They already make millions. Don't they owe it to their fans? Well, yes and no. Most professional athletes work virtually every day, six to nine months of the year. Admittedly, having three to six months of vacation a year would be nice, but giving up part of that time is like going back to work. Plus, why should players go out of their way to appear at card shows during their spare time, giving away autographs that could be resold for profit and helping a promoter make more money off his show? Many players don't mind signing for free during spare moments in public or at the stadium. But some players object when they have to go out of their way to sign. They believe that some compensation is in order.

Still, seeing fans lining up to pay money to millionaire athletes is a rather unsavory sight. When players began appearing routinely at shows in the early 1980s, fans literally handed cash to a promoter or friend of the player sitting next to the star and then presented the item for a signature. (Several players got in trouble with the IRS by using this technique; they pocketed the cash and "forgot" to tell Uncle Sam.) These days, collectors purchase autograph tickets at the entrance of the show or some other part of the show far away from the celebrity guest. That way, they merely present a ticket when they reach the table. The process is not unlike purchasing chips at a casino. The players now receive lump payments up front, along with tax forms.

In 1983, you could go to a show and get New York Yankees great Joe DiMaggio to sign a photo or ball for $8. In 1997, that same signature cost $175 or more. Inflation and DiMaggio's advancing age accounted for part of the increase. Most of it, however, was due to the market. DiMaggio and promoters can charge so much for his signature because people are willing to pay the price.

In sports collecting, a fine line exists between a fan's love of the game and the reality that sports is big business. Sure, it would be nice if all collectors could get an autograph of every athlete. Just 15 years ago, there were so few collectors that players were lucky to get $5 a signature at a card show. But like anything else, when you can find a market for a service, the cost increases according to supply and demand.

Which players appear most often

You may notice that former players tend to appear at card shows more often than current stars. Many old-timers have no other income, although baseball Hall of Famers such as Jim Palmer, Johnny Bench, Joe Morgan, and Don Sutton make lucrative salaries as broadcasters. But ex-stars, particularly from baseball, can make high six- and seven-figure salaries traveling to card shows around the country. The late Mickey Mantle, who retired in 1969, never made more than $100,000 as a player. But when he died in 1995, he was clearing more than $3 million through show appearances and various autograph deals.

Current players, however, are bound by time constraints. Plus, they don't need the money. The average baseball salary in 1997 was $1.3 million. To give up a Saturday afternoon, an active player might require $40,000 — more money that a promoter could ever recoup. Do you think that athletes such as Michael Jordan or Ken Griffey Jr., with their eight-figure incomes, want to spend their free time for any less than $100,000 a shot? Actually, Jordan and Griffey have exclusive autograph deals, which I talk about later in this chapter.

But for an instant star making the league minimum, the card show circuit represents an easy way to supplement income. Some of you may remember that in 1996 Atlanta Braves phenomenon Andruw Jones, then 19, blew through the minor leagues and ended up hitting two home runs in the World Series against the Yankees. Because he had played just a few months in Atlanta, he made "only" a fraction of the league minimum salary, which was $109,000 per season at the time, along with a postseason bonus share. All of the sudden, promoters were lining up to offer him $10,000 and $15,000 for a show appearance. How do you suppose young Andruw spent his winter vacation?

Watch for appearances by players who sign for no charge. Young players, usually those unlikely to have lengthy, stellar careers, often sign for free at card shows. They're getting paid, of course, but their appearance fees are so insignificant that the promoter eats the payment in return for increasing attendance and goodwill at his show. You never know when you may get the autograph of someone who's a nobody today but a star of tomorrow.

Veteran athletes often say something like, "Yeah, I don't do card shows. I just don't like the idea of charging for my autograph." That's easy to say when you're making $5 million a year. But these same guys may have been running around earlier in their careers to every card show that would have them, just like Andruw Jones.

Why autograph fees vary

Not all autograph tickets cost the same price, even for the same player. Unfortunately, the price depends on what you want signed. The price structure wasn't always this way, but after players realized that their signatures were worth more when placed on certain items, they began to alter their fees accordingly. For instance, the cost may be $20 for a signed 8-x-10 photo, $30 for a signed baseball or football or 16-x-20 photo, and $45 for a signed "premium" item such as a bat or jersey. Be sure to buy the proper ticket.

Always have your own item to be signed. Promoters are more than happy to provide official balls and photos, but the markup can be significant.

You probably feel like you're being robbed at an autograph signing. After all, you've spent big money for essentially 10 to 15 seconds of someone's time. Even lawyers don't charge such exorbitant rates! Remember, though, that you've saved time by getting it in person rather than tracking down a player at a ballpark or hotel. Plus, you know that the autograph is legitimate because you witnessed the signing. If nothing else, you know that you received the best possible signature because the player was seated and signing on a flat surface.

Private Signings

A variation on the autograph show is the *private signing,* an event for which the dealer contracts with a player for a period of time and/or a set number of signatures. The dealer provides his own photos, balls, and equipment for future sale. In many instances, he'll accept items from collectors — for a fee, of course — and return them autographed. Many players prefer the private signing because they do not have to meet the public and they can sign at any time of day or night. Some athletes prefer to invite dealers to their hotel rooms as they travel across the country. But there's no set spot for a private signing; it's dictated by the schedule and whim of the athlete.

The disadvantage of a private signing, of course, is that you never get to see the athlete sign. Even though you may spend only a few seconds with an athlete at a card show, at least you have an absolute guarantee that the signature is real. Dealers routinely provide photos of themselves with the athletes from the signing. But how do you know that the dealer didn't include some forgeries? You can never know for certain; you have to trust the ethics of the dealer, which can be a leap of faith in this business. I talk more about forgeries and dealer ethics later in this section.

To Pay or Not to Pay?

Collectors must decide whether they want to pay for an autograph. Many collectors refuse to buy an autograph ticket under any circumstances. For them, collecting is about the thrill of the hunt, of tracking down a player at the ballpark or in public to obtain a freebie. These same people will stand in line for hours at major collectibles shows just to get a few promotional cards.

But if you look at the situation from a time and money standpoint, paying for the autograph ticket is probably cheaper. You'll still have to wait in line — briefly — for the signature, but you will not have spent hours hunting down a player. Plus, because the player is a paid participant in the transaction, you're likely to receive a nicer looking signature.

Another thing to consider is your age. If you're male and older than 16, your odds of getting an autograph at the ballpark or in a public situation diminish considerably. Players can easily blow off adult men; they figure that you're either going to sell it or you need to get a life. No one believes that you're getting the autograph for your kid, even if that's really your intention. But turning down a kid — male or female — is more difficult, and players rarely turn down girls of any age. So for you adult guys out there, the autograph show is your best alternative. Consider it the price of manhood.

I don't mean to imply that all collectors are men, nor that all celebrity sports figures are male. With the success of women's professional basketball, many collectors go after WNBA and ABL stars such as Lisa Leslie and Dawn Staley. And who wouldn't want a photo signed by Chris Evert and Martina Navratilova? Or Tara Lipinski and Nancy Kerrigan? Or volleyball star/fashion model Gabrielle Reece? After the success of the 1992 movie *A League of Their Own,* the stars of the 1940s women's baseball league began appearing together at card shows. Recently, the female stars of *American Gladiators* began appearing at shows. You might argue over whether these "gladiators" are professional athletes, but usually people are waiting in a long line to get their signatures.

Look for opportunities for free signatures at places besides the ballpark and in public. Players routinely appear at auto dealerships, malls, and sporting good stores, either as part of an agreement with a business or on behalf of their team. These signings almost always are free of charge. Does a player appear at a local sports bar for a weekly radio show? That's a great time to grab a signature. Do you live near a golf course that hosts charity tournaments? That's a perfect chance for autographs; the player already is in a charitable state of mind.

Personalization

The casual autograph collector generally prefers to have a photo personalized. For instance, if you ran into the president, you might want him to sign your photo, "To Dave, My Best Friend in Alabama. All My Best. Bill Clinton." But sports collectors prefer a simple signature because it's worth more and easier to sell. After all, if you're trying to sell an autograph that reads "To Pete," you're going to be able to market it only to guys named Pete. (Of course, if your name is Pete and you're the buyer, you can pick up some great bargains).

Show promoters generally do not allow collectors who purchase autograph tickets to request personalizations. This personal touch inevitably slows down the autograph line, and because the guest is contracted for only a limited period, time is money. Restricting personal autographs may seem unfair to the true collector, who may want the signature only for his personal collection. Most collectors prefer the simple signature, however, so promoters generally stick to the no-personalizations rule.

Why some players insist on personalization

Don't be surprised if a player asks you for your name when you approach him in public. He's not being overly friendly, although that may be the case in some instances. More likely, he wants to make sure that you're not looking to sell the item. Ozzie Smith, the former shortstop for the St. Louis Cardinals, insists on personalizing his signatures. This is a reasonable request, but few players actually autograph this way because personalization takes more time. If you're asked for your name, be sure to spell it, especially if you have an uncommon spelling, such as *Bryan* rather than *Brian* or *Erik* rather than *Eric.*

When to ask for personalization

When requesting signatures by mail, requesting a personalization is acceptable. (Figure 3-1 shows a personalized autographed picture of Bob Feller, a Hall of Fame pitcher and prolific signer who played for the Cleveland Indians from 1936 to 1956.) That way, if you're sending two of the same item, the player knows that you really are getting one for yourself and one for a specific someone and that you're not looking to sell the duplicate. For whatever reason, players signing by mail routinely personalize photos but sign only their name to sports cards. Many religious players also list their favorite Bible passages.

Personalized autographs seem to look good only on 8-x-10 photos. With sports cards or smaller photos, the excess verbiage looks unsightly. Avoid personalizations on hats, bats, and balls, especially if you plan on obtaining multiple signatures.

Tough Signers

Some players hate signing. The reasons are many: They don't like the commercialization of autographs, they don't want to be bothered, they're not nice people, and so on. For the most part, you can't do anything to change them. Albert Belle, the volatile star of the Chicago White Sox, rarely signs in public and has been known to be downright hostile to fans who ask. Thurman Munson, the Yankees catcher who was killed in a plane crash in 1979, was a notoriously tough signature. That attitude, along with his accidental death, has made his autograph quite valuable. Some collectors who have received a signature from Reggie Jackson in public discovered

Figure 3-1:
A
personalized
autographed
picture of
Bob Feller.

later that Jackson signed their item "Bugs Bunny" or "Daffy Duck." For years, Bill Russell, the former center for the Boston Celtics, refused to sign for anyone — even close friends. In recent years, he's been more than willing, albeit for hundred of dollars at card shows and private signings. His stinginess created a huge market for his signature and resulted in a lucrative income. Likewise, former Philadelphia Phillies pitcher Steve Carlton generally refused to sign during his career, but he now is a regular on the show circuit.

If a player has a reputation for being surly to autograph collectors, approach with extreme caution.

What Should Be Signed?

Your autograph collection needs a theme. Collectors may debate the merits of which items to have signed, but almost everyone agrees that a common thread should run through your collection.

For years, kids headed to a baseball game to get as many autographs as possible on a single ball. Nothing was wrong with that goal, especially if the kids obtained the players' signatures from one team. But if the young fans got a handful of autographs from one team and several from another, all they really had was a ball with no theme.

The standard: the single-signed ball

During the sports memorabilia explosion of the 1980s, the single-signed baseball became the gold standard. Collectors wanted a ball with only one autograph, written on the *sweet spot,* the narrowest point between the two seams, opposite the ball's logo. Part of this phenomenon related to the business element of collecting; pricing single-signed balls was easier because they had only one signature. But the other reason concerned aesthetics. A display of ten balls each signed by a prominent player looked more impressive than one ball signed by all ten players. (Figure 3-2 shows some sweet spot, single-signed balls.)

Figure 3-2:
Autographed
balls from
Nolan Ryan,
Stan
Musial, and
Ted
Williams.

Photo by Tom DiPace

Knowing when a ball could have been signed

Over the last 15 years, Rawlings has produced balls with special commemorative logos for the All-Star Game and World Series. These have become collectors items themselves. In 1995, a special ball was made for the game in which Cal Ripken broke Lou Gehrig's record for consecutive games played. In 1994, when the World Series was canceled because of the players' strike, many collectors acquired commemorative balls. They make nice conversation pieces, but because more collectors ordered the 1994 ball than during a year in which the Series was played, it doesn't stand to have much lasting collectible value.

Based on the following list of baseball league presidents, you can determine which deceased players could have signed a particular ball. When a president leaves office, it usually takes a few months for a new ball to be produced. The National League generally began using signature balls in 1934, the last year of John A. Heydler's term in office. The American League followed in 1935, not long after William Harridge took office. You might, however, find balls prior to this era with the signature of a league president, although it was hit-or-miss. The league president's signature was applied separately in those days, stamped on a side panel of the ball. It's usually NL balls that can be found without signatures.

These baseball league presidents' signatures appear on balls:

National League

Morgan G. Bulkeley: 1876

William A. Hulbert: 1877–1882

A. G. Mills: 1883–1884

Nicholas Young: 1885–1902

Henry Pulliam: 1903–1909

Thomas J. Lynch: 1910–1913

John K. Tener: 1914–1918

John A. Heydler: 1934

Ford Frick: 1935–1951

Warren Giles: 1951–1969

Charles S. Feeney: 1970–1986

A. Bartlett Giamatti: 1987–1989

William B. White: 1989–1994

Leonard S. Coleman: 1994–present

American League

Byron Bancroft Johnson: 1901–1927

Ernest S. Barnard: 1927–1931

William Harridge: 1935–1959

Joseph E. Cronin: 1959–1973

Leland S. MacPhail Jr.: 1974–1983

Robert W. Brown: 1984–1994

Gene A. Budig: 1994–present

You can't go wrong with the single-signed baseball. If it's not single-signed, you need a theme: all the players from a championship or All-Star team, members of the 500 home run club, Major League brothers, and so on. Single-signed footballs and basketballs are not as popular because they take up more display space. Collectors still go for the single-signed ball, but they're more likely to concentrate on top superstars, such as Michael Jordan or Dan Marino. Always use the official balls of the respective leagues for autographs. Here's some more advice:

- ✔ Baseballs should have the league logo and facsimile signature of the league president.
- ✔ Footballs should be official NFL balls with the commissioner's facsimile signature.
- ✔ Basketballs should be official NBA or NCAA (National Collegiate Athletic Association) balls, depending on what level of the game the player or coach is most associated with.
- ✔ Hockey pucks should be official National Hockey League pucks, although hockey collectors seem to be a little more flexible and accept team logo pucks for autographs.

When you hand a player a baseball to be signed, don't assume that he'll autograph the sweet spot — even if you ask. Just as some players insist on personalizing autographs, some purposely sign elsewhere on the ball to lessen its resale value. Of course, if you pay for an autograph ticket at a show, you have every right to expect a signature on the sweet spot.

Items for various sports

Here's a rundown on the items that should be signed for the various sports. Photos are always acceptable.

- ✔ **Baseball:** Balls, bats, hats, gloves, jerseys, cleats, home plates, pitcher's mounds, bases, lineup cards, batting gloves, and catcher's equipment
- ✔ **Football:** Balls, helmets, jerseys, cleats, mini-replica helmets, down markers, and goalposts
- ✔ **Basketball:** Balls, jerseys, backboards, and rims
- ✔ **Hockey:** Pucks, sticks, jerseys, mini-replica helmets, goals, and goalie's equipment
- ✔ **NASCAR:** Miniature model cars, tires, and sponsor logo baseball caps.

Admittedly, some of this stuff is so large that museums and sports bars are the only places that can display it.

Other sports provide some off-the-wall items to be signed. Some collectors have golf and tennis balls signed, although writing a nice autograph on those surfaces is difficult. Some collectors like to get boxing gloves signed, but they can be tricky to display. NASCAR drivers sometimes autograph the hoods of their cars, but unless you own a sports bar, they're not practical collectibles.

Other items for autographs

If you often run into sports celebrities, you may want to keep a small stack of blank 3-x-5-inch index cards handy. (See Figure 3-3 for an example of an autographed index card from Stanley Coveleski, who pitched for four teams from 1912 to 1928 and was inducted into the Hall of Fame in 1969.) Although they're not that attractive themselves, you can frame the card with a nice photo or magazine cover. Many autograph collectors save issues of magazines such as *Sports Illustrated, Sport, Inside Sports,* and *The Sporting News* (now that it has a glossy cover) to frame with autographs.

Figure 3-3:
A close-up
of Stanley
Coveleski's
autograph
from a 3-x-5
index card.

Other autographs that make for interesting collectibles, albeit difficult to acquire firsthand unless you know a sports figure, include canceled checks (personal or payroll), handwritten correspondence, business cards, and contracts.

Try to avoid getting signatures on cocktail napkins and scraps of paper. Besides having little collectible value, they're impossible to display in an attractive fashion.

The term *cut signature* refers to an autograph that has been cut out of a document. (See Figure 3-4.) There's nothing inherently wrong with a cut signature. It represents a relatively affordable way to acquire a signature of a deceased athlete. You still need to find a way to mount it with a photo or magazine cover. If the athlete is still alive, you don't need to get into cut signatures.

Figure 3-4:
Cut
signature of
Baseball
Hall of
Famer
James
"Cool Papa"
Bell.

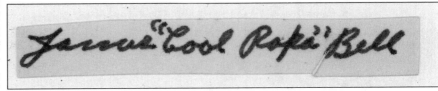

 Sometimes players will add something to their signature, such as their uniform number or career home run total. A Cy Young or MVP winner may add the award and the year to his signature. If that's what you want, it doesn't hurt to ask. Some players find such requests flattering.

Pinpointing Pens to Use for Signing

The universal standard for autograph signing is a black or blue Sharpie pen. These versatile pens, widely available wherever office supplies are sold, write on everything, including bats, gloves, hats, and most cards. (Not even Sharpies write on some of the newer cards, with their gloss and foil stamping, but even here there are few exceptions). Sharpies cost only between $1 and $2 apiece, so be sure to replace them often. The tip of the Sharpie gets fatter over time, which means sloppier signatures.

 When approaching a player in public, have the cap off the Sharpie and pointed toward you. Sharpie ink never comes out of clothing, and nothing ends an impromptu autograph session quicker than staining a player's clothes — even accidentally. Never keep a Sharpie in your pocket; if the top pops off, the pen could stain your clothing. If this happens, console yourself by remembering that your wardrobe is probably not as expensive as the professional athlete's.

 Do not use Sharpie pens for autographing baseballs, because the ink bleeds into the cowhide. Use ballpoint pens instead. When approaching players in public or at the ballpark, have the right pen available for your item and try to avoid having both a Sharpie and a ballpoint pen available. Some players, ever concerned about fans reselling their signatures, will sign balls with Sharpies and photos with ballpoints. Give them only one option. Of course, players can always reach for your neighbor's pen instead.

Basketballs and footballs do not always fall under the Sharpie rule. Although a black Sharpie works fine on either surface, some collectors prefer gold or silver felt-tip markers.

The Hall of Fame Factor

When sports fans talk about the Hall of Fame and sports memorabilia, they're probably referring to the Baseball Hall of Fame, located in Cooperstown, New York. The Football Hall of Fame has a beautiful museum in Canton, Ohio, but few people seem to know how the voting takes place, who votes, who's eligible and when, and the criteria that voters use to make their selection. The Basketball Hall of Fame in Springfield, Massachussetts, has some interesting wrinkles; college basketball coaches are eligible, for instance. And because hockey ranks a distant fourth among collectors, no one pays too much attention to the Hockey Hall of Fame in Toronto, Ontario, Canada.

Those other Halls of Fame

Does the fact that the Baseball Hall of Fame is so popular mean that you should ignore the Hall of Fame lists for football, basketball, and hockey? Of course not. These are, after all, the greats of the game and the most popular players among collectors. But run a list of names past a die-hard fan of those three sports. Chances are, they won't know whether each player is in the Hall or not. (You can test your knowledge by looking at Appendix C, which lists Hall of Fame members for baseball and football.)

The Baseball Hall of Fame

Baseball's Hall of Fame, on the other hand, is the oldest of the halls. Great barstool debates — and a few brawls, no doubt — have taken place over who belongs in the HOF and who does not. Fans closely follow the balloting, conducted by the Baseball Writers Association of America each winter for induction the following summer. And after a player is inducted — or on the verge of being inducted — demand for his collectibles increases, as does the value of his cards, autographs, and memorabilia.

The rules for induction into the Baseball HOF, although many, are straightforward. Players are eligible for the Hall after five calendar years have passed since they stopped playing. The voting body consists of current and former sportswriters who have covered baseball for at least ten consecutive seasons. Each voter can select up to ten players. A player must appear on 75 percent of the ballots for election. A player who has appeared on the ballot for 15 years or who, at any point, does not receive at least 5 percent of the vote becomes ineligible. Those players get a second chance beginning 23 years after their retirement; they become eligible for selection by a Veterans Committee, which also can elect former managers, umpires, executives, and members of baseball's old Negro Leagues.

Much of the value associated with baseball collectibles is determined by whether the player is in the Hall of Fame or has a shot at the Hall of Fame. Baseball has several statistical barometers that seem to ensure enshrinement, such as 300 wins, 3,000 hits, or 500 home runs. As of 1998, every member of these clubs who was eligible for the Hall of Fame was in.

One of the best opportunities for collectors to obtain autographs is during Hall of Fame weekend each July. Many living Hall of Famers return to Cooperstown to welcome the newest members. Because of the thousands of fans who descend on the little town, getting autographs isn't as easy as it was in the pre-collectibles boom period. But you still have plenty of chances to get signatures, both for free and by buying autograph tickets.

Expect to pay a premium for HOF signatures. The biggest reward for making the Baseball HOF is financial. Just ask guys like Phil Niekro and Don Sutton, who, despite winning 300 games apiece, had to wait a few years to get to Cooperstown. Now, their asking price at card shows has doubled. And because their memorabilia is worth more as a result of their induction into the HOF, collectors are willing to pay the price.

Hall of Fame Plaque Postcards

One of the more popular items to have autographed is a Baseball Hall of Fame plaque postcard, which pictures the member's plaque that hangs in Cooperstown. From 1946 to 1964, the HOF manufactured black-and-white postcards. In 1964, the Hall replaced them with a yellow-bordered card that is still sold by the HOF today for about $40 a set, or 25 cents a card.

No one can collect an entire signed set because some players are elected posthumously or died before the creation of the postcards. Some signed plaques are particularly valuable if a player died shortly after his election to the HOF. Babe Ruth, for instance, died in 1948, shortly after the first black-and-white plaques were released.

Always have the postcards signed on the front of the card, in the margin above the plaque, with a Sharpie pen. (See Figure 3-5 for a sample of a plaque postcard signed by Hall of Famer Monte Irvin, a Negro League star in the 1940s who spent eight seasons —1949 to 1956 — with the New York Giants.)

Figure 3-5:
A plaque postcard signed by Hall of Famer Monte Irvin.

For display purposes, postcards of Hall of Fame plaques look very attractive when a dozen or more plaques are framed together, each with their own window in the frame. Some collectors like to have players sign the plaque postcards of players they have a connection to. For example, they may have Pete Rose sign a Ty Cobb plaque or Cal Ripken sign a Lou Gehrig card.

Another popular HOF postcard line is the Perez-Steele cards, produced by artist Dick Perez and business partner Frank Steele. (Figure 3-6 shows a signed Perez-Steele postcard of Hall of Famer Ted Lyons, who pitched for the Chicago White Sox from 1923 to 1946.) These cards aren't quite as popular as the plaque postcards, if only because they're not as plentiful and have been produced only since 1980. That year, Perez-Steele Galleries began releasing the cards in series, roughly every 6 to 12 months. In 1983, the entire set was issued in a special numbered edition of 10,000. The gallery

Figure 3-6:
A signed Perez-Steele postcard of Hall of Famer Ted Lyons.

issues updates each year as new members are inducted into the Hall. The unsigned Perez-Steeles are collector's items themselves, with cards of players such as Babe Ruth, Stan Musial, and Ted Williams valued from $60 to $80. In addition, the gallery has produced a line of Perez-Steele Great Moments cards and Perez-Steele Celebration cards. Both lines are popular among autograph collectors.

Similar cards are available that depict football and hockey greats. Goal Line art cards were first produced in 1989. Five 30-card series of football stars are available. The cards are individually numbered and limited to 5,000 of each player. Legends of Hockey postcards are individually numbered to 10,000. Only five series, each of 18 cards, have been produced thus far. Plans call for additional series until every Hall of Famer has been pictured.

Cards: To Sign or Not to Sign?

Collectors have an ongoing debate about whether sports cards should be signed. The general consensus is that having a player sign lesser-valued sports cards of recent vintage is okay. But after a card is signed, it's no longer looked upon as a card. In other words, you can't consider it part of a set because it's essentially been defaced. What you have is the equivalent of a small signed photo. Of course, if you could somehow get an entire set of cards signed, then you would have a unique collectible with a premium value.

Several years ago, Reggie Jackson was in the process of acquiring 563 copies of his 1969 Topps rookie card — one for each home run he hit. He was planning to sign and number them, from 1 to 563, and market them as limited-edition, signed collectibles the summer before his induction into the Hall of Fame, in 1993. At the time, the card was valued around $450, so people were interested to see what the market would have been for them. (Jackson, being a shrewd businessman, probably would have placed a steep price on the product). But when his Oakland, California, home was destroyed by fire — with the cards inside — Jackson gave up on the project. Still, the value of that collectible probably would not have been equal to, say, an unsigned Jackson rookie card and another signed Jackson collectible numbered 1 to 563. As valuable as the card was, it would have lost much of its value because a signed version could not be included in a set.

As a general rule, if the card is part of a complete set or has significant value, do not have it autographed. Consider a player such as Walter Payton, the great running back for the Chicago Bears. His 1976 Topps rookie card is worth about $80. Don't get that card signed because it would be viewed as a signed photo (worth maybe $20), but it would be worthless as a card. His 1977 and 1978 cards are valued between $5 and $15. You could get those cards signed, but why not find a card from later in Payton's career, valued at only a buck? Because an unsigned 8-x-10 photo of Payton will cost you at least $2 anyway, you really have nothing to lose.

As another example, recently produced cards of Hall of Famer Carl Hubbell and Billy Sample (a 1980s journeyman outfielder) would be worth only pennies unsigned. (Cards of Hubbell from the '30s, however, are quite valuable.) Having the newer cards autographed does not raise their value. (See Figure 3-7.)

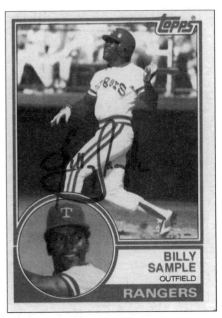

Figure 3-7:
Recently produced cards of Carl Hubbell and Billy Sample; collectors need not worry about having them autographed.

How Do I Know Whether It Is Real?

Sports collectors always want to know how they can tell whether their autograph is real. (This is the second-most frequently asked question in the sports collecting hobby, right after "How much is it worth?") Unless you saw the autograph signed in person, you have no 100 percent absolute way of knowing that the signature is authentic. How could you?

Because of the money involved, the autograph side of the sports memorabilia business has been hit particularly hard by forgers and scam artists. In 1996, the FBI said that 70 percent of autographs on the market were forgeries. The Bureau later amended that statement, saying it meant 70 percent of top-name, star athletes. That figure still is high, so you should be very skeptical when buying signatures secondhand.

The problem of forgeries

Unless you're purchasing signatures of someone who's deceased, do you really want to buy an autograph secondhand? Because of the money involved, almost everyone appears at a card show sooner or later. Even many of those who don't usually appear at card shows can be pursued at the stadium, in another public place, or during some sort of scheduled appearance. Wouldn't you rather get the autograph in person than risk buying a fake?

Forging someone's autograph is not that difficult. Anyone who ever faked a parent's signature as a kid knows this. Some secretaries — and doctor's assistants, regrettably — sign their bosses' signature so often that even the boss can't tell the difference. Try practicing someone's signature a hundred times, and you'll find that you get pretty good at it. Now imagine having the incentive of making a little money at it. You'd probably get even better.

Fortunately, very few sports memorabilia dealers sell autographs that they know are phony. The problem arises when they sell autographs that they *don't* know are phony. Suppose that they purchase a collection consisting of dozens of autographs, some real, some not. All the autographs *look* legitimate, so even if dealers have doubts about a certain item, they can rationalize selling it. They figure that it's probably real. After all, they're experts on sports autographs. They know what signatures are supposed to look like. And if they get burned by buying something phony, they'll just pass it along to the next sucker.

Hobby publications and people in the industry always advise collectors to "find a reputable dealer." That's solid advice, but how do you know who's reputable? You can do research, find the people who have sterling reputations and who have been working in the business for 25 years, and feel pretty comfortable purchasing an autograph from them.

But everybody has been fooled at least once. Anyone who tells you differently is either lying or in denial or hasn't been in the business very long. The lengths that some forgers and con men have gone in the last 15 years to make and market phony collectibles is downright scary. In some cases, no one can tell the difference between some good forgeries and real autographs — not even the athletes themselves.

Unfortunately, in some instances, the athletes themselves are responsible for many of the bogus signatures. Some use rubber stamps. Others employ friends or business associates to sign their autographs, or they let others "sign" their name with an autopen. For years, baseball players have employed batboys and clubhouse attendants to sign their names, a practice that continues today.

The certificate of authenticity

Dealers often offer a certificate of authenticity with each autograph. But it guarantees only that you received an authentic certificate. Someone who sells phony merchandise probably thinks nothing of writing a false claim of its legitimacy. A certificate is really a guarantee; the dealer is putting his good name behind the item. Often, he'll even offer a lifetime, money-back guarantee (insist on it) if, for whatever reason, the item is proven to be fake. But you still don't have a 100-percent guarantee that the signature is real.

True, you'll get your money back if the signature is not real. But when you buy medicine, you expect it to work, right? When you have your car fixed, you expect it to run properly, at least for a while. So why would you pay good money for something that only *might* be authentic?

What to consider when getting a secondhand autograph

If you're buying secondhand, the goal is to remove as much doubt as possible about the signature's authenticity. Buying an autograph second-hand is no different than almost any retail transaction. For example, if you buy a diamond with all the proper documentation from a jeweler, you're still buying on faith and placing your trust behind the reputation of the business. How do you know that the diamond is absolutely what it purports to be? You don't, but you try to remove as much of the doubt as possible.

That's why the FBI's estimate that 70 percent of autographs are forgeries is probably high. Think about it. Every weekend, at card shows across the country, professional athletes sign thousands and thousands of items. Each day, at sporting venues nationwide, players sign thousands more. Forgers would have to crank out a ton of autographs just to account for a modest chunk of the signatures.

Still, you shouldn't underestimate the threat of forgeries. Wherever possible, try to get an autograph firsthand. But suppose that's not possible, and you're going to purchase an autograph secondhand. Here's a list of questions that you can ask to remove some of the doubt.

1. **Is the dealer a close friend or relative of the sports figure?** For the last few years, John Henry Williams, the son of Ted Williams, has handled all of the marketing for his father's signature. Emmitt Smith and his father operate a memorabilia store in Florida. Obviously these sources will have legitimate autographs.

2. **Does the seller have access to a sports figure?** Did he promote a show where the athlete appeared? Did he hold a private signing? Does he have business connections with the athlete? Some dealers have culti-vated relationships with players that go back decades. You can feel pretty good about these sources.

3. **Were the autographs acquired through major businesses that have agreements with players to sign autographs, such as The Score Board or Upper Deck Authenticated?** If the autographs come with proper paperwork supporting their authenticity, you should feel at ease about them.

4. **Does the dealer have a solid reputation in the business?** Is he a sought-after source for authenticating signatures? Is he widely quoted in newspapers and hobby magazines? You're buying on faith here, but buying from the most-respected sources is the best advice.

5. **Is the autograph in question from a lesser athlete?** Sort of a backward logic applies to this theory. Because more money can be made in forging the autographs of stars, few people are going to waste their time with lesser players. Of course, you can argue that these forgeries may be easier to pass off because no one ever suspects fake signatures in these cases. Generally speaking, however, the brighter the star, the bigger the threat of forgery.

6. **Does the signature look right?** Granted, a player's autograph can vary depending on such factors as how it was signed (sitting down, while walking, and so on) and whether the athlete was signing at a show or in public. Players such as Joe Montana, Frank Thomas, and Greg Maddux sign little more than their initials in public but have more intricate signatures when they are being paid for an appearance. Like anyone else, a player's signature can change over time. Know what the various versions look like and determine whether the signature matches.

7. **Is the dealer willing to offer a lifetime, money-back guarantee?** A guarantee does not help prove an item's legitimacy, but it does demonstrate a dealer's faith in his goods. If nothing else, you have peace of mind that you can get your money back if you ever discover — for whatever reason — that the signature is fake.

8. **Is the product legitimate?** Look for the obvious. For instance, Thurman Munson would not have signed a 1980 New York Yankees team ball because he died in 1979. Babe Ruth would not have autographed an American League baseball with Joe Cronin's facsimile signature because Cronin did not become American League president until after Ruth's death. Roberto Clemente died in a plane crash before his career ended, so he could not have signed a Hall of Fame plaque postcard. These examples may be extreme, but you'd be surprised by what people have tried to pass off as legitimate.

If you see an autograph at a card show that doesn't look right, don't question the seller about it in public. Such questioning is a sure-fire way to invite an argument, a physical attack, or a lawsuit. Sadly, these threats keep knowledgeable experts from expressing their concerns. In a business where nothing can be proven 100 percent, you have to weigh one person's word against another. So remaining quiet or walking away is the best action. (And you wonder why I caution against buying secondhand autographs!) If you must express your concern over the authenticity of an autograph, find a way to do so in private.

Does asking those eight questions provide definitive proof that an autograph is real? Of course not. But they help remove a lot of the possibility of forgery. Fortunately, through the efforts of two companies, sports fans can remove another layer of doubt.

The Score Board and Upper Deck Authenticated

In the late 1980s, a New Jersey company called The Score Board Inc., which I mention in Chapter 2, began signing athletes to exclusive autograph deals. The company wanted to become the exclusive broker of signed memorabilia for certain players. According to the deals, the athletes could still sign in public for free and at the stadium. But they generally could not appear at card shows or do private signings. Score Board hired athletes such as Joe DiMaggio, Mickey Mantle, and Cal Ripken to sign thousands of photos, baseballs, and bats, which the company in turn sold through department stores, in-flight magazines, and home shopping networks.

Because the merchandise went through a middleman before reaching a retail outlet, it inevitably was priced higher than what collectors were used to paying when the same athletes appeared at card shows. But many of the buyers of Score Board merchandise were not people who attended card shows; they were simply avid fans who enjoyed the convenience of picking up a Mickey Mantle-signed ball while browsing at their local mall or while watching a home shopping program. Score Board, which offered certificates of authenticity, benefited from being the exclusive provider of memorabilia relating to some of the biggest names in sports.

As this book went to press, The Score Board was experiencing financial difficulties and operating under Chapter 11 bankruptcy protection. That development, of course, takes nothing away from the authenticity of the material it is selling while it reorganizes.

In 1992, Upper Deck took Score Board's concept one step further by forming a sister company called Upper Deck Authenticated (UDA). Just as Upper Deck had been the first card manufacturer to place holograms on baseball cards, UDA used its same technology with memorabilia to ensure authenticity. It too signed up top athletes, outbidding Score Board for players such as Mantle and Ken Griffey Jr., and went to work marketing its goods through catalogs and home shopping outlets. It, too, sent company employees to deliver the memorabilia and watch it being signed. But UDA added an extra step, placing a hologram on each item that can't be removed without destroying the hologram. (Therefore, no one can switch a bad product for a UDA one). Each purchase comes with a certificate of authenticity with a matching serialized hologram. The collector can register ownership of the piece in a company database.

From an authentication standpoint, the process is hard to beat. But the prices for much of the UDA memorabilia are staggering, especially considering that many of the athletes are not signed to exclusive deals. They still can sign in public for free and at card shows for fees, usually for much less than the cost of their signatures through UDA. Collectors can find many of the same autographed products for up to 50 percent less at card shops and shows, although they would not have the same peace of mind that the autographs were legitimate.

This price structure, however, is only logical. At card shows, you're getting a signature wholesale, with perhaps a modest markup by the promoter. Buying through UDA or one of its outlets, you're paying retail.

But what irks some traditionalists is Upper Deck's "manufacturing" of memorabilia. UDA takes replica jerseys and balls and has them signed by the likes of Ken Griffey Jr., Michael Jordan, and, before his death, Mickey Mantle. Such items cost thousands of dollars apiece; a signed replica Mantle bat sold for $1,750, a Jordan-signed basketball goes for $1,299, and a Griffey unframed jersey sells for $599.99. At one time, it marketed a Magic Johnson-signed jersey, basketball, photo, letter, and basketball card in a 4½-foot-square black Plexiglas frame for $3,995. Now, the company does not market these items as "game used." But it prices them almost the same as game-used items to cover the cost of the authentication process and, most importantly, to recoup the staggering fees it pays the athletes.

If you want peace of mind that you've obtained an authentic signature, you can't beat Upper Deck Authenticated or Score Board. But be prepared to pay dearly. And don't expect to sell your item for a similar price. Many collectors view these products, especially the pricey framed jerseys, as expensive wall hangings more suitable for sports bars, not as genuine memorabilia.

Care and Maintenance of Autographs

If you make an effort or spend the money to get the autographs of your dreams, you should take special steps to protect those autographs. Signatures, especially those in ballpoint ink, will fade over time if exposed to direct sunlight. Therefore, keep those signatures away from windows and out of the path of light coming into your home.

Two popular baseball holders are available, a spherical model and a cubed version. Either is acceptable. Whatever you do, don't spray your baseballs with lacquer, varnish, or any other chemical — even if it's clear — that purports to preserve signatures. These sprays will only turn the balls yellow. Many older balls were preserved in this manner, And they're still collectible, particularly if they are signed by Hall of Famers. But to preserve modern signatures, you'll want to keep your baseballs white.

Consider *archival mounting* when framing valuable flat items. This museum term refers to the process of framing items in a manner in which they can be removed looking exactly like they did before they were framed. The memorabilia is not dry-mounted or taped or glued in place. It is positioned in its original form. In other words, if you removed a photo or lithograph from its framing, it would have no tape marks or any other signs that it had been mounted. For valuable sports memorabilia, particularly limited edition prints, insist on archival mounting.

Autographed photos, cards, and Hall of Fame plaque postcards can be placed in plastic sheets, which come in almost every size. Be careful, however, not to place a signed item in a plastic sheet until the ink has dried. Let Sharpie-signed items sit for a few hours — or even a day — before placing them in sheets. Plastic sheets are readily available at hobby shops and at card shows. Be sure to avoid sheets with PVC (polyvinylchloride). PVC tends to melt when heated, which can destroy your precious collectibles.

Chapter 4

The Shirt off His Back (And Other Game-Used Equipment)

In This Chapter

▶ Distinguishing game-worn items

▶ Obtaining jerseys

▶ Telling whether a jersey is really game-worn

▶ Authenticating baseball bats

▶ Getting game-used equipment from other sports

*I*n the 1970s, Coca-Cola made a cute commercial in which a tired "Mean" Joe Greene walked off the field, received a Coke from a kid, guzzled it down, and then tossed the kid his Pittsburgh Steelers jersey. At the time, the game-worn-jersey element of sports memorabilia collecting was only in its infancy. Few collectors sought out uniforms, bats, and other equipment that had been associated with the game. A player wouldn't have thought twice about giving his uniform away.

Heck, even the kid in the commercial wasn't looking for a jersey; he just wanted to help "Mean" Joe, who threw him the jersey as an afterthought. These days, if a player walked off the field with his jersey draped over his shoulder, he'd have hundreds of fans urging him to throw it into the stands. Few superstars do this, of course, knowing full well that their jerseys can command thousands in the collectibles market. If a kid offered a Coke, the player would still take it. But it's unlikely that the kid would get anything more than some used athletic tape, or maybe some gloves.

Then again, if a player walks off the field today with his jersey casually flung over his shoulder, it's a good bet that someone would grab it and run. So much for warm-and-fuzzy interaction between fans and players. The "Mean" Joe Greene anecdote is just one of many examples of how big money — in sports and in memorabilia — has further separated fans from the players they worship. You can still get a game-worn uniform at the stadium; for example, flamboyant National Basketball Association star Dennis Rodman routinely peels off his jersey and throws it to fans. But unless you can afford to pay hundreds of dollars for prime NBA seating, you won't even get a shot at a Rodman freebie, especially if you're not an attractive young woman.

How to Tell Whether an Item Is Game-Used

I frequently use the examples of Greene and Rodman to answer a question that I'm often asked about the authenticity of game-worn jerseys and equipment: How do I know that it's real? Unless a player walks off the field/court/green/ice and hands you his jersey/shoes/golf club/stick, you have no guarantee that an item is legitimately game-used. And someone who attempts to buy it from you later has no way of knowing for sure that you're selling the same item you obtained firsthand.

But wait, you say. You got the jersey from a very reliable source. Perhaps it came from someone who works in the team clubhouse or locker room. Maybe a player's agent, relative, friend, or business associate gave it to you. Or maybe you acquired an item from the team or even the player himself.

Unless a player walks off the field, spots you, his close personal friend, and hands over a uniform or something that he used in the event, you have *absolutely no way* of knowing that an item is authentic. To acquire a game-used item through other channels means taking a leap of faith or, rather, a leap of hundreds or thousands of dollars.

I'm not saying that items you don't obtain directly from a player could not be legitimate. You could acquire a legitimate autograph without seeing it signed yourself, although you'd probably have more peace of mind if you did. The difference, of course, is that collectors can obtain autographs firsthand quite easily, thus eliminating the doubt that comes with purchasing autographs from dealers. That's not the case with game-used equipment. Hardly anyone, except for the rare Rodman-jersey recipient, has firsthand access.

As a general rule, I don't recommend that beginning collectors purchase game-used uniforms and equipment. It's too easy to get burned. But, like any other aspects of sports memorabilia collecting, you can find ways to remove much of the doubt regarding an item's authenticity. It's my job to make you an expert. And in this chapter, I explain how to become one.

The Popularity of Game-Worn Equipment

Over the last decade, game-worn equipment has become more popular as collectors have gotten their fill of cards and autographs, which just aren't as special as game-worn items. People get a magical feeling when they wrap their hands around the handle of a bat that was used by a star slugger and imagine how it would feel to go deep themselves. Collectors also like to put on a jersey belonging to a favorite running back or power forward and pretend that they're making a winning play.

This progression up the sports memorabilia ladder is logical, really. You go from having a picture of a player on a card to something he wrote on to something he actually used in a game. You can guess where this is headed. Pretty soon collectors will be asking for locks of hair and toenails. If you don't believe me, here's a true story that illustrates how ridiculous some people think the memorabilia field has become. Not long before his death, but after Mickey Mantle had received a liver transplant, he asked noted memorabilia collector Barry Halper how much he had paid for his old liver. Mantle was only half joking. Halper didn't buy the organ, of course. But given the scope of Halper's collection of Mantle merchandise, Mantle asked a reasonable question.

What is a game-worn piece of equipment?

The definition of a game-worn jersey should be self-explanatory. It was worn in a game, right? But what about jerseys used for batting practice or spring training? What about jerseys worn by pitchers on days they did not pitch? (On the days that he didn't pitch, Nolan Ryan used to wear the jersey manufactured by a company that supplied jerseys to the entire team, and he wore a different brand of jersey on days he did pitch.) What about jerseys worn by guys in the National Basketball Association like Jack Haley who always seem to be on championship teams but never leave the bench? Do these jerseys qualify as game-worn?

How about baseball bats? What constitutes a game-used bat? Does that category include the bats that players use only in batting practice? These days, dozens of boutique bat manufacturers give players free bats in the hope that they will use them on television, providing free advertising. Sometimes the players do, and sometimes they don't. When players get a shipment of bats, they keep some and discard the ones they believe are of an inferior-quality wood. Plus, players routinely share each other's bats. What if a bat says Ken Griffey Jr. but really was used by Joey Cora? How would you ever know?

Admittedly, I'm splitting hairs here. But the questions point out how difficult, if not impossible, it is to prove game use. What confuses the issue even more is the amount of replica merchandise cleverly marketed as, say, an

Can a player identify game-worn equipment?

Even players often don't know whether a jersey is game-worn, because the replicas look identical to the real thing. A few years ago, I attended a card show where four different dealers were marketing Mike Piazza road jerseys from the same year. All four swore that their jerseys, priced between $800 and $1,500, were worn by the then-Los Angeles Dodgers catcher in an actual game, and they were willing to provide me with certificates of authenticity attesting to that fact. A few weeks later, I was interviewing Piazza and asked whether those four jerseys could possibly be his. He said that he kept both of his road jerseys each season, giving one to a close friend and putting the other in storage. He suggested that maybe someone had stolen jerseys out of his locker stall or the laundry and replaced them before he realized that they were missing. Or, of course, the jerseys simply were replicas being passed off as the legitimate item. But even if he saw the jerseys, he wouldn't be able to tell, because they likely were his size and bore the appropriate tags. So the buyer of that merchandise spent big money for something either fake or stolen!

A baseball player can identify his game-used glove (or *gamer*) easier than he can identify his jersey, especially if he's used it for a while. Many players can identify their gloves blindfolded, just by the feel, because they often go years without breaking in a new glove. Not surprisingly, game-used gloves are among the rarest collectibles in the market.

"official game jersey." Is that misleading or what? Now, the people who use such sales pitches are not lying or doing anything unethical. If a jersey is officially licensed by the appropriate sports league, it is indeed official. If a jersey is just like the one worn in a game, then it's definitely an official game jersey. But it hasn't been any closer to a professional sports arena than the T-shirts hanging in your closet.

Although no one is claiming that these items are game-worn, a novice collector may assume that they are, especially if they're legitimately autographed and priced at hundreds of dollars. But why pay that kind of money for a jersey that you can buy yourself at a sporting goods store and have signed? With so many signed replicas out there, telling the real uniforms from the replicas is almost impossible.

 Never buy anything marketed as an "official game jersey," at least not for collectibles reasons. There's nothing wrong with purchasing a replica jersey of your favorite player to wear to the stadium or for backyard games, as long as you've paid only between $80 and $120. Never pay hundreds of dollars more just because it's signed.

Just because an item is legitimately signed does not make it game-worn, although many collectors make the mistake of believing it's real because a player was willing to sign it. But athletes, particularly those signing at card shows, will sign almost anything for the proper fee. Several baseball players have told me that they've been presented gloves at card shows that they know were stolen from them. Rather than make a scene, they sign the item while doing a slow burn. Of course, those gloves are actually game-worn, but it's unfortunate that collectors have resorted to stealing such memorabilia.

The supply of jerseys

Jerseys are a very common commodity. (See Figure 4-1 for some samples.) Now, you might ask just how many jerseys of a particular player are available. The answer is, nobody knows. Athletes, especially baseball and football players, can order as many as they want. (Dennis Rodman, for example, must order in bulk because he tosses so many of his into the crowd.) Major League Baseball players typically receive two sets of home uniforms and two sets of road uniforms each season, which are returned to the team at the end of the year. There's no need for more than two sets; the durable fabric is more than capable of withstanding the rigors of a 162-game season. But players are allowed to order as many as they want to give to friends, relatives, and charity auctions. A player making the league average of $1.3 million thinks nothing of dropping a big chunk of change on jerseys priced at "only" $100 apiece.

But few baseball players actually do order extra jerseys. Players are used to getting what they want right away, and they dislike dealing with — and paying for — things that may take weeks to arrive. Some clubhouse attendants, however, think nothing of ordering extra jerseys on their own dime, or just taking extras out of lockers and the laundry. Imagine if you worked 18-hour days cleaning and scrubbing for a modest salary in a place where everyone made millions playing sports. Even the most scrupulous employee may be tempted. Heck, many athletes condone the phenomenon, even giving jerseys to clubhouse employees. Some people look at this practice as a form of tipping. Although most of these jerseys are game-worn, who's to say that they are? And do you want to acquire something that may have been stolen?

I use the words "jersey" and "uniform" interchangeably. Although sometimes jerseys and pants are sold together on the collectible market, you'll usually find only the jersey. Because baseball and football pants, along with basketball and hockey shorts, have no team logo and look pretty generic, there's little market for them.

A 1976 L. C. Greenwood game-worn jersey from the Pittsburgh Steelers

A 1968 Reggie Jackson rookie jersey from the Oakland A's

Photos courtesy Leland's Auctions

Figure 4-1: Interesting jerseys are not too hard to locate.

A 1987 Larry Bird game-worn jersey from the Boston Celtics

A 1993 Mario Lemieux game-worn jersey from the Pittsburgh Penguins

How Do I Obtain a Game-Worn Uniform?

If you want to purchase a game-worn uniform for your collection, here's how to remove some of the doubt about its authenticity:

- First, consider the source. Is the seller a personal friend or family member of the athlete? Does he have a business connection to the player or assist in his charitable endeavors? If so, he's more likely to have legitimate material.

- Second, know your dealer. This is shaky advice because even some of the most reputable dealers have been duped by fakes and forgeries. Plus, the more an item is sold and resold, the more difficult it is to trace its authenticity. Remember that grade school game in which everyone sat in a circle and whispered a secret from one person to another? By the time the message got around the circle, the original phrase was unrecognizable. A similar thing is true with dealers. They may know from whom they bought the item — and can speak to his credibility — but they likely can't trace the sale past four or five previous owners. Unethical behavior is always possible in such a situation.

If you collect game-used uniforms, always be skeptical of a dealer who has only star players. Many teams sell their entire inventory of uniforms at the end of the season to the highest bidder, who must then try to sell the lesser players along with the stars. If a dealer has the unifroms of the entire team, he's more likely to be legitimate. Although ordering replica jerseys of stars with all of the proper tags and lettering is a common practice among dealers, who would take the time to do it for every last benchwarmer? Many teams have long-standing relationships with certain dealers who buy out their entire inventory after each season. Although I never want to unconditionally say that something is infallible in this business, you're generally safe buying from such sources.

Team and charity auctions

Team and charity auctions can be a mixed bag. If an item came from a team, you can assume that it's game-used, right? Not necessarily. Generally speaking, if the auction is hosted by the team, the items are more likely to be game-used. But because teams get hundreds of requests for donations to charitable auctions, inevitably they send along some extra bats or uniforms that were not used. Clubhouse attendants routinely order extra uniforms on behalf of the team to have signed for these auctions. So how do you know for certain that the item you acquired was used in a game? Unfortunately, you don't.

Things really get blurry at auctions that include items donated by professional teams but that are not run by the teams themselves. Maybe the jerseys are game-worn — or maybe they're not supposed to be — but rarely is the distinction made. Usually, auction officials find it sufficient to announce that the jerseys came directly from the team. At charity auctions, where audiences typically consist of more noncollectors than collectors, no one ever presses the issue.

Use extreme caution when buying sports memorabilia at charity auctions — and not just because of concerns over the authenticity of a game-worn item. Often you're bidding against people who aren't collectors, just wealthy folks willing to make a sizable donation. At such auctions, memorabilia is grossly overpriced whether it's game-worn or not.

> ## Give shoes a try
>
> If you don't want to roll the dice with jerseys, why not try game-used shoes or cleats? You can easily tell whether footwear has been used, although you won't necessarily know whether all the use occurred in games. Granted, players get dozens of pairs of shoes each season; many National Basketball Association players wear a new pair in each game. But they're more likely to get rid of the ones that show wear. Many baseball collectors prefer cleats belonging to noted base stealers.

The turn-back-the-clock uniform

One type of game-used jersey that has been a popular collectible in recent years is the turn-back-the-clock uniform. In baseball and basketball, this uniform typically was worn for only one game, but National Football League teams played much of the 1994 season in retro uniforms. Even though these uniforms may not have seen much action, at least you know that they were used, especially if they were purchased at a team auction. Of course, collectors know this, so the jerseys usually go for huge sums. Opinions differ on whether you should buy the uniform of a player who did not dress for a turn-back-the-clock game, because the uniform obviously is not game-used. In that situation, if you collect that player, you still may want that item for your collection. But don't pay a premium for it.

Baseball Uniforms

If you're going to buy a game-used jersey — or try to authenticate one — you may need to understand a little about the history of uniforms. Like other areas of sports collecting, baseball dominates. Yes, uniforms are available from the earliest stages of professional football, basketball, and hockey. But baseball uniforms are available in greater quantities. And because baseball has a more storied history, uniforms belonging to the greats of the past seem to command the most attention and dollars. (See Figure 4-2.)

Until the mid-1980s, non-baseball sports memorabilia attracted little attention in the collectible market. Even in the late 1970s, football and basketball teams thought nothing of using old jerseys as practice gear until the clothing fell apart.

Figure 4-2:
A 1969
Roberto
Clemente
game-worn
jersey.

The appeal of flannel

Many baseball uniform collectors prefer to buy flannel jerseys. (See Figure 4-3 for a classic flannel jersey.) With the mass production of modern knit jerseys, along with replicas that look identical, proving authenticity is very difficult. Does this mean that collecting flannel uniforms doesn't have problems? Of course not, and some very resourceful scam artists have "produced" old jerseys by switching numbers or, worse, by finding old fabric and making "new" jerseys.

Uniforms in the early 1900s were either 100 percent wool flannel or a blend of wool and cotton. Imagine exercising in a burlap sack, and you'll get a pretty good idea of what it was like to play baseball before the knit fabric revolution. Gradually, in the 1970s, double-knit fabrics were introduced that were lighter, cooler, and more comfortable (see Figure 4-4). They also held up a lot longer, which is more than can be said for some of the hideous fashions designed in the 1970s for baseball uniforms. Admittedly, double knits do not provide the classic, well-tailored look of flannel, but they are more practical.

The rise of knits

If you really want to know your flannels, you should know that, in 1970, the Pittsburgh Pirates became the first team to wear knit uniforms. They were joined by the St. Louis Cardinals at the beginning of the 1971 season. At the

Figure 4-3:
A 1938 Lou Gehrig road jersey from the New York Yankees.

Photo courtesy Leland's Auctions

Figure 4-4:
A 1977 Frank Robinson jersey from the Cleveland Indians.

Photo courtesy Leland's Auctions

All-Star break that year, the Baltimore Orioles followed suit. In 1972, everyone was wearing knit except the New York Yankees; the Boston Red Sox, Kansas City Royals, and Montreal Expos switched over during the season. By 1973, everyone was wearing knits.

This timeline is important for two reasons:

✔ First, you're less likely to find fakes from the flannel era because very few uniform collectors existed before the 1970s. Thus, people trying to pawn off fakes as game-used uniforms didn't have much of a market for their merchandise. Plus, companies did not manufacture replica jerseys to the degree they do today. Even those that did produced shirts that were easily distinguishable from the real item.

✔ Second, and perhaps more importantly, knowing the design and fabric of jerseys through the years may help you avoid buying a nonauthentic jersey. This information can help you authenticate a jersey. You can check to see whether the player played for the team during the era in which the team wore that particular style of uniform. You'll be able to recognize whether the uniform you're looking at is identical to the style of that year. Books are available that picture baseball uniforms through the years, such as *Baseball Uniforms of the 20th Century,* by Marc Okkonen (Sterling Publishing Co.). It's out of print but still can be found at used bookstores. It's also new enough that you can still find it occasionally at new bookstores.

Identifying a uniform by its number

Another great book to pick up is *Baseball by the Numbers,* by Mark Stang and Linda Harkness (Scarecrow Press). Tireless researchers, Stang and Harkness searched far and wide to come up with the definitive list of baseball players who have worn each number on each team through the years. This list is particularly impressive when you consider that the first team to wear numbers full-time was the New York Yankees, way back in 1929. The Cleveland Indians previously had experimented with uniform numbers, on the sleeves. By 1931, all players in the American League wore numbers on their backs. By 1932, all players on every team in the National League wore numbered uniforms. This book is a little pricey and weighs about ten pounds, but it could easily pay for itself if you use it to discover that some unnamed uniform really belonged to a star player that a dealer had not bothered to research.

Just as card collectors believe that cards produced after 1980 never will be worth much, some uniform collectors shy away from post-1980 uniforms. It's not that these uniforms aren't collectible; who wouldn't want a jersey that belonged to Jim Palmer, Nolan Ryan, or Mike Schmidt in the early '80s? It's just that knit jerseys are much easier to replicate; thus there are more fakes from the knit era. And because players knew, even in the early '80s, that a collectible market existed for their jerseys, they ordered more for themselves and donated more to auctions than their predecessors. Collectors should keep this in mind when authenticating knit jerseys and understand that the value of flannels is often more than knits, not only because flannels are older, but because there are fewer pitfalls in determining their authenticity.

How to Know Whether a Uniform Is Real

To authenticate a uniform, ask yourself the following questions.

Is the jersey the right size?

Making sure that the jersey fits the player sounds like obvious advice, but you'd be surprised how many people are fooled. For several years, a Babe Ruth jersey in a size 38 was floating around. Obviously, Babe grew out of that size in grade school, but at least a few people failed to notice. For an average-size player, you may not know whether he wore size 42 or size 44, but you should at least make sure that the jersey in question is approximately a size that could have fit him.

Some players order their jersey with a few inches of extra length so that their shirttails do not come untucked. The jerseys are marked accordingly, but you may need to do some detective work to find out which players do this. Some players have told me that the extra length is the only way they can tell whether a jersey marketed as one they used in a game, a *gamer,* is really theirs. Of course, not all players order their jerseys with extra length. Even the players who do so may not have done so consistently.

Does the uniform have an appropriate patch?

Many teams have worn patches on a shoulder of the jersey to commemorate an anniversary season or to pay tribute to a recently deceased member of the organization. Many of these patches have become collectibles themselves. Unfortunately, unscrupulous individuals have taken the patches off the jerseys of lesser players and sewn them on superstar jerseys. So verifying patches is not a foolproof way to authenticate. Of course, jerseys with patches are not the norm. But if you find a jersey that *should* have a patch, you should make sure that it does. For example, if you find a Pittsburgh Pirates jersey from 1973, it should have a number 21 patch on the left sleeve in recognition of the uniform number of Roberto Clemente, who died the previous winter in a plane crash.

Is the name spelled right?

A few years ago, an auction house was selling an Oakland A's jersey, allegedly game-worn, of Dennis Eckersley. The problem was, it was misspelled Dennis "Eckersly." Wanting to get to the bottom of the story, I approached the "Eck" in the A's clubhouse one day with the auction catalog. He said that he never wore such a jersey — obviously he would have remembered if his name was misspelled — and didn't remember ever seeing it. I relayed this to the auction house, but it stood by its "sources." I don't know whether the item was pulled from the sale or not. I do know that the auction company is now out of business, perhaps from too many questionable sales such as this.

Occasionally, however, players intentionally wear misspelled jerseys. Either that jersey is the only one they have, or they just want to poke fun at the manufacturer for getting their name wrong. Usually, they wear them in only one game.

The value of such jerseys is debatable. On one hand, if you know that it's been worn in a game, it's a unique collectible. On the other hand, do you want a misspelled jersey, one that's been worn in only one game? Most collectors would rather have a properly spelled jersey that's seen more extensive game use, and values of jerseys reflect that.

Some baseball jerseys, particularly from the 1970s and early 1980s, had multiple owners. After a major league team was through with them, it sometimes stripped the nameplates off the back and shipped them to one of its minor league clubs. The jerseys are still game-worn, of course, but they may be missing an original patch or nameplate. This practice has pretty much died out now that minor league teams have come up with their own nicknames, thus requiring distinctive, original uniforms.

Just because a dealer or auction house says an item is authentic, don't assume that it is. Do your own research.

Is the tagging appropriate?

One of the important ways to identify a jersey is through its "tagging," the patch that identifies the company insignia, size of the shirt, and year. Unfortunately for collectors, tagging has been inconsistent through the years. In the early days, the player's name, but not the year, was stitched into the jersey. For some years, the uniforms had no taggings — no name, no year.

Taggings have become a little more confusing since Russell became baseball's official uniform manufacturer in the early 1990s. Now, uniforms for the same team may have three or four different taggings. Because of all these reasons, never use tagging as a sole means of authenticating a jersey. However, tagging can help remove *some* of the doubt.

Whenever teams switch uniform manufacturers, inevitably a few teams are stragglers. Although Russell became baseball's official uniform manufacturer in the early '90s, as of 1998, the St. Louis Cardinals still were using St. Louis-based Rawlings, baseball's previous jersey maker, to produce its uniforms. The White Sox use a mix of Russell and Wilson, a Chicago company. The Blue Jays also stuck with Wilson for a few years before switching to Russell.

The New York Yankees do wear Russell but have refused to let the company place its logo on the shoulder of the jersey. Team owner George Steinbrenner says that he doesn't want to desecrate the sacred Yankee pinstripes. At the same time, he's battled his fellow owners for the rights to sell that same spot to Adidas.

Is the appropriate number displayed?

For authenticity purposes, collectors should make sure that a jersey has the appropriate style of number. Some jerseys use 7-inch numbers, and others use 8-inch numbers. Teams also can choose from three different styles of number: fancy block, full block, and regular block. Experts prefer to compare a jersey in question to one from the same era they know to be legitimate, sort of like cross-matching blood.

The Not-So-Authentic "Game" Jersey

One of the biggest problems in authenticating jerseys is the authentic "game" jersey, an exact, non-game-used replica readily available through memorabilia companies and some sporting goods stores.

Over the last 15 years, several memorabilia companies have been licensed to sell "game" jerseys. These shirts obviously aren't game-worn. Unfortunately, they look identical to genuine game-worn jerseys. (They don't, however, come with the extra length. This difference helps, in some instances, to distinguish between the game-worn jerseys and the "game" jerseys.) This practice was particularly widespread in the mid-'80s, when several companies sold hundreds of game jerseys of players such as Dwight Gooden, Bo Jackson, and Darryl Strawberry.

The companies included letters of authenticity stressing that the jerseys were not game-worn. But nothing prevented other people from writing their own letter saying that the jerseys were game-worn. And after such a jersey has changed hands a few times, tracing its origins becomes very difficult — especially if the letter has disappeared.

Watch out if you're buying what you think are game-used National Basketball Association jerseys. You can purchase jerseys that look identical to the real things in larger sporting goods stores. One Chicago dealer did just that, buying more than 1,500 jerseys of Michael Jordan, Scottie Pippen, Grant Hill, and Dennis Rodman, forging their signatures, and selling them as legitimate game-worn jerseys. He even donated some of them to charity auctions, giving them an air of legitimacy. Fortunately, the authorities caught up with him. But even though he won't release any more of these bogus items into the marketplace, hundreds of fakes are already circulating.

Another pitfall to avoid is the *salesman's sample.* Each year, companies produce sample jerseys to show to clubs, usually when a team is changing uniforms or a club is wearing a new patch. Somehow, these salesman's samples always make it into the hands of dealers or collectors. Fortunately, dealers market them as salesman's samples. But after they're sold once, people are often highly tempted to resell them as legitimate game-used jerseys.

The best advice when searching for a game-worn uniform is to look for the dealer who has the entire team's uniforms. Remember, though, that if you try to sell it, people will question the authenticity of the item — even if you have documentation stating that it came from the team.

Baseball Bats

Game-used bats have exploded in popularity in recent years. Several reasons account for this interest among collectors. A bat has a more direct link to the game than a uniform. A player used a bat to do something, whereas a uniform was something he just happened to be wearing at the time. Plus, people get a bigger thrill from swinging a bat that belonged to a famous slugger than from putting on the jersey of a famous slugger. And don't forget that a huge supply of bats is available. Players go through dozens each year, but they may use only two pairs of jerseys each season.

You know that bats must be popular when players collect them. Whenever I'm in a player's home, I know that I'll inevitably find a row of bats neatly displayed in the trophy room or family room. Such a display is a tribute to all the players they've competed with and against. (See Figure 4-5.)

Figure 4-5:
A bat autographed by Babe Ruth, Mel Ott, and Jimmie Foxx.

Photo courtesy Leland's Auctions

Proving game use

The only problem with bats is proving game use. Some players have *gamers* that they use for games and others that they only swing in batting practice. Because they often keep more than a dozen bats in a rack, even they don't know which bats were used, or when. (Ballplayers are a superstitious lot, so they will stick with a hot bat until it breaks. But because even the best players fail 70 percent of the time at the plate, they're forever switching bats.)

When determining whether a bat is legitimate, don't assume that it must be a Louisville Slugger made by Hillerich & Bradsby of Louisville, Kentucky. Though Hillerich & Bradsby continues to provide the vast majority of bats to major leaguers, a number of smaller companies, such as Kissimmee Stixx, Young Bat Co., Glomar, and Carolina Club, have started producing bats in recent years. These companies usually start by giving players some bats for free, hoping that the players will enjoy the product and order some more. Sometimes the player does, and sometimes he doesn't. Sometimes he just puts them into the rack and uses them occasionally. Or he may just use them for batting practice.

Sometimes the quality of wood can help a collector determine whether a bat is game-used. When a player gets a shipment of bats, he examines them closely. Most players believe that the fewer rings in the grain of the bat, the older and better the wood. They'll set aside bats with more rings to give away to team auctions, friends, or other players. (Players themselves don't care where or whether a bat was used. They just want a signed bat with the player's signature logo on it.) So if you see a bat with fewer rings and noticeable game use, it's more likely to be an authentic, game-used bat and thus have more collectible value.

Note: Don't be surprised if you see far more bats of today's players than those of yesterday's stars. It's not just because there were fewer collectors years ago or because many years have passed. Inferior wood quality also accounts for the increasing number of bats from today's players. The quality of northern white ash lumber that is used to make bats has declined over the years. Some players in the '40s and '50s often went through an entire season with three or four bats. In recent years, however, players may go through four bats in ten minutes of batting practice.

Repairing broken bats

Memorabilia collectors debate whether a cracked or broken bat should be repaired. Obviously, a cracked or damaged bat has been used at some level. Many hobbyists feel that sports memorabilia should not be restored. In fact, only the most unscrupulous card dealers try to repair a card and pass it off as a card in better condition. Bats, however, are a different story. The general consensus is that gluing or fixing a broken bat is permissible, as long as you tell potential buyers that the bat has been restored.

Authenticating bats

Unlike the jersey market, where a collector must make sure that a game-used jersey is not one of the thousands of replica "game" jerseys, bat collectors don't have to worry as much about replicas. There's little market for replica bats. In fact, few wooden bats are produced outside of professional baseball, because they're not used in college, high school, or youth competition.

You still need to watch for pitfalls to avoid when purchasing a game-used bat. Ask yourself the following questions when authenticating bats.

> ✔ **Is the bat the right length, weight, brand, and model number for the particular player?** Players routinely receive bats not tailored to their specifications. These, obviously, are discarded. Knowing what bat company a player uses takes a little research, especially with all the newer bat companies coming along. Barry Bonds, for instance, started using bats from the Young Bat Co. in 1997. That does not mean that he used Young exclusively or that he'll continue to use Young. But if a collector knows that Bonds has used Young, at least a good possibility exists that the bat is legitimate.

> I know what you're thinking. *How the heck am I supposed to know what brand of bat a guy uses?* Finding out this information is easier than you think. Just pay close attention when you watch television. If you familiarize yourself with the various brand logos, you can recognize them when the camera focuses closely on the batter, especially between pitches. I didn't believe that this advice would work until representatives from bat companies told me that's how they determine whether a player is using their bats. You need a little patience and a keen eye, but it works.

> ✔ **Is the player's name printed on the bat?** In the case of Louisville Slugger bats made since the early '90s, the player's team name has been block-printed beneath his embossed signature on the barrel of the bat. This identification can help put a date on the bat. But because players change teams so frequently, they may still be using bats from two teams ago. Some bat companies print team names, others don't, and some do so inconsistently. Louiville Slugger, however, prints the team name on each bat.

✔ **Does the bat show wear?** Obviously, someone else besides the player could have taken the bat and played softball with it for the weekend. Or another player could have used a bat. So just because a bat shows wear does not make it legitimately game-used. On the other hand, if it shows no wear whatsoever, it probably was never used.

✔ **How close are the grains on the bat?** Because most players discard bats with too many grains, a bat with very close grains probably was never actually used.

Other Game-Used Equipment

If a piece of equipment is used in a sporting event, you can bet that someone's in the market for it. Although baseball dominates the game-used market as it does the rest of the sports memorabilia field, numerous items from other sports are also highly collectible. (Every so often, you'll see a jockstrap or athletic supporter find its way into an auction. Don't look to me for advice on how to authenticate such items. I'm not going to, um, touch that. You're on your own.)

Football

Game-used helmets are rare, if only because a player often goes through an entire season with just one. (See Figure 4-6.) Plus, a proper football helmet is expensive even if wasn't used by someone in the National Football League. So prepare to pay accordingly. Fortunately for collectors, the steep cost scares away some of the unscrupulous people who would pass off a replica helmet as the real thing. A collector should look for signs of helmet wear; linemen naturally have more scratches and marks on their helmets than wide receivers.

Figure 4-6: Helmets from the Buffalo Bills and the Detroit Lions.

Photos by Tom DiPace

Cleats are fairly common collectibles, as are gloves used by linemen or wide receivers. Not many collectors are interested in pads, because they don't have a logo on them. Other items to consider collecting are any types of documentation used by coaches during the game, including "play cards" that list and diagram a team's offensive plays.

Basketball

Basketball doesn't provide many collectible opportunities because the players don't wear much besides uniforms and shoes. Warm-up suits are pretty common (see Figure 4-7), but not many collectors are interested in them. In many instances, warm-up suits have no distinguishing features — other than size — that give you an indication of who used it. Plus, so many of these outfits through the years have been just plain cheesy (see Figure 4-8).

Figure 4-7: A 1980 Kareem Abdul Jabbar warm-up jersey from the Lakers.

Photo courtesy Leland's Auctions

Hockey

Hockey sticks are very popular among collectors (shown in Figure 4-9), and helmets also appeal to some collectors. Goalie masks, especially the elaborate ones of recent years (see Figure 4-10), are very rare because players can use them for long periods. Like football helmets, they're expensive to begin with, so players go through only a few. Because of the cost of making replica masks, it's not worth it for someone to purchase a replica and try to pass it off as a game-used item.

Figure 4-8:
A 1994 Karl Malone All-Star game game-worn jersey.

Figure 4-9:
Game-used sticks from Gordie Howe and Bobby Hull.

Figure 4-10:
A 1995 Bill Ranford goalie's mask.

Chapter 5

Unusual and Oddball
Sports Collectibles

*M*any sports collectors limit their memorabilia to cards, autographs, and game-used equipment. They assume that not much else is available — at least not much worth saving.

But wait just a minute. Many collectors, especially in recent years, have abandoned the Big Three niches of sports collecting — cards, autographs, and game-used equipment — in favor of oddball memorabilia. Many people have become interested in this catch-all category of figurines, publications, and bric-a-brac. Unfortunately, wherever there's a market, someone inevitably has published a price guide on the topic. Still, the great thing about oddball memorabilia is that it remains relatively uncharted territory, with few price guides and few collectors.

For example, suppose that you have a cardboard movie display from the film *Bull Durham,* starring Kevin Costner and Susan Sarandon. The display is the type that may have stood in the lobby of a movie theater for a few weeks before the movie was released in the summer of 1988. How rare is it, you may ask? Is it worth anything? And is there a market for it? The great thing about oddball merchandise is that the answer to all three questions is "maybe." Someone may price it at $10. Someone else may try to get $100 for it. But, unlike cards, memorabilia, and jerseys, the cardboard cutout really is rare because few people have access to movie stand-ups and few people collect them. Of course, those same reasons help explain why there may be little market for such items. But because your mission is, first and foremost, to assemble a unique collection for a modest price, you can't go wrong with oddball merchandise.

The Strength of Collecting Oddball Merchandise

You're probably wondering whether collecting oddball merchandise does not go against the general rule of having a theme to your collection. Actually, it fits in perfectly with the rule because oddball collecting is one of the easiest ways to specialize. You can specialize by collecting a piece of oddball merchandise from every niche related to a certain player. Or you can specialize in the niche itself.

For instance, suppose that you're collecting Cal Ripken memorabilia. This task is daunting, given the amount of available Ripken-related merchandise and the many Ripken collectors you will be competing against. Suppose that you've managed to collect hundreds of Ripken cards. Plus, you've obtained a couple legitimate autographs. Perhaps you've even purchased a game-used jersey through legitimate channels that left you feeling very good about its authenticity. For many collectors, these possessions may be enough.

But is your collection complete? Hardly. You can expand by collecting Cal advertising pieces. Maybe you can find a Cal's Choice milk carton or a Cal candy bar wrapper from the early '90s. (See Figure 5-1.) Over the years, Ripken also served as a spokesperson for everything from the Mid-Atlantic Dairy Marketers to Coca-Cola to True Value Hardware to the Adventure World amusement park in Maryland. These advertisements generated posters, packaging, and life-size cardboard stand-ups of Ripken that were set up in stores.

Because Ripken is the Baltimore Orioles most recognizable player, he's been included on the cover of several media guides, along with advertising for Home Team Sports, a regional cable network that carries Orioles home games. When I lived in northern Virginia, my cable bill occasionally included a flyer or schedule of upcoming televised games with Cal featured prominently.

Ripken has appeared on more than 100 magazine covers, ranging from *Sports Illustrated* to *GQ* to *The Washington Post Sunday Magazine*. He has appeared once or twice a year on the cover of *USA Today Baseball Weekly* since its inception in 1991 and has made several appearances on the cover of *The Sporting News*. Ripken's picture has been featured in several of the annual preseason baseball magazines that come out each spring, along with the *Baseball America* almanac and several in-depth statistical books produced by Stats Inc. Publishing. Plus, Ripken has written his autobiography, *The Only Way I Know* and a coffee-table-sized book called *Cal on Cal*, and cowritten a book on fantasy baseball. And several writers have written unauthorized books on Ripken. The point here is not to make you feel

Figure 5-1:
The Cal Bar candy wrapper.

overwhelmed, but to help you realize that numerous "oddball" items are available at card shops and shows beyond the familiar realm of cards, autographs, and game-used memorabilia.

With many players, the amount of memorabilia produced decreases as their career winds down. Not so with Ripken. When he broke Lou Gehrig's consecutive-games-played streak in 1995, a cottage industry sprung up around the event. Commemorative newspapers, T-shirts, and lithographs were produced. Scalpers sold the tickets to the record-tying and record-breaking games at Oriole Park at Camden Yards for hundreds of dollars, and collectors were paying premiums for the tickets — which were not torn at the turnstiles — after the game. Coca-Cola produced a commemorative bottle. The American League even produced a special baseball for the game, with Ripken's No. 8 emblazoned in orange. Many collectors feel that anything even remotely related to their favorite player is an integral part of their collection.

But that's not the end of the Ripken merchandise. Any baseball product licensed in the last decade is likely to have included Ripken. You can find Starting Lineup sports figures, bobbin' head dolls, Ripken plaques, commemorative plates, pins, buttons, pennants, and photos.

Yes, the list seems endless, but it does have a theme: Ripken. You can also organize your collection by focusing on one aspect of oddball collecting, such as Starting Lineup figures, sports-related Coca-Cola bottles, programs, or ticket stubs.

Even narrowing your collecting goals in this manner can present a daunting challenge. The key to preserving your sanity and assembling a worthwhile sports memorabilia collection is to focus. This advice is especially valuable in oddball collecting.

How Oddball Items Become Collectibles

The great thing about oddball collectibles is that they became collectibles by accident. This makes perfect sense. If everyone had collected baseball cards in the 1950s with an eye toward their investment potential, keeping them in pristine condition as opposed to flipping them and placing them in bicycle spokes, would the Bowman and Topps cards of that era be worth anything? A little, to be sure, but not nearly as much as they are today. But because most people looked at cards as playthings rather than collectibles, ultimately throwing them away, relatively few remained, with certainly precious few in mint condition. Hence, they became rare collectibles. (Turn to Chapter 2 to find out more about sports cards.)

The problem with so much of today's sports collectibles market is that everything is produced with the investor/speculator in mind. Yet, the term "new memorabilia" is really an oxymoron. The term memorabilia implies something that reminds us of yesteryear. Of course, if you save something long enough, you'll have a memory of yesteryear. These days, everyone saves things with the hope that they will increase in value. But it doesn't work that way anymore. If you bought a set of Fleer baseball cards in 1981 for $15 — the going rate at the time — you'd now have something worth just $35.

Nothing's wrong with collecting recently produced memorabilia that won't appreciate significantly. Even if you're not in sports collecting for the money, you still may want to focus your efforts on things that years from now will be regarded as unique and unusual. To do that, you often need to travel off the beaten path, into the realm of oddball collectibles.

The unlikely collectible

You're probably wondering whether you should collect newly-produced sports memorabilia. After all, almost everything may have some investment potential if you wait long enough. For example, 30 years ago, few people thought baseball cards would be worth anything.

The Starting Lineup figures are another example of collectibles that were slow to show any value. In 1988, Kenner Products introduced this line of goofy plastic sports figures amid very little fanfare. The figures included a baseball series of 124 players, a basketball line of 85 players, and a football series of 137. (Hockey came along later.) These figures, which came neatly packaged in plastic and cardboard, much like a Matchbox toy car, sold for a mere $3.97 each. Today the entire baseball series is worth $3,000. The basketball set is valued at $5,000, and the football edition can fetch $7,000.

In 1988, however, nobody thought of Starting Lineups as collectibles; they were silly toys. Many stores couldn't give them away, and several dealers with foresight bought up the extra stock. Today you can find Starting Lineup price guides and collector's clubs. Starting Lineup collectors gather for regional and national conventions. This product is one of the more popular niches in "oddball collecting."

Remember that most memorabilia with true, lasting collectible value came about by accident. If everyone is collecting it, chances are that everyone will have it years from now and it will never be worth much.

Photo by Tom DiPace

Duke Snider and Dale Murphy as Starting Lineups

The important thing to remember about oddball memorabilia is that it's no longer that unusual, especially now that many collectors have gotten their fill of cards, autographs, and game-used merchandise. If anything, oddball collecting has gone mainstream in recent years, with many hobbyists focusing their attention on a growing number of niches off the beaten path.

Your goal is not to make money in sports collecting, because sports memorabilia is a terrible investment. Instead, you should try to put together a unique collection of modestly priced merchandise that *could* increase in value because it's relatively rare.

Stadium Seats and Fixtures

For years, no one thought to save old stadium seats. When the wrecking ball was taken to such classic ballparks as Brooklyn's Ebbets Field, The Polo Grounds in New York, and Pittsburgh's Forbes Field, no one was clamoring for seats, signs, and fixtures that were part of the stadium. Not surprisingly, relatively few seats from such parks are around, and those that are available sell for thousands of dollars at auction. (See Figure 5-2.)

Figure 5-2: An original Ebbets Field triple seat.

Photo courtesy Leland's Auctions

These days, with new sports facilities springing up across the country, old stadiums are being torn down. And because teams realized that they could find a market for anything attached to the facility, they began to sell off just about anything. As a result, sometimes fans got some remarkable bargains, even in recent years. In 1987, the Detroit Tigers booster club sold original Tiger Stadium seats for $5! A year later, the Chicago Cubs removed many of the original wooden seats from Wrigley Field and sold them for $15.

By 1990, the market had changed. Jerry Reinsdorf, the owner of the Chicago Bulls and White Sox, made sure that his baseball team wasn't giving away any part of Old Comiskey Park after it was torn down. Seats were sold for $250. The club sold bricks, signs, fixtures, and vials of infield dirt encased in plastic cubes and marketed as Christmas ornaments. Unfortunately for collectors, those prices have set the tone for stadium sales that have taken place since.

Seats usually are sold individually or in groups of two, three, or four. However, most ballpark seats are fastened to concrete so that they do not stand by themselves. You may have to fasten them to wooden platforms to make them functional in an office or family room.

Find out well in advance what a team plans to do with the fixtures in a ballpark scheduled for demolition. When the Atlanta Braves demolished Fulton County Stadium in 1997, hundreds of potential collectibles were buried in rubble. Because the stadium seats could not be removed easily from their original home, only a few hundred seats were made available to collectors. The Braves, for whatever reason, did not put too much effort into selling off stadium fixtures. Perhaps the team has so much money that it figured saving the seats wasn't worth the time. A few persistent collectors, however, lobbied the team for items. Several dealers actually went to the demolition site and struck a deal with construction workers for signs and fixtures. You never know what a little resourcefulness will yield.

Don't forget about all the other collectibles that you can salvage from a stadium. (See Figure 5-3.) Look for locker room signs, press box signs, yard markers, advertising pieces, scoreboard parts, aisle signs, clubhouse lockers, restroom signs, and turnstiles. The best way to authenticate such items is to get a letter from the club. Another idea is to photograph a fixture in the stadium while it's still in use, but you need to plan ahead.

I'm not forgetting the other sports here. However, the collectible interest for National Football League arenas and indoor basketball and hockey facilities has never been as great. Many indoor arena seats seem no different from the ones you sit in at a movie theater. (But check out Figure 5-4.) In addition, collectors don't seem to get attached to NFL stadiums, because they don't have the history of baseball parks. And besides, fans sit in football stadium seats for only eight games a season.

Figure 5-3:
A Yankee
Stadium
sign —
complete
with graffiti.

Photo courtesy Leland's Auctions

Figure 5-4:
Who
wouldn't
want a
Boston
Garden
aisle seat?

Photo courtesy Leland's Auctions

Figures

If you think that toy statues and action figures are just kiddie playthings, think again. In the sports collecting hobby, they account for some of the most popular and valuable collectibles.

The bottom line on seat collecting

Unless you have deep pockets and plenty of storage space for your collection, you may not want to become a serious stadium seat collector. Seat collecting, however, is one of the most unique sports collectibles. After all, it's one thing to show visitors to your home a card collection or a bunch of framed autographed photos. It's quite another to invite them to sit down in a seat from an old, classic ballpark.

Die-hard seat collectors believe that wooden seats from older stadiums are more legitimate, much like jersey collectors prefer flannels over knits. Seat collectors also debate whether or not repainting or restoring a seat is permissible. Most collectors seem to think that repainting is fine, as long as you match the paint color to the original color. Other collectors believe that painting alters the seat's integrity and collectible value. You'll get an argument either way. Ballpark seats are best when they look nice and can be used, so I'd go with the restoration route.

Photo courtesy Leland's Auctions

A Yankee Stadium seat from the 1923 opening

Hartland statues

Some of the more popular collectibles from the 1960s are Hartland baseball figurines. Because they were regarded as toys initially, many of them were discarded or damaged through heavy handling.

Hartland Plastics manufactured the figurines between 1958 and 1963 as a way to avoid layoffs during winter production lulls. The line consisted of 18 baseball stars along with 2 smaller statues known as the bat boy and the minor leaguer. (The bat boy and the minor leaguer were frequently used by bakeries as birthday cake decorations.) The 8-inch statues sold at ballpark concession stands and retail outlets for $2.98. The set consists of Hank Aaron, Luis Aparicio, Ernie Banks, Yogi Berra, Rocky Colavito, Don Drysdale, Nellie Fox, Dick Groat (see Figure 5-5), Harmon Killebrew, Mickey Mantle, Roger Maris, Eddie Mathews, Willie Mays, Stan Musial, Babe Ruth, Duke Snider, Warren Spahn, and Ted Williams.

Figure 5-5:
Dick Groat
as a
Hartland
statue.

Photo courtesy Leland's Auctions

The two most valuable players in the set, ironically, are the two of the lesser players. Only 5,000 figurines were made of Groat, the Pittsburgh Pirates shortstop, and only 10,000 were produced of Colavito, an outfielder for the Detroit Tigers. By contrast, up to 150,000 figurines were made of players such as Aaron, Mays, Mantle, Ruth, and Williams.

Prices of the Hartland statues vary depending on condition. Hartlands have a tendency to yellow over time. The whiter a Hartland, the higher its value. Hartlands were packaged in cardboard boxes and came with a name tag attached to the player by a string. Because people often discarded the box and the tag, they can add to a Hartland's value. A collector hoping to assemble a complete set of Hartlands in top condition should plan to pay up to $6,000. But you can pick up Hartland figurines of mass-produced players, such as Fox, Mathews, and Spahn, in lesser, yellowed condition, for as little as $100 apiece.

In 1988, Hartland produced a 25th anniversary edition of the statues. Ten thousand of each of the original 18 figurines were reproduced and sold for $25 each. The new Hartland figurines came with a 25th anniversary label on the back of each player's belt.

The new Hartland figurines are fine, but why settle for less than the original? For the price of a few reproductions, which now sell for $50 to $100 in the secondary market, you can buy the real item, albeit of a lesser player. Things that never were intended to be collectibles usually are the ones that have lasting memorabilia value.

Bobbin' head dolls

Like Hartland figurines, bobbin' head dolls were not viewed as collectibles when they were first produced by a Denmark-based company in the 1960s and imported by Sports Specialties of Los Angeles. The funky dolls had heads connected to the base by a spring. When the heads were tapped, they had a tendency to bob.

Bobbin' head dolls were not built to last, and many that remain are chipped or dinged up. Originally made of papier-mâché, the dolls sold for $2.95 or less at ballpark souvenir stands or by mail order. They're a prime example of how the thing that you may least expect to become collectible actually does so. Many "bobbers" came with magnetic bases and were placed on the dashboards of cars.

Initially, the figures were not of players, but of mascots in team uniforms. For example, the Cubs doll had a bear head, and the Pirates doll had a buccaneer head. The mascot dolls had bases in different colors, depending on when they were produced, which contributes to their value. From 1961 to 1962, dolls of Roberto Clemente, Mickey Mantle, Roger Maris, and Willie Mays were released (see Figure 5-6), with a plastic version of Hank Aaron made in the mid-1970s when Aaron was finishing his career with the Milwaukee Brewers. Because Clemente was the least popular of the group at the time, fewer of his dolls were produced and saved. Now, however, Clemente is one of the most popular players among individual collectors, so his doll is the most valuable.

Each of the player dolls came on a white base with a facsimile autograph reproduced as a decal. Other lines of dolls showed baseball players in uniform with a cartoonish boy face. As the bobbin' head doll fad began to fade in the late '60s, so did the number of dolls being produced. The papier-mâché dolls were replaced with plastic replicas that were easier to produce. Hockey and football dolls also were produced at various times during the '60s.

Figure 5-6:
Mays,
Maris, and
Mantle as
bobbin'
head dolls.

Individual teams continued to produce generic bobbin' head dolls into the '90s. (Remember the Joe Piscopo bobbin' head doll skit on *Saturday Night Live* in the '80s?) Not until 1992, however, did a company enter the business on a grand scale. That year, Sports Accessories and Memorabilia (SAM) began selling hand-painted, ceramic figurines produced in a factory in Taiwan. Its first line consisted of Ken Griffey Jr., Babe Ruth, and Tom Seaver. SAM is now licensed by all four major sports leagues, and its figurines have depicted Kirby Puckett, Mike Schmidt, Ted Williams, Troy Aikman, John Elway, Brett Favre, Roger Staubach, Gordie Howe, Wayne Gretzky, Mario Lemieux, Larry Bird, Michael Jordan, David Robinson, and Dale Earnhardt, among others. (See Figure 5-7.)

Figure 5-7:
Emmitt
Smith and
Brian
Leetch
immortalized
as figurines.

Bobbin' head dolls are one of the few vintage collectibles that you can find regularly at flea markets, antique stores, and estate sales. People have a tendency to overlook the dolls, with their generic, goofy look and flimsy construction, and not realize that many of them are worth hundreds of dollars. Always be on the lookout for the '60s bobbers. The SAM dolls, although hardly vintage, have received a positive response from individual player collectors. The dolls are unlikely to have any lasting collectible value, but they bear a strong likeness to the actual players and make a good addition to any single-player collection.

Starting Lineup

Even after the success of Hartlands and bobbin' head dolls, most collectors dismissed the collectible value of Kenner's Starting Lineup figures when they were first released in 1988. Most collectors thought of the figures as playthings, but they quickly developed a cult following. Starting Lineups took a while to catch on with collectors. Once they did, the earlier, undercollected editions soared in value. Consider the complete set values of the football lines, according to *Tuff Stuff* magazine: 1988 ($7,000), 1989 ($6,000), 1990 ($2,000). In 1991, Kenner cut the football line from 75 to 26 players. The 1991 set, according to *Tuff Stuff,* is worth $650.

Kenner began with baseball, football, and basketball in 1988, not adding hockey until 1993. Kenner has compensated for sagging interest by making its regular set smaller and producing more lines. Its 1997 basketball products, for instance, included an 8-player "extended set," a 6-man "backboard kings" edition, and a 5-player set of 14-inch figures, as opposed to the standard 4-inch figures — all in addition to the standard set of 38 players.

Many of the early lines were distributed regionally, making it difficult for a fan in Miami to find a John Elway as easily as a Dan Marino. Some areas apparently had little distribution at all.

Some of the most valuable Starting Lineup figures are four Utah Jazz players from 1988. According to *Tuff Stuff,* future Hall of Famers Karl Malone and John Stockton are worth $700 and $500, respectively. Even long-forgotten Thurl Bailey and Mark Eaton are worth $250 apiece.

In many of the earlier editions, some of the lesser players are more valuable because the stars were more widely distributed. Some of the more valuable members of the 1990 baseball set, according to *Tuff Stuff,* include infielder Jack Howell ($100), pitcher Mike Witt ($120), and outfielder Devon White ($140). Like the 1988 Utah Jazz, the 1989 Angels Starting Lineup figures were not widely circulated. Of course, now that Kenner has decreased the size of its sets, few figures count as "lesser players."

Starting Lineup collectors want figures only if they're in their original packaging. That quest has contributed to the value of the early editions, because many buyers took the figures out of the boxes. Many of the 1988 and 1989 figures that were sold were opened, further limiting the collectible supply from that era. Unfortunately, unopened Starting Lineup figures are a little unwieldy to display or store.

When *Tuff Stuff* started publishing a Starting Lineup price guide, some of the innocence of collecting was lost. Now numerous price guides, both published and online, are available. Fans gather for Starting Lineup conventions and collectors clubs. At most major sports memorabilia shows, you can see at least a couple booths devoted solely to the figures.

Starting Lineup figures are a nice addition to any individual player collection. Be prepared, however, to pay dearly for 1988 and 1989 versions of such popular players as Cal Ripken, Dan Marino, Joe Montana, Tony Gwynn, and Nolan Ryan. If you're collecting the whole line of Starting Lineup figures, remember that everyone has jumped on this bandwagon. Still, always be on the lookout for older Starting Lineup figures that have been on store shelves for years. You never know what some mom-and-pop toy store may still have lying around.

Publications

It seems like everyone collects publications, whether by intention or just because they were left lying around. Because publications are mass-produced, they usually have limited memorabilia value. But in many cases, they have become sought-after collectibles.

Magazines

Any magazine that has a sports figure on the cover is somewhat collectible. Hobbyists like magazines for their content and cover image but also because they're suitable for autographs. Magazines don't have much collectible value, however, because everyone saves them. Even magazines from the '40s and '50s routinely show up at yard sales.

Still, magazines are a good, affordable addition to any themed collection. The two most popular periodicals among collectors are *Sports Illustrated* and *The Sporting News.*

TIP

Putting your issue of *Sports Illustrated* to work

It pays to be creative if you're an autograph seeker. While covering the baseball strike in 1994–95, I witnessed a collector approach Donald Fehr, the executive director of the Players Association, with a copy of the June 22, 1981, edition of *SI*, which featured a story on that summer's baseball strike. Fehr, who was second in command to Marvin Miller during that work stoppage, shrugged and signed. Most fans don't like to think of strikes and lockouts, but I guess this collector appreciated the historic significance of having Fehr's signature.

✔ The first issue of *The Sporting News (TSN)* was published in 1886, although it was not printed with a large color cover photo until 1964. Before then, *TSN* looked much like a regular broadsheet newspaper. Until the late '80s, *TSN* focused its efforts on baseball; for a long time it was referred to as "The Bible of Baseball." Some people collect *TSN* for its content, which is a little odd considering that it's widely available on databases and library microfiche. The magazine is more popular among collectors focusing on individual players. Unfortunately, because it was printed on newsprint before 1998, old copies of *TSN* have a tendency to yellow over time.

✔ The premier issue of *Sports Illustrated (SI)* was released August 16, 1954, and has become quite a collectible, valued around $300. *SI* is very popular among autograph collectors, so much so that Upper Deck Authenticated markets framed *SI* magazines signed by athletes it has under contract.

You'll have no problem finding old copies of *SI*. (See Figure 5-8.) Although several price guides are available, you don't need to pay book value; you can find back issues of *SI* for less than $1 a copy at flea markets, antique stores, and library sales. Many collectors prefer copies without mailing labels attached to the cover. The most valuable copies of *SI*, ironically, are the only ones that don't feature professional athletes. The annual swimsuit issue, of course, is the most popular among readers *and* collectors.

Numerous other magazines, particularly those that feature individual players on the cover, interest collectors. *Sport* and *Inside Sports* have beautiful covers each month. The annual yearbooks produced by publishers such as Street and Smith's, Athlon Sports, and others usually feature the top stars on the cover. In early 1998, ESPN launched its own magazine, which

Figure 5-8:
A vintage
copy of
*Sports
Illustrated,*
featuring
Mickey
Mantle,
from June
18, 1956.

will be published every other week. Many sports franchises put out their own magazines, and countless unofficial or "underground" pubs are produced. Hobby magazines such as *Beckett's, Tuff Stuff,* and *Sports Cards* are popular as collectibles themselves because they usually put only big-name stars on the covers.

A magazine does not have to focus on sports to attract the interest of sports collectors. Through the years, sports figures have appeared on the covers of numerous publications, including *Time, Life, Newsweek,* and *GQ. Playboy* regularly includes interviews and feature stories on athletes, although they never appear on the cover, of course.

Newspapers

Newspapers have never been popular among sports collectors. Perhaps it's because newspapers yellow and crumble over time. Perhaps it's because they're tough to display and store. Perhaps it's because they're still mostly black and white. These days, many papers produce commemorative issues of historic events on slick glossy paper that are suitable for framing. The availability of those special editions has contributed to the decline of sports collectible interest in newspapers.

Still, as a writer for *USA Today Baseball Weekly* since 1991, I know that some sports collectors have an interest in newspapers. Whenever the paper features a popular player such as Cal Ripken or Ken Griffey Jr. on the cover, a handful of collectors call and ask for a dozen issues. My colleagues at *USA Today* get similar requests. (Before you grab the phone, please note that the paper charges for back issues, and you may not get them for several weeks. If you see a player featured prominently in either publication, you're better off just buying a stack of them at the local convenience store.)

Baseball Weekly (shown in Figure 5-9), like the pre-1998 version of *The Sporting News,* is printed on newsprint and has a tendency to yellow over time. Another tabloid sports publication that was printed on newsprint but that has gone largely unnoticed by collectors is *The National Sports Daily.* Printed from January 1990 until June 1991, *The National* had an all-star cast of sportswriters and offered readers a heavy dose of sports every day. It had beautiful color covers, but only a few were saved. Perhaps collectors looked at it as a newspaper rather than a magazine, even though it had more daily content than many thick monthly periodicals.

Figure 5-9:
*USA Today
Baseball
Weekly.*

Programs, scorecards, and yearbooks

Programs from baseball, football, and basketball games and scorecards from baseball games are among the most commonly purchased and saved collectibles, even by noncollectors. Programs and scorecards are only of modest value, unless they're at least 30 years old. Super Bowl and World Series programs, for instance, have been so widely sold outside the stadium through newsstands and on television that they're pretty common.

Collectors debate whether or not scorecards should be scored. Collectors who prefer things in mint condition want them left blank. Others like to see what happened during the game, especially if something noteworthy took place. Personal preference is what matters, of course. But because everything in the sports collecting hobby has a price, many experts will tell you that scorecards are more valuable when they're blank.

Some collectors like team yearbooks, but teams don't seem to produce yearbooks like they did in the 1970s and early 1980s. Because many of them began cranking out team magazines and monthly programs over the course of the season, they probably figured that they didn't need a yearbook, too. Yearbooks, however, make great collectibles from past seasons and can be had for very affordable prices. (See Figure 5-10.)

A 1963 New York Yankees program and scorecard

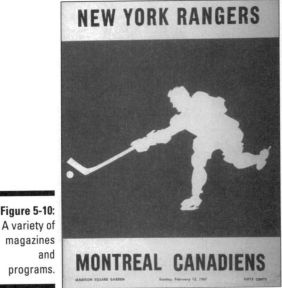

Figure 5-10:
A variety of
magazines
and
programs.

A New York Rangers program from 1967

A 1979 World Series program
(Baltimore Orioles and
Pittsburgh Pirates)

Photos by Tom DiPace

Media guides

Some people may classify media guides as publications, but other collectors place them in their own category. Mass-produced in recent years, they're readily available — and not just to members of the working press. (See Figure 5-11.) Many teams sell them at stadium souvenir stands and at stadium stores, usually priced from $6 to $10, and distribute them free to season ticket holders. Baseball guides almost always are $4^{1}/_{2}$ x 9 inches; football, basketball, and hockey guides often are smaller. Because they're the complete reference tool for journalists, the guides are chock-full of player biographies, photos, organizational charts, and every statistic imaginable.

As collectibles, media guides are most popular among individual player collectors; a franchise player is likely to appear on the cover of a guide every three years or so. Other collectors prefer to put together a complete run of their favorite team, and a few fans try to collect them all. Media guides have been widely distributed over the last 30 years, so they generally have not appreciated in value. Older guides, however, can be worth $75 to $100. A special premium is given to the roster sheets and booklets, the precursors to media guides, that were produced in the 1920s and 1930s.

Figure 5-11:
Media guides from the 1997 Oakland A's (with Mark McGwire) and the 1997 New York Yankees.

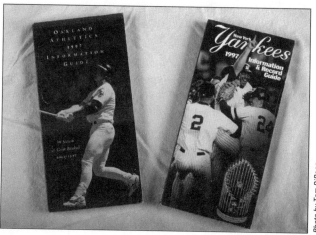

Photo by Tom DiPace

Press Pins

Unlike media guides, press pins are given only to members of the media covering the Super Bowl and baseball's All-Star Game, World Series, and Hall of Fame inductions. The World Series pins were first produced in 1911, with the All-Star pins coming along in 1938. The All-Star Game pin is created with the host city in mind, and each World Series participant produces its own pin. Generally, the winning team's pin becomes more valuable than the losing team's pin, although sometimes one team may produce more pins than the other team. During the 1997 World Series, for instance, the Cleveland Indians press pins seemed to disappear quickly, with late-arriving members of the media getting shut out. Press pins are well constructed and preserved in boxes, so don't compromise when it comes to condition.

Hall of Fame press pins were not produced until 1982. In 1990, the Hall also began issuing "retro" pins, beginning with a pin for 1936 — the first year of Hall of Fame inductions. In 1991, a 1937 pin was issued. In 1992, the Hall issued pins for 1938 and 1955 and has issued two retro pins a year since.

For the first three Super Bowls, beginning with Super Bowl I in 1967, members of the press were issued commemorative "tie bars" that attached neckties to dress shirts. For Super Bowls IV and V, patches were issued. Pins have been issued since Super Bowl VI.

The National Basketball Association has never issued press pins for either the NBA Finals or the All-Star Game. The National Hockey League has issued press pins for its Stanley Cup final since 1970 and its All-Star Game since 1976. More information on press pins can be found at www.recollectics.com.

Because press pins are distributed only to the media, they're relatively rare and yet relatively affordable. Collectors can buy many of the pins produced since 1980 for about $100.

Be sure that you're buying an authentic press pin and not a reproduction. The reproductions often vary little from the real things. (See Figures 5-12 and 5-13.) During the 1997 World Series in Cleveland, the pins sold at souvenir stands looked nearly identical to the ones distributed to the media.

Figure 5-12:
A 1923
New York
Yankees
World
Series pin.

Photo courtesy Leland's Auctions

Figure 5-13:
Recent
World
Series and
All-Star
game press
pins.

Photo by Tom DiPace

Tickets and Stubs

Even if you've never collected sports memorabilia, chances are that you
have some tickets or ticket stubs in a wallet or desk drawer. Everyone likes
to hang onto them as a memory of games attended and as a depressing
reminder of how much less it used to cost to attend sporting events. (See
Figure 5-14.)

Figure 5-14:
A ticket
stub from
Yankee
Stadium,
July 24,
1983.

Unfortunately, because tickets and stubs are so commonplace, the only ones with lasting collectible value are from major events such as the Super Bowl, World Series, National Basketball Association Finals, and NCAA Final Four. Collectors would much rather have the entire ticket than just a stub. (See Figures 5-15 and 5-16.) Why are complete tickets even available? A large percentage of tickets to major events are distributed to rich corporate honchos who show up only at big events, so inevitably some tickets go unused. (Meanwhile, you can't get any closer to the game than your television set!)

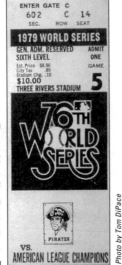

Figure 5-15: A ticket stub from Game 5 of the 1979 World Series in Pittsburgh.

Photo by Tom DiPace

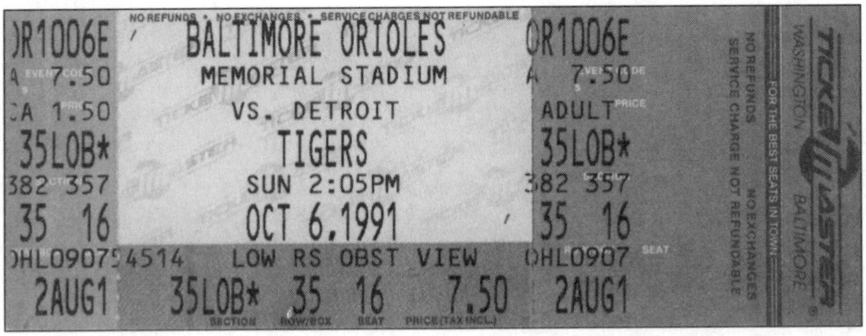

Figure 5-16: A ticket to the last game played at Baltimore's Memorial Stadium on October 6, 1991.

Complete tickets are available for another reason these days. Some teams realize that everyone has the collector mentality, so ticket takers may stamp the backs of tickets instead of tearing off the bottom. At the Tampa Bay Devil Rays home opener at Tropicana Field in 1998, fans even received a hard plastic holder for their ticket as they came through the gate.

When buying tickets from the 1940s and 1950s, always make sure that they have seat numbers. Back then, seat numbers usually were stamped in a different color ink on a separate press run. Tickets without seat numbers most likely were artist's proofs and have little collectible value.

Sometimes tickets become collectible by accident. What if you're at a game where Michael Jordan scores 100 points? You'd have an instantly collectible ticket stub. Late in Nolan Ryan's career, people attended games just because of the possibility that he might throw a no-hitter. If someone is approaching 3,000 hits, the chance always exists that he'll break the record during a certain game. If he's five hits away from a record, he may go 5-for-5 (5 hits in 5 at-bats). Of course, he could be one hit away and then go a week without reaching the milestone.

Not long ago, if a collector was at a game that suddenly became noteworthy — a Ryan no-hitter for instance — he might have approached the ticket office and asked for unused tickets. This approach is still worth trying, but team officials have caught on to this trick and usually will find a way to sell them later to the highest bidder.

Phantom tickets

Phantom tickets are tickets that are produced in anticipation of an event that, for whatever reason, does not occur. As playoff time approaches, teams try to get a jump on planning by selling tickets, just in case. Of course, not everyone makes the playoffs, so teams must offer refunds. Usually, teams insist on getting the tickets back, and given the high cost of postseason tickets these days, few fans keep them as collectibles. But some phantom tickets slip into the market because some fans forget to return theirs or because the team sells them all to a dealer.

You may find phantom tickets from many events through the years, especially baseball.

You may also find phantom press pins. Some phantom items are quite valuable, and they can make wonderful additions to a collection if they fit your theme. For example, if you're a long-suffering Cubs fan — if that's not redundant — you may want a phantom Cubs ticket to the 1984 World Series. That year, of course, the Cubs reached the playoffs but lost to the San Diego Padres.

Try to make friends with the people who work in the ticket offices of professional sports teams. They can help you get your hands on phantom tickets and unused ducats from significant events. Plus, they can help you get tickets when you actually want to attend!

Schedules

Like ticket stubs, schedules tend to pop up during spring cleaning. Even sports fans who aren't collectors usually hang onto them. Schedules are a nice complement to any team or individual player collection. Some collectors even specialize in *skeds*.

The common schedule is a wallet-sized trifold that's given out at the ticket office or to fans requesting information by mail. But you also can find schedules printed on items such as magnets, posters, television schedules, cups, and glasses. Many team sponsors also produce schedules that you can find at gas stations, grocery stores, sports bars, liquor stores, and cable television offices. (See Figure 5-17.)

The next time you see a big cardboard schedule display when you're out shopping, ask the store manager if you can have it when the season is over. Be sure to leave your name and phone number. Better yet, ask if you can write that information on the back of the display. That way, employees will be reminded of your request before they throw it in the trash. You may be surprised to find out how many managers will give you the schedule on the spot.

Figure 5-17: The schedules of the 1986-87 Washington Bullets and the 1978 New York Yankees.

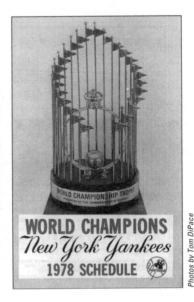

Photos by Tom DiPace

Foods and Beverages

For years, no one thought to save food and beverages that came in sports-themed packaging. If you finished a box of Wheaties or can of Coca-Cola, you simply threw the container away. These days, many "oddball" collectors focus their attention on food and beverage products that feature a sports theme.

Coca-Cola

Coca-Cola has produced some fabulous sports advertising pieces through the years. Unfortunately for sports hobbyists, Coke has its own legions of collectors. Many Coke items, especially vintage advertising pieces, seem grossly overpriced by sports memorabilia standards. Coke has produced commemorative bottles and cans for sporting events for years, and although they're not particularly rare or unusual, they make nice collection pieces.

Coca-Cola produces an amazing number of collectibles commemorating different sports events. (See Figure 5-18.) In 1996, the company produced a bottle when John Smoltz of the Atlanta Braves won the Cy Young Award. The fact that Coke is headquartered in Atlanta and an official sponsor of the Braves probably had a lot to do with the production of the special bottle. But the event also exemplifies Coke's heavy involvement with sports and sports memorabilia.

Figure 5-18: A Coke can commemorating Don Shula's NFL record 325th coaching win.

Photo by Tom DiPace

If you ever attend the Super Bowl or the fan-related carnival known as "The NFL Experience," you'll find lots of Coke-related sports memorabilia. As the title sponsor of "The NFL Experience," Coke produces banners, cans, bottles, and numerous other trinkets commemorating the event.

If you're ever in Atlanta, check out the "World of Coca-Cola" museum downtown. It's a great historical tour of Coca-Cola in its own right, but it has a section on Coke memorabilia, much of it related to sports. You can see promotional pieces related to the Mean Joe Greene campaign of the '70s and get ideas for your own collection. Plus, at the end of the tour, you get to drink all the Coke-related products you want from around the world!

Be very careful about unopened Coke cans. Over time, the soda will eat through the aluminum, creating a sticky mess. Many collectors prefer to drain the cans from the bottom or through a pin prick somewhere in the can.

Canned collectibles

In 1997, sportscard manufacturer Pinnacle Brands issued football and baseball cards in a can. Each can contained ten cards and featured a prominent player on the can. The cans could be opened, with the help of a can opener, but many collectors — especially single-player collectors — preferred to keep them unopened. The cans were considered oddball collectibles more so than cards.

Photo by Tom DiPace

Wheaties boxes

Appearing on a box of Wheaties, the so-called "Breakfast of Champions," is quite an honor. Through the years, Wheaties has pictured everyone from Mary Lou Retton to Pete Rose to Michael Jordan to Cal Ripken. Wheaties is also fond of picturing entire teams, especially Super Bowl and Olympic champions. As with Coca-Cola cans, collectors debate whether or not Wheaties boxes should be opened. Any stale food item is likely to attract bugs and rodents over time, so keep that in mind when making your decision. Some collectors prefer to open the box from the bottom, eat the cereal, and reseal the box. Some collectors even insert wood chips so that the box still seems like it contains cereal. (See Figure 5-19.)

Beer cans and related memorabilia

Beer can collecting isn't quite the fad it was in the '70s, so at least you won't be competing with beer can collectors for sports-related cans. Actually, not too many sports-related beer cans have been produced. Iron City beer has produced cans commemorating the Pittsburgh Steelers and Pirates in the '70s. (See Figure 5-20.) Schmidt's issued four "Casey" beer cans in 1980, featuring Richie Ashburn, Whitey Ford, Monte Irvin, and Duke Snider. In 1990, Old Style beer created cans of Chicago Cubs greats Ron Santo, Billy Williams, and Ferguson Jenkins.

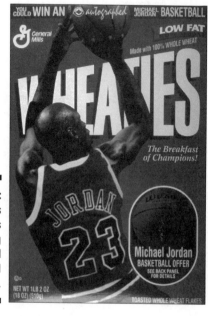

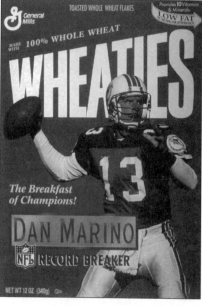

Figure 5-19: Wheaties boxes featuring Michael Jordan and Dan Marino.

Photos by Tom DiPace

Figure 5-20:
The 1979 Pittsburgh Pirates commemorated on an Iron City beer can.

Plenty of beer-related advertising memorabilia is still available. Remember those great Lite Beer ads of the '70s and early '80s that featured everyone from Rodney Dangerfield to Bob Uecker to Mickey Mantle? You also can still find advertising pieces featuring the "Miller Lite All-Stars."

As with Coca-Cola cans, open beer cans from the bottom, so that they at least look new.

Candy bars

Many players have been featured on candy bars through the years, perhaps the surest sign of athletic and celebrity success. In the late 1970s, Standard Brands produced the Reggie! Bar with New York Yankees slugger Reggie Jackson on the wrapper. (See Figure 5-21.) In the early '90s, Pacific Trading Cards marketed a Ken Griffey Jr. bar, and a Maryland company produced candy bars featuring several athletes, including Cal Ripken.

Chocolate bars do not preserve well, so just keep the wrappers. Look for related collectibles, however, such as store display boxes and advertising pieces.

Photo by Tom DiPace

Figure 5-21:
A wrapper
from a
Reggie!
Bar.

NASCAR memorabilia

Because NASCAR is not a stick-and-ball sport, its memorabilia is inherently oddball. Among the popular NASCAR collectibles are racing suits and helmets worn by drivers during races, autographed car hoods and tires, and miniature models of the cars.

Sports Movie Memorabilia

Memorabilia from movies with a sports theme is in plentiful supply. Here's a list of some movies categorized by sport:

- ✔ **Football:** *North Dallas Forty, The Longest Yard,* and *Brian's Song*
- ✔ **Basketball:** *The Fish That Saved Pittsburgh, Hoosiers, White Men Can't Jump,* and *Blue Chips*
- ✔ **Hockey:** *Slap Shot* and *The Mighty Ducks*
- ✔ **Baseball:** *Bull Durham, Field of Dreams, Major League,* and *A League of Their Own*
- ✔ **Golf:** *Caddyshack* and *Tin Cup*

Movie posters autographed by actors make wonderful display items, although the signatures of many actors are worse than those of athletes. Some collectors make a distinction between official movie posters and those sold commercially or produced for video store advertising. Movie posters from the last 20 years have been mass-produced, so they're probably not that collectible because, like recently-printed sports cards, they won't appreciate much in value. Many original posters from '40s and '50s movies, however, are worth hundreds of dollars.

Movie studios also produce cardboard standees that appear in movie theater lobbies and "lobby cards," 11-x-14-inch ad pieces featuring multiple photos. In recent years, memorabilia from the movies themselves has found its way into major auctions. The uniform that Madonna wore in *A League of Their Own,* for instance, sold for $9,000.

Uncut Card Sheets and Proofs

If you're looking for uncut sheets of sports cards from the '70s and '80s, plenty of them are available. In the early '90s, numerous stories circulated about employee theft at card production sites and about executives who covertly directed the sheets into the marketplace themselves. Whether or not those stories are true, avoid overpaying for uncut sheets just for the sake of novelty. So many uncut sheets are for sale that you shouldn't have to pay a premium. Uncut sheets look especially nice when they're framed.

Uncut sheets can easily fit into the theme of your collection. If you collect a particular player, you may want an uncut sheet that features him prominently. Remember, though, that the more valuable the cards in a sheet, the pricier the sheet will be.

Printer's proofs, on the other hand, are a little different from uncut sheets. They're printed on flimsy, slick paper rather than cardstock, to test for ink distribution and registration. Printers mark them up and send them back to press operators to make adjustments. Usually, proofs are tossed out, but when something has a collectible value, inevitably it makes its way into the hobby. Proofs are less common than uncut sheets, but the demand seems to be minimal for something that can look as marked up as a bad term paper. But if they fit the theme of your collection, they're worth picking up.

Sports Advertising Pieces

One of the more popular oddball niches, sports advertising pieces include everything from classic tins of the '50s to posters and promotional items of today. Their cheesy charm makes these items attractive. Many ads, in hindsight, are just hilarious. Remember those goofy Aqua Velva television commercials of the '70s? No doubt you've probably also seen some low-budget local spots featuring hometown heroes in your area. Usually, there's a "print" version of these ads, with the athletes appearing in magazine and newspaper ads. Many baseball players endorsed cigarette and tobacco products in the '50s, and you can still find them, albeit for a premium.

Many quality reproductions have been made of classic advertising pieces. Although seasoned collectors can easily tell the difference, many novices can be fooled. As always, do your homework and make sure that you're really getting the old item that you think you're buying.

Personal Memorabilia

Pick up any major auction catalog, and you're likely to see items that you can't believe a player would want to sell. You'll find championship rings (see Figure 5-22), awards (see Figure 5-23), mini-Super Bowl and World Series trophies, and even personal effects. An interesting story usually is associated with how the items got in the auction. Maybe the player has fallen into financial difficulty or lost the items as part of a divorce settlement. Maybe he gave the items away years ago, and the recipient is now selling them. Maybe the player does not have the collector mentality — you'd be surprised how many don't — and is simply cleaning out a closet. Some athletes sell their belongings to raise money for charity.

Figure 5-22: A 1981 New York Yankees World Series Ring.

Photo courtesy Leland's Auctions

Figure 5-23: Keith Hernandez's Gold Glove Award from 1978.

Photo courtesy Leland's Auctions

Whatever the reason, auctions are a great opportunity to pick up something for your collection, albeit at a steep price. Who wouldn't want a Gold Glove award or a Super Bowl ring?

Many championship rings and trophies are merely salesman's samples, created to give players and team officials a preview of what the real item will look like. Fortunately, auctions distinguish between the samples and the genuine articles. Although salesman's samples make great conversation pieces, the real items have a truer collectible value.

Pennants

The pennant, particularly the baseball pennant, is probably one of the most genuine pieces of Americana. Generations of kids have taken these triangular collectibles home and tacked them onto their bedroom walls. Some collectors and dealers do specialize in pennants, but most look at them as mere novelty items rather than collectibles because they've been produced in large quantities through the years. A strong interest is found in pennants produced before 1960, however.

Pennants are among the most unwieldy collectibles out there. Fortunately, you can buy plastic sleeves or hard Lucite covers to protect them.

Going National

I'm often asked what I collect. As a sportswriter, I'm always interested in things relating to my profession. Perhaps that's why I collect *The National Sports Daily,* a fabulous newspaper that was published from January 1990 until June 1991. The newspaper, the first daily sports publication ever launched in the United States, debuted on January 31, 1990, at the peak of the sports memorabilia explosion. *The National* featured some of the best sports writing and photography anywhere but struggled financially. Because of its short existence, the publication's 400 or so issues are not available on any database or Internet service.

Consider that for a moment. Collectors and fans can find the entire runs of *Sports Illustrated* and *The Sporting News* on microfiche at any public library. But *The National* exists only in the few remaining copies still in circulation. So even though 250,000 copies of *The National* were produced five or six times a week, it ranks as one of the rarest sports collectibles of the past decade because so few were saved. Of course, there's little collectible market for *The National.* Because the publication was the same size as *The Sporting News* and was printed on newsprint, many collectors don't want the hassle of storing it and dealing with yellowing and deterioration. Few sports memorabilia dealers carry old copies of *The National.* Many dealers, as I've discovered, have never heard of it. But it's a publication that I've been collecting for a while — perhaps because as a sportswriter, I appreciate great sportswriting.

I even have a *National* newspaper vending machine that I acquired five years ago, along with about 50 copies of the publication. Every few months, I rotate a different issue through the display window of the vending machine. I don't even have to feed it three quarters, the price when the paper folded. (The paper originally cost 50 cents.) But I'm finding it increasingly difficult to find "new" issues to put in the window. It's one of those rare sports collectibles that isn't included in any price guide.

Plenty of *National*-related memorabilia, including a promotional card picturing Michael Jordan and Patrick Ewing, plus caps, T-shirts, jackets, and other logo merchandise, was produced — the problem is finding the stuff. The promotional cards, handed out the day before the launch date, used to be listed in some price guides for $75 to $100 apiece. One of my favorite *National* collectibles is a promotional placard that I occasionally place in the display window of my machine. It reminds me of the perils of the publishing business. The card reads: "Coming Soon: The National Sports Daily. Changing the Way America Reads Sports."

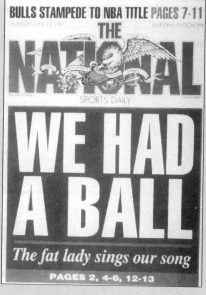

BULLS STAMPEDE TO NBA TITLE PAGES 7-11
THURSDAY, JUNE 13, 1991   OUR FINAL EDITION 75¢
THE NATIONAL SPORTS DAILY
WE HAD A BALL
The fat lady sings our song
PAGES 2, 4-6, 12-13

Photos by Tom DiPace

Part II
Acquisitions: From Shows to Shops to TV

The 5th Wave   By Rich Tennant

"What do you mean, everyone on the bus has to sign the speeding ticket?"

In this part . . .

The chapters in this part show you how to put your sports memorabilia collection together. I tell you how to get the most out of a visit to your neighborhood card shop and explain how sports cards are distributed and how you can get the most for your money. I give you some tips on finding hidden treasures at places such as antique stores, yard sales, and estate sales.

Next, I take you to a sports memorabilia show. You can find out how to prepare for the show so that you will make the most of your time and money. I also explain which shows are worthwhile and which ones aren't worth your time, and I let you know the best time of the show to buy.

You take a "tour" of the sports auction process, read about examples of buying strategies to employ, and find out exactly when to raise your bidding paddle and when to stand pat. I explain the nuances of mail-bid and phone auctions. Finally, I describe how television shopping programs try to unload mostly worthless sports memorabilia on unsuspecting viewers, and I tell you why you should almost never buy sports memorabilia from television.

Chapter 6

The Hunt for Sports Memorabilia Treasure

● ●

In This Chapter

▶ Getting new cards

▶ Finding old cards

▶ Using a dealer

▶ Exploring alternative avenues

▶ Networking toward a collection

● ●

*A*s recently as the early 1980s, a card shop was a rare and unusual place. A collector was likely to find vintage sports cards and loads of oddball merchandise. A collector would not find piles of rookie cards, stacks of unopened boxes of new cards, and recently manufactured memorabilia. Because there were only a few shops in each city, they tended to have a deep inventory and the resources to locate what they didn't have in-house. Many dealers kept their stores so packed that they risked a visit from the fire marshal. They almost always had what collectors were looking for, although they probably had to dig for it.

But like card shows, card shops proliferated in the mid-1980s, and not always for the better: Card shops became watered down, with dealers selling the same freshly minted cards, autographed plaques, and manufactured memorabilia. These days, your neighborhood card shop may have little more than cards from the '80s and '90s, with perhaps a display case full of star cards from the '60s and '70s. You now have plenty of room to walk around because most dealers don't have the financial resources to amass inventory.

Most serious collectors have little use for the typical strip mall card shop. Actually, because of the downturn in the market, only a fraction of the stores open just five years ago still remain. Unfortunately, the downsizing has claimed some of the best card stores. The survivors have to diversify with toys and other hot kiddie products. These days, it's not uncommon to see a sign advertising Beanie Babies in a card shop window.

Does this mean collectors should bypass card stores? Of course not. Just as you can find worthwhile card shows and some quality merchandise on television shopping shows, you can discover many good places carrying sports memorabilia. Just as there are some quality card shows and some quality merchandise on television shopping shows, there are many good places to find sports memorabilia. In this chapter, I show you how.

How New Cards are Distributed

New sports cards, which account for a good chunk of card store sales, often go through several hands before you get a crack at them. Card manufacturers, like food and candy producers, sell by the vending case. Because most card stores cannot sell an entire case of 12 to 20 boxes, each with roughly 30 packs, they buy from distributors. By the time the unopened packs are placed on the shelves for sale, they've taken at least two markups: one from the distributor and one from the card shop owner.

Card stores

I'll never understand how card stores stay in business, especially these days, by relying on new card sales. For instance, if a store owner buys a box of unopened packs of sports cards for $40 a box from the distributor and sells the packs for $75 a box, he makes $35. Of course, it may take months to sell the contents of the box just to make that $35. In the mid-1980s, at the height of the sports card boom, dealers could make a healthy living this way because new cards sold quickly. Many collector/investors bought by the box, not the pack. But not anymore.

Actually, before Upper Deck started producing cards in 1989, most card shop owners had to buy their cards for resale from retail outlets. When the market boomed in the mid-1980s, some owners made arrangements to buy entire shipments from toy or grocery stores. Upper Deck, realizing that a huge market of dealers were willing to buy direct from the company, started distributing directly to card stores. Other manufacturers followed suit.

But even though card store owners now received cards directly from the manufacturer, the shopping clubs could afford to price their cards at lower prices because they bought in greater quantities. Not surprisingly, card dealers complained to the manufacturers. How could they possibly expect to compete with the shopping clubs and retail chains? After all, the dealers were the ones educating consumers on collecting and promoting the hobby. Yet, they were being undercut by the larger companies. The manufacturers tried to remedy the situation by creating "hobby" versions of card sets distributed only to card stores. These have had only modest success. Because collectors are already overloaded with all of the different card lines, this distinction tends to make things even more confusing.

Don't get hung up on "hobby" only card sets. They're just another attempt by the card manufacturers to create a false sense of rarity. Even if these cards are in limited supply, they'll never have any lasting collectible value.

Other outlets

Today's card store has more competition than ever before. Just 15 years ago, card companies distributed cards primarily to grocery, drug, and convenience stores. Today you also find sports cards at shopping clubs, sporting goods stores, newsstands, and toy stores. In many of these places, a collector can buy unopened boxes and sets sealed in cellophane. Because shopping clubs buy in bulk, they can pass the savings on to the customer. Why pay more at a card shop? Of course, like everything else at these outlets, you have to buy a large quantity — you can't expect to purchase only a few packs.

Although shopping clubs may not have much selection when it comes to sports cards, their prices often are very competitive. Why pay more at a card shop because the owner doesn't have the financial resources to buy large quantities?

Shopping clubs may not have much selection in sports cards, but their prices are usually very competitive. I recommend getting what cards you can at a shopping club, and paying the higher prices at card shops only for the items you can't get more cheaply elsewhere.

Finding Older Cards at Card Shops

Unfortunately, locating older cards at a card shop can be difficult. For the most part, card dealers acquire older collections from sellers unfamiliar with the card market. With very little discretionary income to buy vintage inventory, shop owners must rely on naïve customers who wander in with a stash of recently discovered, vintage cards they're looking to unload. Even though almost every sports collectible has a well-publicized price tag, many people who fall into this category still have no idea of the market. So when a dealer offers $100 for a stack of cards from the 1960s and early 1970s, it sounds like a great deal to someone unaware of the sports card market.

If only those people would come knocking on your door! This is how many card store owners stay in business — by buying cards dirt cheap and selling them for a huge profit. Of course, the number of gullible sellers has dwindled in recent years. And because there's little market for anything produced after 1980, a seller probably has to be at least 30 or have acquired a collection from someone that age, to have anything worthwhile. Because fewer of these people are selling, less of this inventory is coming into card stores.

Negotiating

The best part about a card shop is that almost everything is negotiable. If a store owner has a card or memorabilia item marked at $50, chances are that he'll take $35, maybe even $25. Can you realistically expect such a discount when shopping for any other product? Even automobile and diamond dealers will only budge so far. But smart collectibles dealers understand how soft the market is and the importance of turning over inventory to survive, so they are very willing to negotiate.

Unless you're buying packs of new cards, always haggle at a card shop.

A dying breed of card dealers

A thing of the past is the card shop with boxes and boxes of "commons" meticulously sorted and categorized. One of the best things about card shops in days gone by was that collectors could go in with their wish lists and easily locate the last few cards to complete a set. Heck, collectors could just drop off their want list and come back later that day to find their orders filled and waiting. Now, mostly because there are so many card lines, a dealer can't possibly sort all of the cards out there. Fortunately for collectors trying to complete sets, some shop owners still have at least all their cards from the pre-1990s period neatly arranged.

If you do find dealers who specialize in vintage material, treat them like a dying breed, for that's what they are. The past two years have been particularly tough on shop owners. Many deal only at shows or by mail order, or have gotten out of the business completely. But those who remain can be very helpful. Which is why it's important to know your dealer. (See "Knowing Your Dealer," in this chapter.)

Using the bid board

Another way to find a bargain is through a store's *bid board,* where customers can place cards and memorabilia up for auction. The items, with accompanying bidding tags, are generally on display in hard, Lucite plastic holders or in plastic sheets. A deadline is set, generally a week, after which time the item is awarded to the highest bidder, with the store owner taking a commission. Collectors looking to sell prefer this route because they can unload cards the shop owner doesn't want, or at least doesn't want for the price the seller wants. Buyers can purchase the cards for less than they may cost from the dealer. Unfortunately, bid boards aren't as popular as they used to be because of the downturn in the market. Most shop owners find they're not worth the trouble.

Knowing Your Dealer

The best thing about dealers is that almost all of them are collectors themselves. They understand what it's like to have a particular area of interest and how great it feels to locate that elusive item. They realize that everyone works within a budget. Sports memorabilia collecting is one of the few areas left where a customer really does get personalized service.

Find out what the dealer collects. Maybe you have access to items that he doesn't. It's always more fun — and less costly — to trade than to buy and sell.

Of course, the better a customer you are, the more likely you are to receive a high level of attention. A dealer has a way of remembering the names and faces of people who spend money in his shop. Some stores become neighborhood hangouts. Because the owner spends so much time there, he often installs cable TV and tunes the set to a sports channel. All he needs is a liquor license. (If you think about it, there's a fine line between a sports bar — with all of its memorabilia — and a card shop.)

Let a dealer know what you're willing to pay for certain items. He may see one of those items in his travels but not have a chance to contact you. If he knows what you're willing to spend, he can buy the item for you on faith. Of course, technically, you're under no obligation to purchase the item, but you probably should if you want to maintain the relationship.

Many of the nation's larger dealers operate mail-order businesses and offer catalogs on a monthly basis. Although shopping in person is best, buying by catalog can be an effective way to acquire things for your collection. Like anything else you order by mail, be sure to find out the return policy before you buy. The Internet has an impact on the sports collectibles hobby as it does on everything else and can be a great place to locate those hard-to-find items. I talk more about collecting online in Chapter 17.

But even a quality card shop in your area isn't sufficient to build a collection. Because so many collectors are looking for only a few available vintage items, you can't limit your search to the well-traveled channels. Sometimes the best items are found well off the beaten path.

Beyond the Card Shop: Antique Stores, Yard Sales, and Rare Finds

If you spend any time in the sports collectibles field, you start to hear stories of collectors who bought wonderful items for just pennies. Not all these stories date back to the early 1980s, when valuable, old memorabilia started popping up everywhere. You can still make tremendous finds today. You just have to know where to look and be patient.

Many people do not have the collector mentality — even athletes. These people get rid of things as they move and change jobs, not feeling any sense of nostalgia. Whoever said "one man's trash is another's treasure" may have been thinking about sports collectors.

Antique stores

Antique stores are a mixed bag. Most antique dealers don't have a good handle on the sports memorabilia market. When in doubt, they just over-price and hope for the best. It's not unusual to see virtually worthless cards from the 1980s and 1990s displayed under glass at an antique store, as if they're rare and precious commodities. Antique dealers, like everyone else it seems, go by strict price guide figures when it comes to cards.

An antique store can be a great place, however, to find oddball merchandise — advertising pieces, programs, sports-related Coca-Cola memorabilia, and so on — at affordable prices, because antique dealers have a hard time getting a handle on the oddball market.

Some of the best card stores aren't really card stores at all, but parts of antique stores. Because antique dealers naturally gravitate toward vintage merchandise, they're less likely than card shop owners to get hung up on recently manufactured memorabilia. Antique dealers get much of their inventory from walk-ins and estate sales. Because dealers often buy entire estates, they inevitably end up with sports memorabilia.

Auctions, estate sales, and yard sales

Of course, you can just skip the middle man and attend estate sales and auctions yourself. For a list of these, just check your local newspaper. Generally, the older the estate, the more likely you are to find vintage sports memorabilia. So concentrate your efforts on the older parts of town.

Recently, Mastro and Steinbach Sports Auctions of Illinois acquired a huge stash of Mike Ditka's memorabilia. When the former Chicago Bears coach moved to New Orleans, he wanted to start fresh. His wife hired a disposal service to clean out their Chicago home, which included hundreds of trophies, plaques, photos, and knickknacks from his tenure as the Bears coach. With Mrs. Ditka's permission, the trash haulers took the stuff right to the auction house. A portion of the proceeds went to charitable organizations designated by the Ditkas.

This is not unusual. A few times a year, a huge collection of a player's personal memorabilia lands in an auction. Often, the sports personality claims it was stolen. Usually, it's either memorabilia he discarded or told someone to discard for him. Or it's from an ex-wife who got it in a divorce settlement or because her ex-husband never came back to claim it.

It's not unheard of to find quality sports memorabilia at a yard sale. I know people who have found everything from vintage programs to game-used jerseys this way. From a time investment standpoint, yard sales can be a little frustrating; for every good piece you find, you have to sort through a ton of junk at a ton of sales. But you never know. People hold yard sales because they absolutely want to get rid of things at any price. They get into the anti-collector mentality, wanting to simplify their lives and unload everything.

Sports teams

Another great source for memorabilia is your local sports team. Now, because of the popularity of collecting, teams are a little wary about requests from collectors. Most team executives realize that anything can be sold, and in this era of million-dollar salaries, they are reluctant to give anything away. That said, most of them don't realize that almost anything connected to the team has value to a collector. When the Atlanta Braves moved from Fulton County Stadium across the street to Turner Field in 1997, they tossed most of their files into the dumpster. Left for the garbage hauler were more than 30 years of contracts, letters, and other documents. One resourceful collector went into the dumpster and came up with a treasure trove of Braves memorabilia.

Now, I'm not advocating dumpster diving. But always be on the lookout for discarded memorabilia. Try to develop contacts in the front offices of your local sports teams. This is easier than you might think, especially if you're a season ticket holder. Get to know the person who handles your account. Attend season ticket holder functions and introduce yourself to club employees. Casually mention that you're a collector. Offer to volunteer in the front office or at games. If a team moves into a new ballpark, offer to help go through old files. Be up front about your interest, of course, and don't take anything without permission. Like any business, sports franchises do not want sensitive company documents in circulation.

Don't forget minor sports and maverick sports leagues. There's a strong market for memorabilia from the old United States Football League (USFL), as well as for the World League of American Football and the Canadian Football League. Major League Soccer attracts a huge following, and numerous professional soccer leagues have come and gone. Growing interest in the WNBA and ABL women's basketball leagues is something to keep in mind also.

Person to person

If you have current or former sports personalities living in your area, try to get to know them. Send them birthday cards. Say hello if you see them in public. Several dealers have become such good friends with older sports figures that they were hired by the family to handle the sports portion of the person's estate.

Do you have elderly friends and relatives? Ask them if they have any old sports memorabilia. It's amazing what people hold onto through the years.

The possibilities are endless. Do you have a major college in your area? Get to know the people in the marketing and sports memorabilia departments. Heck, get to know the athletes themselves. Many colleges are small, tight-knit communities, and one often overlooked aspect of collecting is college memorabilia. Imagine if you had a Michael Jordan uniform from his days at North Carolina. Of course, only a few college athletes go on to have noteworthy professional careers, but if nothing else, you'll have some nice college memorabilia.

Some of the best sports memorabilia is found outside the "Big Four" of baseball, football, basketball, and hockey.

Networking

By now, you've probably figured out that building a collection is similar to building a career. It takes a lot of networking. The more people you meet and the more who know of your collecting interests, the more likely it is that you're going to find rare and unusual memorabilia at an affordable price. Plus, you meet more people with whom you can trade, which saves money for everyone and is a lot more fun than just buying and selling.

You have to walk a fine line if you want to be known as a tireless, resourceful collector and not just a pest. When sports memorabilia had little value, no one thought twice about giving away collectibles. If someone doesn't want to sell or give you something, don't push it. Unfortunately, the business side of sports collecting has jaded many people, who would just as soon never deal with collectors. But if you're honest about your collecting intentions and maintain a pleasant, professional demeanor, you'll find that you'll have a lot of luck landing those rare, unusual items.

Chapter 7

Showtime: Surviving Card Shows

. . . .

In This Chapter

▶ Finding the best card shows

▶ Learning the value of card shows

▶ Discovering those card shows that aren't really card shows

. . . .

*O*nce upon a time, a sports collectors' convention or show was a huge event. As recently as the early 1980s, shows were held only regionally, so even if you lived in a major city, you'd get a chance to attend only four or five shows a year. Not that this was necessarily a bad thing. Because shows took place so infrequently, dealers went out of their way to attend them. Plus, they inevitably accumulated lots of great stuff in the months between their major shows. The dealers involved tended to be people who worked full time at it, specializing in vintage cards and tough-to-find memorabilia.

Like everything else in the sports collectibles field, shows have changed, and not always for the better. These days, hundreds of shows take place each weekend. No matter how small your community, chances are you can find a show — if not several — within a 30-mile radius. Unfortunately, many of these shows are the same, full of the same dealers selling the same freshly printed cards at the same inflated prices.

However, shows remain perhaps the best places to locate sports memorabilia, if only because you find many dealers under one roof. The trick is to find the worthwhile shows, and then know how to bargain for merchandise. In this chapter, I show you how to do both.

The Best Card Shows

The term *card show* is out of date. At a modern sports collectibles show, you're likely to find cards, autographs, game-used memorabilia, and every imaginable oddball item. (You're also likely to find Beanie Babies, although I'll never understand why dealers think that the same crowd that purchases sports memorabilia is also interested in Beanies.) But because the shows originated in the 1970s when people were interested only in cards, they're still called card shows today.

Finding a show is as easy as looking in your newspaper under antiques/collectibles. Many show promoters take out ads in the sports section, especially if there's an autograph-signing guest involved. You may also see a show advertised on the marquee of your local shopping mall. Many shows are held in the ballroom of a budget hotel. You also find shows at high schools, colleges, flea markets — even at sporting events. Even if you had no involvement in sports collecting prior to buying this book, chances are that you stumbled upon a show somewhere.

The trick is to find a show that's worthwhile. Ninety-five percent of card shows consist of 30 or so dealers set up in a hotel ballroom, all selling the same recent vintage cards. The display tables even look the same. (Many of the dealers even look the same: 300 pounds, lots of gold jewelry, and body hair.) Boxes of cards in stiff plastic holders are lined up neatly, with perhaps a display case full of the pricier cards. Chances are, even the prices on the cards are the same, because all the dealers flipped through their own dog-eared copy of the latest issue of *Beckett Baseball/Football/Basketball* or *Hockey Card Monthly.*

 Always clip the classified ad promoting the show out of the paper. Usually, it's good for a buck off admission. Even if the ad doesn't say that, bringing it is still worth trying. Because giving a discount is common practice at many shows, the person working the door might give you a buck off just for the effort.

Shows have evolved over the years. In the early to mid-1980s, many collectors came to shows searching for individual cards to complete sets. Dealers knew this, and brought dozens of boxes of commons and binders of stars. Then, when Rookiemania hit, dealers began bringing huge display cases filled with rookie cards in plastic holders. Once Rookiemania died down, collectors focused on stars, and dealers began arranging their cards alphabetically by last name, with all of a player's cards grouped together. In recent years, as collector interest has shifted to the memorabilia side, you see fewer cards at shows and more autographed and oddball memorabilia.

The True Value of Most Card Shows

Would you attend an auto show if it had hundreds of the same car? Would you shop at a supermarket that offered only one brand? Of course not. That's why you should avoid most card shows, unless your idea of collecting is concentrating on new cards that sell for outrageously inflated prices.

The business of show promoting

Understand what's going on here. A show promoter pays a modest sum to rent a hotel ballroom. He, in turn, charges dealers $35 to $100 to set up a table. With 30 dealers, that can yield up to $3,000. Tickets sell for $2 or $3, which puts another $200 to $300 in the promoter's pocket.

Many dealers are weekend warriors — people who hold full-time jobs during the week and try to make a little money on the side by setting up at card shows. There's nothing wrong with this; some of the best dealers are weekend warriors. Unfortunately, the majority of dealers traffic in brand new cards, buying a few boxes from wholesalers and trying to turn a profit by selling the star cards for the top dollars prescribed in *Beckett*.

I'll never understand how this is profitable from a time/money standpoint, but there seems to be no shortage of people who find it worthwhile.

Hopefully, you develop an interest in a unique area of collecting, requiring more than the average weekend warrior show at a budget hotel. I'm not saying there's nothing to be gained from attending one of these shows. Every so often, if I see one as I'm driving along on a Saturday afternoon, I'll stop by, if only to see what the market for new cards looks like. But I usually leave disappointed, having seen the same new cards at every table. These shows, because of their low table fees, naturally attract dealers hawking new cards. Dealers who specialize in rare and unusual merchandise know better than to waste their time at a hotel ballroom show.

So where does a collector turn? Generally speaking, when it comes to card shows, bigger is better. The larger, regional shows usually are promoted by dealers who have been in the business a long time. Because of the rental fees at large, modern conference centers, where these shows are often held, promoters must charge hundreds of dollars per table, which scares off the weekend warriors but attracts the top-name dealers specializing in rare and unusual sports memorabilia. You may pay $5 to $8 to get in, and you may have to drive a little farther to attend, but it's worth it. No matter what your field of interest, chances are that you'll find it at a regional show.

One promoter, Bob Schmierer, has conducted a popular quarterly show in the Philadelphia area for years. Another group, Tri-Star Productions, holds from four to six large, regional shows a year in cities such as Chicago, Houston, St. Louis, Phoenix, and San Francisco. *Tuff Stuff* magazine holds semiannual shows at the Virginia State Fairgrounds in Richmond, Virginia.

No matter what show you attend, get on the mailing list. You'll receive information on future shows, often with coupons for discounted admission. Registering for prize drawings as you enter the show puts you on the mailing list.

Some shows are limited to a certain aspect of collecting. Starting Lineups have become so popular that there are Starting Lineup shows. A group of dealers and collectors in the Washington, D.C./Baltimore area gather each September for a uniform, equipment, and memorabilia show.

One of the best parts of attending shows is meeting dealers and fellow collectors. Most dealers understand that theirs is a competitive business and will go out of their way for a steady customer. They are happy to keep an eye out for a certain item for a customer they know is willing to pay for it. Plus, shows are a great place to meet collectors with similar interests. It's a lot cheaper to complete a set of, say, 1952 Topps baseball cards by trading your doubles to fellow collectors than by purchasing the missing cards from dealers.

Card Show Strategies

You don't have to prepare to attend a card show. But doing so can help you make the most of your time. Some of the larger, regional shows are so vast that you can become a victim of sensory overload. So it helps to make a list of items you're looking for and the approximate prices you're willing to pay.

Making the rounds

No matter what card show you go to, here are a few things to remember. Of course, you're always free to walk in completely unprepared. Some people just like to browse.

✔ **Walk the entire floor before buying anything.** There's nothing worse than purchasing something at one table and then finding it for a fraction of the cost elsewhere in the show.

✔ **Work one dealer against another.** You sometimes hear dealers say that they won't get into bidding wars. That's completely false. Feel free to settle on a price with one dealer and then see whether another dealer will beat it. If he does, go back to the original guy and see whether he'll beat that. Remember, you're the one with the leverage.

✔ **Always remember that everything is open to negotiation.** With cards, if a dealer won't budge from the prices listed in *Beckett Publications,* go elsewhere. It's not insulting to offer as little as 50 percent, especially for a big ticket item or if you're willing to buy in bulk. If the dealer is insulted, who cares? Sports memorabilia is a competitive market; those not willing to make reasonable deals won't survive.

> ✔ **Don't be afraid to introduce yourself.** Explain your collecting needs. You'll be surprised at how quickly you develop a rapport with a dealer. But use this to your advantage; let him feel guilty about not coming down to your price.

Because card shows are temporary, there's less accountability. With card shops, the customer always has the option of going back if he becomes dissatisfied with his purchase. Not so with a card show. If you purchase a card set at a show, make sure that the dealer guarantees that all the cards are included. If you buy an autograph and want a lifetime guarantee of authenticity, make sure that you receive one when you purchase the item. Another good idea is to pick up dealers' business cards — if only to keep in touch with those who can help further your collection.

The best deals come at the end of the show. That's when dealers start calculating their profits, or lack thereof, and are most willing to cut prices. Sometimes dealers want to get rid of things at any price just to avoid carting them back home. Another school of thought says you should arrive early, before the best deals disappear. You can always do both. Just make sure to get your hand stamped at the door.

Autograph guests

In Chapter 3, I explain the significance of autograph guests appearing at card shows. Although paying for autographs may seem wrong, at least you know you're getting a legitimate signature. For what it's worth, you'll also be able to say you had a fleeting moment with a famous sports figure, even if he never looks up from the table.

A signature on a "premium" item such as a bat or jersey may cost more. Always make sure you buy the right ticket.

Sometimes an autograph guest shows up and few people buy tickets, either because of lack of interest or because the ticket is overpriced. The guest is left twiddling his thumbs, and the promoter inevitably is crushed because he's paid the fee up front.

This benefits you in two ways:

> ✔ If you're literally the only person in line, you can feel free to ask questions and see whether the guest will pose for photos. You may have a genuine conversation as opposed to a brief sign-and-go transaction. Because there's plenty of time, any restrictions on personalizations will be lifted. You won't, unfortunately, be able to ask for additional autographs.

> ✔ You may be able to cut a deal with the promoter — not in the presence of the guest, however. Offer to pay a fraction of the autograph ticket price for multiple signatures. What does he have to lose? At this point, he's losing lots of money. Any little bit he can sell will offset his losses.

Selling at card shows

I talk more extensively about selling your collection, or part of it, in Chapter 12. For now, it's important to realize that a card show can be either the best or the worst place to sell. At a typical weekend warrior show, you're rarely able to sell anything. Dealers at these shows, for the most part, operate under a narrow profit margin. They merely want to sell what they have. They opened hundreds of packs to sort out the gold-foiled, holographic, super premium, deluxe, die-cut, limited edition star cards they display before you for $10 to $20 each. The last thing they want to do is pay you $5 to $10 for the same cards. And these are not the dealers who have the financial resources to buy vintage cards.

Say it until you believe it: I will not make money buying and selling sports cards. Cards are a terrible investment. No matter what a price guide says, you will not make significant money selling your cards unless you stumble upon a stash in mint condition from the early '70s or before. If you doubt this theory, open a few dozen packs of new sports cards. Take out the ones worth $5 or $10 apiece according to a price guide. Then take them to a show and see how much you get for them, if anything. You'll find precious few takers.

At larger shows, however, you may have some luck, especially if you have older cards and memorabilia. But unlike buying memorabilia, it's more difficult to play one dealer off of another. A dealer will calculate how much he can sell your cards for and then make his offer accordingly. You may be able to haggle with him initially, but chances are, he's not going to raise his offer just because his neighbor did.

Perhaps you want to go the dealer route yourself. Remember, it's a tough market out there. I don't know about you, but I have better things to do with my weekend afternoons than spending them trying to sell cards. Remember, when you set up at a show, you have to sell enough to cover your $35 to $100 table fee before you start making money. From a time/profit standpoint, you're much better off selling to an individual dealer.

The National Sports Collectors Convention

Since 1980, the leaders of the sports collectibles hobby have held an annual National Sports Collectors Convention. Through the years, it's been hosted by cities such as Los Angeles; Anaheim; Chicago; Arlington, Texas; Atlanta; Cleveland; St. Louis; and Houston. Back in 1991, at the height of the sports card explosion, more than 100,000 collectors attended the National at the Anaheim Convention Center near Disneyland. The event attracts top dealers from around the country and represents every niche of the sports collecting hobby. The National also offers collecting seminars and a full slate of autograph guests signing for a fee. If you can't find what you're looking for at the National, you probably can't find it anywhere. If the National ever comes to your area — or at least within driving distance — don't miss the opportunity to attend.

Some of the larger shows, including the National, attempt to lure collectors by offering tons of promo cards. This practice almost literally caused riots in the past. Although the promo craze has died down, you still find cards given out at some shows. Don't obsess over promo cards. They have little lasting value, either collectible or otherwise. Spending your time at shows searching for what you really want is a better idea.

FanFests

Each of the four major sports puts on a carnivallike "FanFest" in conjunction with its All-Star Game. The exception is the National Football League, which holds the NFL Experience the week before the Super Bowl. These events are chock-full of interactive exhibits for kids and include a card show featuring many prominent dealers. At the NFL Experience, kids can toss a football through targets and race through an obstacle course. At Major League Baseball's FanFest, fans can have themselves taped doing play-by-play commentary; watch gloves, bats, and hats being produced; and view memorabilia on loan from the Baseball Hall of Fame.

The primary purpose of these events is to help the leagues sell tons of officially licensed, logo merchandise to fans in the host cities, especially to those fans unable to attend the game. The leagues charge steep prices for dealers to set up at the shows, which means that only the top dealers can hawk their wares. Next to the National, the card show at MLB's FanFest may be the best one of the year, even though it naturally focuses solely on baseball memorabilia.

Because the major FanFests are run by the leagues as promotional events, all their official licensees — such as the card companies — hand out promotional merchandise. This sets off a frenzy, and some fans wait in line at one booth after another, not even caring what they receive. If this is your idea of fun, go right ahead. You'll have a better time, however, if you bypass the promo area and go right into the card show.

In recent years, baseball teams started holding their own FanFests, usually in the winter as a way to sell tickets for the upcoming season. Often players are required — or at least made to feel required — to attend the FanFests and sign autographs for free. The team often brings back former players; the Chicago Cubs FanFest frequently includes the likes of Ernie Banks, Ferguson Jenkins, and Ron Santo. These FanFests can be great opportunities to get free autographs, although you may be competing with thousands of your fellow collectors and you're not guaranteed a signature. Many clubs also put on a card show in conjunction with the FanFest.

Unofficial Card Shows

Some of the best shows aren't sports card shows at all. You may find rare and unusual sports items at antique shows. Great oddball stuff can be found at paper collectibles shows. You may come across bargains on sports autographs at shows focusing on autographs of entertainment figures. Even Coca-Cola shows offer an occasional bargain, although usually any sports-related Coke merchandise — except for recently printed bottles, cans, and advertising pieces — comes with a premium price tag.

Be extra careful when it comes to authenticity. An antique dealer may not know the difference between a legitimate advertising piece and a reproduction, a game-used jersey and a replica, or an authentic autograph and a blatant forgery. On the other hand, you can pick up bargains if you come across a dealer who doesn't know the difference between sports memorabilia junk and something with huge value in the sports collecting world.

Chapter 8
The Auction Block

In This Chapter

▶ Finding out about auction merchandise

▶ Discovering how to do your bidding by phone, by mail, or in person

▶ Bidding with the high rollers without losing your shirt

▶ Attending a charity auction

*N*othing gets a collector's blood pumping like an auction. There you are, putting your cash on the line, competing with dealers and fellow collectors for that much-desired piece of memorabilia. You're not only looking to buy memorabilia; you're participating in a sport of sorts. The stakes, however, can be high.

Like card shows and card shops, sports memorabilia auctions have proliferated in recent years. Once the sole domain of such big-name art auctioneers as Christie's and Sotheby's, dozens of sports auctions are now held each year, with varying ticket prices. Some, such as Leland's, routinely sell game-used jerseys for six figures. Others, held by individual dealers, offer more modestly priced goods.

Most people are familiar with only one type of auction — the live, in-person sale. If you want to buy a house, car, or antique, you almost always have to be there yourself, or at least hire someone to bid for you. Not so with sports memorabilia, which offers at least three types of sales. In addition to the live sale, some auctions feature mail bids only, and other auctions accept only phone bids. Many auctions offer some combination of the three. Some live auctions accept mail or phone bids. Many phone auctions accept mail offers filed in advance. Some mail auctions have a designated period for phone submissions before the bidding closes.

This chapter concentrates on the buying end of auctions, which can be intimidating for beginning collectors. (Turn to Chapter 12 for a discussion of selling collectibles via the auction.) In this chapter, I transform you from a 98-pound auction weakling into a strong, confident auction-goer. Coming to the sale with a thick bankroll helps, of course. But even if you don't, here's how to avoid getting sand kicked in your face.

The added costs of auctions

Policies on auction commissions vary. The standard commission is 10 percent, but some auctioneers add it to the buyer's price while others subtract it from what the seller receives. Naturally, if you're the buyer, you're hoping that the commission comes from the seller; otherwise you're paying 110 percent of what you bid. Of course, if you're the seller, you'd like to see it added to the buyer's price.

If not, you get 90 percent of the selling price. The important thing is to feel good about the auctioneer you're dealing with. These days, more auctioneers seem to take their cut from the seller, which makes sense. If the auctioneer does an effective job marketing his sale, the 10 percent commission will be more than fair for the consignor.

What to Know Before You Go

The best advice to heed when attending a sports memorabilia auction is the boy scout motto: Be prepared. The more you know about the market, the merchandise and the rules of the auction, the better off you will be.

How items arrive at an auction

Some beginning collectors assume that all the items at an auction belong to an auction house, which searched far and wide and spent hundreds of thousands, even millions, of dollars to purchase the collectibles that it will then sell at a substantial profit.

Actually, that assumption is partially true, because some people would rather dispose of an item quickly than wait through the consignment and auction process. Most larger auction houses make a distinction in their catalog between consigned items and those they own. From a buyer's standpoint, it doesn't matter.

The auction catalog

The marketing of auctions varies. The big houses, like Leland's, Christie's, and Mastro's, produce beautiful full-color books featuring every item or *lot* in the sale. Because these sales bring in six- and seven-figure totals, the houses can afford to spend big money on printing. Of course, they sometimes pass the cost along to collectors, unless they have purchased big ticket items in the past, in which case the house usually provides future catalogs at no charge.

The major auction houses announce their sales in publications such as *Sports Collectors Digest* and *Tuff Stuff*. If the auctions involve high-priced or notorious items — Leland's once had dozens of items that Pete Rose's ex-wife had obtained in a divorce settlement — you might have read about the sales in national publications such as *USA Today*. And if you've ordered an auction catalog in the past, you'll get postcards announcing future auctions and inviting you to send away for the catalogs.

Other catalogs are more modest. Some auctions limit their marketing to a few pages of advertising in *Sports Collectors Digest*. Nothing's wrong with that approach, of course, although some collectors feel that they get a better look at an item in a glossy sales catalog than on the thin paper of *SCD*. Many small auctioneers, some of whom are sports card shop owners, simply send out mimeographed catalogs.

Catalogs from the major auction houses make great reference tools. Always call the house and obtain a copy of the auction results and place it in the catalog. This record is a great way to determine the value of an item in the future. And because some collectibles reappear in future auctions, it's important to know the previous price paid.

Keep in mind the following advice before you attend an auction:

- ✔ **Try to avoid bidding without at least seeing a picture.** You can't really get an idea of the condition of sports memorabilia, especially cards, unless you at least see a photo in an auction catalog. Sometimes, however, you may not be able to judge the condition even with a photo, because items tend to look worse after photos of the merchandise are reproduced in catalogs, especially those printed on newsprint.

- ✔ **Be sure to take a close look at photos of team-autographed baseballs in auction catalogs.** If the signatures of the star players are not visible, chances are that they're not of the same quality as the lesser players pictured. The star signatures may have faded or may not be as legible as those of the lesser players. A reputable auctioneer thoroughly describes the item, including its deficiencies.

Bidding

There are two methods of bidding at auctions — either in person or by phone or mail. Here's how to take either approach:

How to bid by phone or by mail

If you've seen a photo of the item you want to bid on and feel comfortable enough with its condition and authenticity to make a bid by phone or through the mail, the process is fairly simple. But here are some points to remember.

- ✔ **Read the entire auction catalog or advertisement thoroughly.** Rules vary from house to house and from state to state. You may owe additional taxes or charges depending on where you live.

- ✔ **To make sure that your mail bid is received on time, send it by registered mail, return receipt requested.** If fax bids are accepted, follow up with a phone call to make sure that the auction house received your bid.

- ✔ **Registration for phone auctions is handled in advance.** You'll be assigned a number, which you give when you call to bid on merchandise.

- ✔ **Phone auctions generally accept bids "until the phone stops ringing" so that bidders don't panic when they get a constant busy signal.** To avoid spending hours on the phone — to say nothing of long-distance charges — it's a good idea to submit a maximum or *top limit* bid. You can also submit such a bid for mail or live auctions. The auction will bid for you, at typical 10 percent increments, until your top limit is reached. If your top limit is not reached, then you win the bidding. For example, if you make a top limit bid of $200 and the other top bid is $120, you pay $132 (which is 10 percent above the last top bid), plus any applicable commissions.

- ✔ **Try to avoid calling the auction house to check on results immediately following a sale.** Auction employees have numerous details to attend to and won't have time to give you an update. Sit tight. You'll usually find out the following day if you've won.

Sometimes buying something by phone or mail isn't worth the hassle. You also may have to pay long-distance or shipping charges. Ask yourself whether you're really saving money. Even if you are saving money, buying in person may be a lot less trouble.

Attending in person

There's no substitute for attending an auction in person. You can examine the collectibles thoroughly before bidding. You can assess the mood and the bankrolls of the bidders and determine whether things are going high or low. And, perhaps most importantly, you can see who is bidding against you.

Your first auction

One school of thought about auctions says that you should not bid for anything during the first auction you attend. That's not bad advice. You can instead use the opportunity to become acquainted with the auction process and determine the best times to get bargains. If you're attending one of the big New York auctions, where items sell routinely for four and five figures, staying on the sidelines the first time around is probably a good idea. You'll be up against well-heeled, experienced collectors who have a much better idea of whether something is overvalued or undervalued.

But at many other, smaller auctions, most items may sell for less than $100. So, no matter how inexperienced a collector you are, you can't get burned too badly at one of these sales.

Rules of conduct

Auctions have a unique set of rules that must be followed. Otherwise, you might find yourself inadvertently buying something you did not want. Here then are some guidelines to follow when attending an auction, regardless of its size and scope of memorabilia.

- ✔ **Register properly.** Auctions require that bidders register beforehand and receive a bidder's number. At this time, you should receive a document outlining information such as whether sales are cash only or if credit cards are permitted, whether items must be paid for immediately or if you have several days, and when the items can be picked up. If you are unclear about any of these variables, ask *before* bidding.

- ✔ **Learn the rules.** Bidding may be done by voice or by hand raising. Other sales issue wooden or cardboard "paddles" the size of hand fans. Find out how the auctioneer acknowledges bids. Remember that shampoo commercial where a guy mistakenly purchases something when he raises his hand to scratch his dandruff? That type of occurrence is not as uncommon as you might think.

- ✔ **Go early and check out the goods.** Make sure that the actual condition and description match what you read in the catalog. Get a good seat, either in the back or in the middle. You want to be able to see who's bidding against you.

  Many sales offer items "as is" and take no responsibility for the item's condition or description. The best defense here, as always, is to educate yourself and be confident about an item's legitimacy and condition. If the item is an autograph or game-used item, check to see whether it comes with a lifetime guarantee of authenticity.

- ✔ **Remember that the worst time to buy is generally at the beginning of a sale.** Auctioneers realize that everyone's finances are at their highest at the beginning, so they start off with the high-ticket items. The best time to buy is often after this initial flurry, when all the bidders are catching their breath and marveling at the huge sum that the winning bidders just paid. Many times these next few items don't attract much interest. Of course, auctioneers know this and often position lesser lots at this point. The end of the sale, when people are cashed out, is also a good time to pick up bargains.

✔ **The best time to enter the bidding for an item often is at the end, when the bidding seems to be dying down.** At this point, the remaining bidders — who have been competing all along — may drop out after they realize that another bidder may push the price even higher.

✔ **Focus, focus, focus.** Don't start bidding on something just because it seems like a great buy. Ask yourself whether it fits into the theme of your collection. If not, the money you spend on the item will take away from something that does fit into your collection. Remain calm, focus on a few lots, and don't be discouraged if you don't win anything. The future always holds other auctions and other lots.

✔ **Sometimes, making a preemptive strike against your competition is a good idea.** If you're willing to spend $200 for an item that you think could sell for $300, make $150 your opening bid. You never know when your brashness may pay off. Some people, especially as the auction drags on, feel more comfortable bidding in 10 percent increments. They may let you have the item. The flip side to this, of course, is that you should feel very confident about the market for the item. Nothing is worse than overpaying — and knowing that you overpaid.

✔ **Don't be afraid to make a bid after the sale.** Sometimes an item won't sell or meet its minimum reserve, and you'll find yourself wishing that you had bid more. After the sale, approach the auctioneer and make an offer — or raise the last one. If it's reasonable, the auctioneer may go back to the consignor and ask whether your bid is acceptable. The dealer wants the commission and also wants to avoid the hassle of returning the lot. Leave your phone number. You never know.

If you're the consignor, be sure to read all the fine print in the agreement and make sure that you understand the ramifications of what you're signing.

Auctioneers have rights, too

Auctioneers reserve the right to pull an item from the sale if it does not receive a minimum reserve bid. They also have the right to insist upon a minimum increment for a bid to be raised. If an item does not sell or meet a minimum reserve, the consignor is charged a fee.

Auction fever can be costly

Don't let the auction adrenaline rush get the best of you. Winning a bidding war may seem an effective way to demonstrate your manhood or womanhood, but you'll only be left with a serious case of buyer's remorse if you overpay. One reason that auctions have proliferated in recent years is because dealers have found that collectors will pay more for something at an auction than they will at a card store, for example; it's worth a premium for collectors to be able to say they won something. Dealers have found that they can sell almost at an auction. Some dealers actually collectibles back for an auction instead of trying to sell them at their store or at a show.

Taking on the Heavyweights

Most of us will never get involved in a five-figure bidding war at a big-time New York sports auction with some rich collector or dealer. That's probably just as well, because many pitfalls can await you.

Fortunately, auctioneers prohibit consignors from bidding on their own stuff. After all, what would a consignor have to lose, other than perhaps a 10 percent commission? But people have accused dealers through the years of acting together to drive up the price of an item.

For example, suppose that Dealer A has purchased a rare, vintage flannel jersey of Lou Gehrig or Babe Ruth from a collector for $35,000. Dealer A wants to get at least $100,000 for it, so he instructs his friend, Dealer B, to bid it up for him at auction. If Dealer B ends up stuck with it, Dealer A agrees to give him the money to buy it.

Dealer B then gets into a frenzied bidding war with Dealer C and ends up buying the jersey for $90,000. Dealer A gives Dealer B the money. What if it's the type of sale where the commission is deducted from the consignor's money? Dealer A, in effect, pays $90,000 for his own jersey and only gets $81,000 back. He's out $9,000. Pretty dumb of him, right?

Not necessarily. The next day, the New York newspapers run stories on the jersey that fetched $90,000 at auction. Over the next month, the hobby trade publications print more in-depth stories. Suddenly, everyone's heard of this jersey. Not coincidentally, the uniform resurfaces in the next big New York auction. This time, amid more hoopla, it sells for $125,000. Dealer A now nets $112,500 after commission.

Auction houses have cracked down on this process. But because big-time sports collectibles dealers are such a small, close-knit fraternity, things can get a little incestuous. In some instances, dealers have served as consultants and authenticators for auction houses that accepted their goods on consignment. In effect, they authenticate their own merchandise.

Making sure you get the real thing

The authentication process for auctions is a double-edged sword. Because these items are being sold publicly, the auction house must be especially sensitive to an item's authenticity. After all, it's going to be displayed and sold in public. Most houses go overboard to make sure that their lots are legitimate. But many collectors may assume that an item is the genuine article just because it's in an auction. They let their guard down when verifying authenticity.

You can feel pretty comfortable when dealing with the major auction houses. They are run by veteran collectors and dealers who know the industry. If they're not 100 percent sure about the authenticity of an item, they have colleagues who can back them up or pronounce the item bogus. To their credit, they're not afraid to pull items that they have even a little doubt about, even after the auction catalog has gone to press.

Outfoxing Wayne Gretzky and Charlie Sheen

Sometimes you never know who will be bidding against you. In 1991, hockey star Wayne Gretzky and Bruce McNall bid successfully over the phone against live bidders at a Sotheby's auction and landed a T206 Honus Wagner card for the then-record price of $451,000. A year later, actor Charlie Sheen of *Major League* and *Platoon* fame paid a whopping $93,500 for the infamous baseball that rolled through the legs of Boston Red Sox first baseman Bill Buckner during Game 6 of the 1986 World Series. One of the underbidders was Keith Olbermann, who is best known for his broadcast work with ESPN and MSNBC.

Unless you have deep pockets, you're probably not going to be facing collectors such as these at auctions. But if you do attend a major auction and decide to get into the bidding, chances are you may go up against dealers and collectors with loads of experience and cash. In fact, much of the audience at the major New York sales consists of well-heeled collectors and dealers who are buying for clients.

Knowing your competition

After you arrive at an auction, chat up some of the people sitting around you. Try to figure out the major players in the audience. If possible, try to distinguish between the collectors and the dealers. That can't be done by appearance, of course. Ask around.

Many collectors get intimidated when they go up against dealers. They figure that the dealer has more cash, which usually is the case. The difference is that the dealer usually plans to flip the item for profit. You, on the other hand, may be willing to pay a little more because you'd be buying it for retail price elsewhere anyway. As always, don't go beyond your limit. But realize that your threshold for spending may actually be higher than the dealer with a bigger wad of cash in his pocket.

The time to worry that the bidding is getting out of hand is not when dealers are bidding, but when collectors are the only ones raising their paddles. Chances are, the collectors have probably gone far beyond the retail price.

Charity Auctions

Charity auctions featuring sports memorabilia can be a mixed bag. Usually, serious collectors want to avoid them because they attract wealthy non-collectors who are prepared to make a sizable donation anyway and are unconcerned about the actual value of an item. Plus, many items donated by teams to charity auctions tend to be of the signed, replica jersey variety rather than game-used equipment that interests collectors.

Sometimes, however, the flip side of that situation is true. Teams have been known to donate game-used equipment, basketball shoes, and baseball spikes. Wealthy noncollectors will shy away from these items. They'd rather have something that they can frame and display in their marble and ma-hogany offices. The shoes are all yours.

Don't forget about the auctions and FanFests hosted by the teams them-selves. These events are often a great way to get autographs for free, or at least for a modest charitable donation. Plus, you'll know that the memora-bilia in the auction is legitimate because it comes directly from the team.

Buying sports memorabilia at a charity auction might be tax deductible depending on the charity and your financial situation. It's worth looking into before you attend the auction.

Charity auctions may yield bargains

Sometimes the organizers of charity auctions miscalculate their target audience, a mistake that can work to your advantage. A few years ago, I attended an auction hosted by The Marriott Corp. in Washington, D.C. Attendance was sparse, although a few members of the Washington Redskins showed up and made sizable contributions. Near the end of the sale, a hood from a race car belonging to NASCAR driver Rusty Wallace was being auctioned. The black hood was emblazoned with the familiar gold logo of Wallace's chief sponsor, Miller Genuine Draft, and had been signed boldly by Wallace with a silver marking pen.

Now, this auction was in the early 1990s, before the demand for NASCAR merchandise really took off. In addition, Washington, D.C. was anything but a NASCAR hotbed. When the item came up for sale, snickers could be heard throughout the room. The audience was a typical D.C. lawyer-and-lobbyist crowd. The same item may have commanded thousands of dollars in Charlotte or Daytona Beach. Instead, the auctioneer struggled to get a minimum bid. I might have offered something, but I had no idea how I would get it home, let alone where I would put it.

The hood finally sold for $100, a fraction of its worth. So never let it be said that a collector can't find a bargain at a charity auction. Actually, because regular sports memorabilia auctions have become so popular and so well attended by educated collectors, you're just as likely to get a good deal at a charity auction as anywhere else.

Items available at charity auctions hosted by professional sports teams tend to be prohibitively expensive because the events attract passionate sports fans, wealthy noncollectors, and collectors. This audience is a great mix if someone wants to raise lots of money for charity. But it's a terrible place to pick up a bargain. However, sometimes the opposite is true.

Chapter 9

Don't Believe Everything You Hear on TV!

In This Chapter

▶ Discovering how sports memorabilia gets on television

▶ Figuring out what stuff to avoid and what to buy

▶ Understanding why you can't always trust your sports heroes

Home shopping channels do not always conjure up pretty pictures. Many people probably think of cheesy cubic zirconium jewelry, hideous fashion leftovers from the 1970s, and goofy gadgets that you probably can do without. Much of the stuff is hawked by big-haired, overly made-up women and smooth-talking, blow-dried male barkers who try to convince you that you can't live without it. Most of you probably watch these shows with a detached amusement, thinking that no one really buys any of this stuff, do they?

Yet, many people lose all common sense when buying sports memorabilia on television. People who would never buy anything on a shopping program can't dial the phone fast enough when they have a chance to buy some autographed sports photo plaque. Some viewers are especially eager to buy if one of their favorite sports heroes is appearing on the show.

Most serious collectors would invest in Florida swampland before purchasing sports memorabilia over the air. And although serious collectors generally should avoid buying sports collectibles from television, in this chapter I show you what merchandise may be worthwhile.

Sports Memorabilia on Television

Sports memorabilia television programs actually have improved over the years. When the shows first aired in the mid-1980s, they were a dumping ground for some of the most worthless products in the industry. Television shopping executives found that they could sell any sports collectible over the air with the help of a hard sales pitch and a celebrity sports guest. Because most television viewers were not experienced collectors, they were easy targets. Today's sports shopping shows still feature over-the-top sales pitches, but the quality of the memorabilia has improved overall.

The television mark up

Here's an example of how some television shopping shows market their sports memorabilia. In 1992, several enterprising dealers offered to serve as middlemen for the shopping networks. They found out what some fellow dealers had in excess inventory. The middleman dealers found tons of leftover sets of 1988 Topps baseball cards, virtually worthless at about $12 a set. They bought thousands of card sets for $5 a set and sold them for $8 to $10 apiece to a shopping network.

The TV hosts then came up with sales pitches that, while true, were not the whole truth. They emphasized that these 1988 sets were no longer in production. What the show hosts didn't tell you is that probably enough of these cards were available for every man, woman, and child in the U.S. The hosts breathlessly noted that the set included many top rookies, including Matt Williams and Tom Glavine. The show hosts neglected to tell you that, like so many '80s cards, these sets were so overproduced and so overcollected that Williams and Glavine rookie cards would never appreciate. The hosts even mentioned that the cards were no longer available in stores, as if retail outlets would still be carrying 1988 cards four years later. (Card store owners and dealers, of course, still had plenty left over.)

The shameless hype artists emphasized the investment potential of baseball cards, mentioning how cards from the '50s and '60s were worth hundreds, even thousands, of dollars. But this investment-quality set from 1988, which was *no longer in production and no longer available in stores,* and chock-full of *many top rookies,* was available for the low, low, can't-beat-it-with-a-stick price of just $39.95! Over the next few minutes, they slashed the price several times, all the way down to $19.95. Unsuspecting viewers figured that they were getting a great deal, a 50 percent discount no less. In reality, they could have purchased the same set at any card store for $10 or less because most card shop owners would have taken any offer to unload four-year-old inventory.

Of course, no educated collector was going to purchase a set of 1988 Topps cards — unless it was 1988, and the collector happened to maintain a complete run of Topps sets. But for a viewer who didn't know better, it sounded like a great deal. Many collectors had the misfortune of receiving a gift set of 1988 Topps cards from relatives who thought that they had gotten a true collectible bargain. This is one of just many examples — which continue today — of the hawking of virtually worthless memorabilia to an unsuspecting viewership.

Not all sports memorabilia sold on television is junk, just as not all the merchandise sold on non-sports programs is junk. After all, QVC and the Home Shopping Network haven't made billions without selling some decent merchandise. But most sports memorabilia on shopping programs is recently manufactured, not the rare and unusual items that you want for your collection. Plus, because the memorabilia is being sold at a retail price — despite all of those last-minute discounts the hosts offer — it's often priced higher than it would be at a card show or shop.

Never, ever, take anything you hear about sports memorabilia during a television shopping program at face value.

In defense of the shopping programs, they do not say anything untruthful. And even though card shop owners moan about how they can't get $10 for the same set of cards that sells on TV for $30, who can blame the TV networks for capitalizing on their broad, naive audience? Of course, many dealers are just upset because they aren't in the privileged network of suppliers who can dump their worthless inventory over the air.

When buying sports memorabilia on television, the advice that "if it's too good to be true, it probably is" is very applicable.

Recognizing the Good Stuff

The shopping networks aren't quite as shameless anymore when it comes to sports collectibles. They still use aggressive sales pitches and focus mainly on products that no serious collector would want. But over the last five years, they've added some merchandise with legitimate collectible value.

Manufactured memorabilia

The Score Board and Upper Deck Authenticated (which I talk about in Chapters 3 and 4) specialize in legitimately autographed, manufactured memorabilia and now account for much of the sports stuff that you see on the shopping networks. These companies have shrewdly marketed their signed replica jerseys and equipment to sports bar owners and corporate executives who want nothing more than a lovely framed item with a legitimate signature for display. Most serious collectors want nothing to do with these items; they prefer actual game-used uniforms and equipment. But clearly a market exists for the recently manufactured memorabilia — there's an oxymoron for you.

Unsuspecting viewers may be misled into thinking that the network is selling game-used items, especially when replica uniforms are touted as *game* jerseys. But to the credit of Score Board and UDA, along with the networks, they make a distinction between the two terms. And because the television audience consists mostly of non-collectors who may want only a display item or a set of 1988 Topps baseball cards to flip through, the programs provide companies such as Score Board and UDA with a perfect target audience.

But you, the educated sports memorabilia consumer, will want to avoid most of the memorabilia sold on home shopping programs. Even if you do want to go the Score Board or UDA route, you'll often get a better price by dealing with the companies or their official dealers directly. Of course, the point of home shopping is convenience, for which you should be willing to pay a modest premium.

How exclusive is exclusive?

The shopping networks often try to draw you in by offering products "exclusively available through (insert name of network) tonight only!" Do not buy into the notion of manufactured rarity. So what if it's available for one night only? Does that make it more collectible than, say, sports cards from the 1960s that were widely available in stores for months? Of course not.

Manufacturers can always create rarity. Heck, they can just produce one of something and have the rarest of collectibles. That does not mean that the item has any true collectible value.

These exclusives can create a dilemma for some collectors, however. For example, suppose that you collect memorabilia of young Los Angeles Lakers star Kobe Bryant. If you're channel surfing one evening and stumble upon a program offering an exclusive Bryant card set for one night only, your natural inclination is to reach for the phone. After all, you want to have the definitive Bryant collection.

You have to draw the line somewhere, and this is as good a place as any. Don't let a memorabilia company or shopping network appeal to your collector mentality by creating false rarity and availability. Even if the merchandise is being touted as a television exclusive, you'll always be able to find the products in the future. Have you ever seen one of those commercials for wacky gadgets that supposedly are not available in stores? Inevitably, you see them in stores. They may not appear for weeks, or even months, but they almost always find their way into the retail market. And why not? Unless a company is completely satisfied with its television sales — and who would ever be satisfied if the potential for more sales were available? — it would be foolish not to place more products in stores.

Sports memorabilia merchandisers are especially eager to sell their products in stores. Many of the card shops, shows, and dealers, which make up a huge secondary market, are in the same supplier network that provides collectibles to home shopping programs. In other cases, the retail outlets may have purchased the memorabilia directly from the television channels and want to resell.

Always ignore the phrase "for a limited time only" when it applies to sports memorabilia.

Be Wary of Your Sports Heroes on Shopping Channels

When athletes appear on shopping networks, viewers assume — incorrectly — that the athlete is endorsing the product. Why, if Joe Superstar is right there with the product, it must be a treasured collectible, right?

Not so fast. Athletes appear on shopping networks for one reason — to make money. Many have never met the hosts of the shows until they walk onto the set. Many have no idea what specific products will come up on the show, although they have a general idea that they're likely to see memorabilia relating to their career, products they've signed as part of a personal services contract. Many players do not understand the collectibles market; all they know is that, besides being a huge business, home shopping networks enable them to make obscene amounts of money.

Huckstering heroes

Next time you watch a sports memorabilia shopping program, wait for the host to ask the celebrity the inevitable question about the market.

> **Host:** Joe, when you were a kid, could you ever have imagined that cards and memorabilia would become such big business?

> **Guest:** I tell you what, Bill — I mean, Bob — I wish I had held on to some of the stuff I had growing up. I'd have a fortune right now!

I've seen this exchange so many times that I'm convinced it's part of the script. But chances are, the athlete is being entirely truthful. After all, who among us doesn't wish that we had kept some of the collectibles from our childhood, or at least maintained them in better condition?

Catcher gets caught

In 1993, Hall of Fame catcher Johnny Bench was charged by the New York Office of Consumer Affairs with making misleading claims on a shopping program. Now, Bench was probably no more at fault than any of the hundreds of other athletes who have appeared on such shows. He just had the misfortune of being the millionaire sports figure on the air when the Consumer Affairs people were conducting their investigation. (The matter was later settled; Bench paid a $5,000 fine without admitting any wrongdoing.) Before you make a decision to buy merchandise from a shopping channel, consider what Richard Schrader, the acting commissioner of the New York Office of Consumer Affairs office, said at the time: "These athletes misuse the trust and adulation of their fans by enticing them to buy today's collectibles even though these bats, balls, and photos are more likely tomorrow's discardables."

But when an athlete speaks, he's making a very subtle sales pitch. *Why, if Joe Superstar collects memorabilia, so should I,* the viewer thinks. *And if I just hold on to it for a few years, I might have a fortune 20 years from now. Joe said so himself!*

Well, that's not exactly how it works. But you can see why people may make that sort of link. Fortunately, most hosts of shopping shows focus the discussion on an athlete's career. But athletes can really get in trouble when the hosts lure them into shilling for the products. Because many athletes have no sense of the market, let alone knowledge of all the subtle tricks that sports marketing shows employ to avoid false claims, they sometimes get themselves in trouble. (See the sidebar "Catcher gets caught" for an example of the trouble that one athlete encountered.)

But many sports fans see only the good side of their hero. Some viewers feel that it's worth buying the product just for a chance to speak to the athlete, although viewers have no guarantee that they'll be that lucky. Even when they do get to speak to the athlete, they just become part of the sales pitch. Most callers are delirious because they're actually talking to one of their heroes, so they're more than happy to help promote the product. The conversation usually goes something like this:

Host: I think we have a caller.

Caller: Um, hello, Joe?

Guest: Hey, how you doin'?

Caller: Oh my God, this is . . . just . . . wow, this is amazing. I, I'm your biggest fan and I just, um. . . .

Host: Caller, what do you think of your limited edition, Joe Superstar, autographed plaque?

Caller: Oh, it's just fabulous.

Host: I bet that's going right up on your mantel, huh?

Caller: Definitely.

Host: It's a pretty good buy at $39.95, don't you think?

Caller: It sure is. I'm just glad I got through in time.

Host: Okay, thanks for calling. Now, moving right along. . . .

Tacky plaques

You see an awful lot of gaudy merchandise on shop-at-home television, and the shows that focus on sports memorabilia are no exception. In fact, if your only exposure to sports collecting was these shows, you might assume that many collectibles were presented and sold as plaques. Of course, you'll see plaques at card shows and card stores, but they seem especially prevalent on sports shopping shows.

For the most part, plaques went out of style in the 1970s. Who wants to display some cheesy, lacquered, simulated wood-grain eyesore? No matter how attractive the photo or collectible, it looks terrible when displayed as a plaque. And yet, you'll see everything imaginable offered as a plaque — especially NASCAR collectibles — on television shopping programs. With the success of NASCAR, drivers are frequent guests on shopping programs. Sometimes they'll bring the tires, hood, or even an entire car from a winning race to the network and have the parts sliced up to be sold to collectors. Unfortunately, these products are usually presented as plaques!

The continued popularity of plaques seems to reflect poorly on the overall sophistication of sports memorabilia collectors. If you wouldn't normally buy a plaque, don't make an exception for sports memorabilia.

Don't Touch That Phone, Unless . . .

The true collector, someone who is interested in relatively rare and unusual merchandise, probably won't have much interest in many of the goods hawked on home shopping programs. Some of these shows do have legitimate merchandise. Indeed, much of it comes from Score Board and Upper Deck Authenticated, so you can rest assured that the autographs are legitimate, albeit on freshly produced uniforms and equipment. So for some collectors, home shopping shows may be a good place to look.

If you fall into any of the following categories, feel free to buy sports memorabilia from home shopping programs:

- ✔ You're a sports bar owner or corporate executive who wants an autographed item as a conversation piece, even if the signature does appear on a freshly minted uniform, ball, or piece of equipment.

- ✔ You're a collector of individual team or player memorabilia, and you're concerned that you'll never be able to find a certain item elsewhere. Your fears are probably unjustified, but if you insist on buying, make sure that you're not overpaying just because you believe that the item is rare. Sometimes the manufacturer's marketing techniques lead viewers to assume that the item is rare, when it really doesn't have any true collectible value.

- ✔ You're absolutely convinced that the product has true collectible value and won't be available elsewhere. I'm allowing this exception for folks interested in the pieces from a NASCAR automobile, for instance.

- ✔ You understand that the items you see may be more expensive than you can find elsewhere, but you're an impulse shopper and appreciate convenience.

- ✔ You like plaques. After all, I'm just a sports memorabilia expert, not an interior decorator.

Part III

Pricing and Selling: Is This Stuff Worth Anything?

The 5th Wave   By Rich Tennant

In this part . . .

If you want to know how sports memorabilia is priced and valued, check out the material in this part. I show you how to interpret a sports card price guide and explain some of the factors that influence the value of a card or memorabilia item. You discover why I believe that sports memorabilia, contrary to reports, is not a good investment and why you shouldn't get into this hobby to make money. Finally, I give you tips about how to sell either part or all of your collection. You may never want to sell, of course, but if you do, this chapter tells you how.

Chapter 10

The Myth of Sports Collectible Investing

. . . .

In This Chapter

▶ Discovering how sports memorabilia came to be regarded as a good investment

▶ Understanding the economics of the sports memorabilia market

▶ Interpreting the Beckett price guides

▶ Finding out why most cards and memorabilia are worthless

. . . .

*W*hen I began writing this book, several of my colleagues wondered aloud why people are foolish enough to collect sports memorabilia. However, there's nothing foolish about indulging in an innocent pastime. This hobby becomes a problem only when people believe that they can make a sound investment in sports collectibles. Collectors of all levels, especially beginners, can enjoy sports memorabilia as long as they don't get hung up on the financial aspects of it. In this chapter, I explain the myths surrounding sports collectible investments.

Some people have made money in this business, and I explain how they did it. But it's virtually impossible for a newcomer in sports memorabilia to turn a profit. Unfortunately, the people who work in what's left of this market thrive on this false notion of sports memorabilia as a blue-chip investment.

Hopes and Dreams versus Cold, Hard Reality

You've probably heard countless stories of people making a fortune in the sports memorabilia market. You've seen books with titles such as *How to Make Millions Collecting Sports Cards!* You have a stack of well-respected price guides that list eye-popping prices for cards — even for those produced in the last few months.

So you probably don't want to believe me when I say that sports memorabilia is a terrible investment. You're skeptical of my advice. You want to think of yourself as an educated consumer, yet the evidence in support of sports memorabilia as an investment seems to be overwhelming. After all, this book explains that a tremendous, highly lucrative market exists for rare and unusual memorabilia with lasting collectible value. Furthermore, you know that you can still find such items if you're willing to tirelessly search antique stores, flea markets, estate sales, and yard sales.

True, very true. But unless you unearth some long forgotten treasure and manage to acquire it for a modest sum, making money in this hobby is next to impossible. Today's cards are so overproduced, overhyped, and overcollected that they'll never be worth anything. Most sports figures sign so many autographs in person and at shows that the value of their signatures barely rises — even after their deaths. And companies continue to crank out so much manufactured memorabilia for athletes to sign that it will never have lasting collectible value.

Still, you want to believe that you can get rich by collecting sports memorabilia. After all, you see so many collectibles for sale for such high prices that you probably think they must be worth something, right? Again, very true. Some dealers can earn a modest profit in the business, but collectors who think that they can become wealthy simply by investing in sports collectibles will be disappointed.

How Sports Collectibles Became "Investments"

Sports fans who were fortunate enough to have kept their baseball cards from the 1950s and 1960s in pristine condition found themselves with some valuable cardboard when the market for sports cards exploded in the early 1980s. Cards that had cost pennies suddenly were worth a small fortune.

The economy was booming, and speculators were looking for places to build their fortunes even further. The headlines generated by the sale of older cards caught their attention. Business writers jumped on the bandwagon, without really analyzing the unique dynamics of the market. No less a source than *Money* magazine chimed in with a study showing that baseball cards were the top investment of the '80s, returning an average of 42.5 percent, outperforming corporate bonds (14 percent), common stocks (12.7 percent), and Treasury bills (7.2 percent).

Some people, of course, were making money. The card companies saw sales rise continually through the '80s, peaking in 1991. Dealers made money as collectors bought cards by the box, scrambling to pick up the next hot rookie cards. Even some collectors made money if the players featured on rookie cards they picked up for pennies blossomed into stars. With the market booming for cards, the demand for autographs and memorabilia soon increased as well.

The hype was fueled by the hobby press and several price guides, particularly the universally followed Beckett Publications of Dallas, Texas. Many articles on the booming business compared the sports card business to the stock market. Under this analogy, each new card line was like a company's initial public offering. But collectors weren't investing in the stocks of companies they viewed as having the most potential; they were investing in the players they thought were most likely to become stars.

This investment analogy, however, had a problem that *Money* magazine and others failed to consider. The study showing huge investment returns on cards assumed that collectors could sell their cards for the amounts listed in the price guides. This assumption was anything but true.

The Fallacy of the Stock Market Analogy

Try some comparison shopping to discover why comparing the sports card business to the stock market is not logical. Suppose that you buy 100 shares of a stock. Each share costs $100 a share, so your cost so far is $10,000. When you add on a $29.95 commission, your total investment is $10,029.95. Then a week goes by, and you discover that you need the money for something else. The stock price hasn't moved, and you're able to sell your stock back for roughly $10,000, minus another $29.95 commission. So basically you're out $60.

Now suppose that you buy 100 copies of the same baseball card, worth $100. You've again spent $10,000. A week goes by, and you discover that you need the money immediately. First, you must find a dealer who wants the cards. If the cards were produced before 1978, you may have a chance of finding one. For example, suppose that the card is a 1975 Topps rookie card of George Brett of the Kansas City Royals, and you're fortunate enough to find a dealer. But like most dealers, he buys cards for, at most, only 50 percent of the value listed in *Beckett Baseball Card Monthly*. (He needs to make a profit and will do so by selling the cards to someone like yourself for $100 apiece.)

The dealer offers you $5,000, just half of your initial investment. Fortunately, your financial crisis passes, and you don't need to sell right away. But the episode has you wondering what the cards really are worth. You could consign them to a major auction house. The cards probably wouldn't sell there for $10,000. Dealers probably would bid up to $5,000, maybe $6,000. A wealthy collector/investor might bid $7,500, realizing that's still 25 percent less than he'd be able to buy them from a dealer. Plus, some auctions take their commission off the seller's gross receipts. So if the cards sell for $7,500, a 10 percent commission would leave you with only $6,750 — only 67.5 percent of your investment.

But you're in this for the long haul, you say. You would not spend money that you may need right away. You strongly believe that George Brett will be inducted into the Hall of Fame in 1999 and that his card will appreciate at that time. Okay, maybe you're right. But assuming that you'll receive only 67.5 percent of the amount listed in a price guide, you'll have to wait until the card reaches $148 — if it ever does — just to be able to get back your original $100 a card!

Would you make any other investment like this? Would you purchase a stock for $100 if you knew that you'd be able to sell it for only $67.50 and then only after you found a buyer? Would you spend $200,000 on a home that you could sell for only $135,000, but only after you found a buyer? At least when you buy a $100 savings bond for $50, it's always worth at least $50.

Investing in sports cards seems less like purchasing a stock and more like purchasing a new automobile, which drops 20 percent in value the moment you drive it off the lot. But cars are not investments; we buy them for practical reasons. True, the cost of depreciation can be taken as a tax deduction if the vehicle is used for business purposes. But most people never think that they're going to make a profit on their automobile. So why would you make an investment that performs, at least initially, like an automobile purchase?

Even if your baseball memorabilia triples in value, you still have to find a buyer for it. Months may pass before you find a buyer for your memorabilia, or you may have to wait for the next auction to sell it.

The Beckett Price Guide Phenomenon

Perhaps you think that sports memorabilia collecting is all very confusing. Indeed, the economics of this market seems very contradictory. Which is why you may find yourself asking, "Who died and made this Beckett guy boss?"

A study in sports memorabilia

In the March 1998 issue of *Beckett Baseball Card Monthly,* George Brett's 1975 Topps rookie card was priced between $120 and $200. In the May 1992 issue, it was priced between $130 and $200. So if you bought it for $130 in 1992, you now can get $87.75 for it, based on the 67.5 percent formula explained in the section "The Fallacy of the Stock Market Analogy."

Congratulations! I'm sure I don't need to remind you of how well the stock market performed during the same period. But Brett's cards have not increased in value, which perhaps is not surprising, because he retired after the 1993 season. But Brett will probably enter the Hall of Fame in 1999, an honor that usually triggers a rise in card values. Yet, Brett's cards have gone slightly *down* in value since 1992.

The Brett card is one of many examples of how the sports card market has soured. (Until recently, for instance, card values would rise in anticipation of a player's induction into the Hall of Fame.) The Brett example also shows how overblown the investment hype surrounding sports cards was. But don't fret about your failed George Brett investment. You could have instead purchased Robin Yount's rookie card, which also was included in the 1975 Topps set. Brett and Yount had very similar careers, both reaching the 3,000 hit plateau and both retiring after the 1993 season. For a long time, their rookie cards were identically valued. In May 1992, Yount's rookie card also was valued between $130 and $200. In May 1998, according to Beckett, it was worth between $50 and $100.

For whatever reason, Yount is viewed as less of a sure bet to reach the Hall of Fame, at least when he's first eligible for the Hall in 1999, and that opinion is reflected in the value of his rookie card. The first-time nominees for the Class of 1999 also include Nolan Ryan and Carlton Fisk, and given the fickle nature of the Hall of Fame voters, Yount might have to wait a few years to be elected.

Of course, if you happened to save a George Brett or Robin Yount rookie card from a pack of Topps baseball cards that you purchased for 15 cents in 1975, you could have made a tremendous return on your investment. For example, if you sold one of those cards in 1992 for $65 — 50 percent of book value, a dealer's standard purchase price — your 15-cent "investment" yielded an amazing return over a 17-year period. (Plus, you still must factor in the other cards that came out of the pack.) By this barometer, the folks at *Money* magazine were right when they said that it's difficult to find an investment that performed as well as baseball cards.

This kind of analysis presents a few problems. For example, very few people viewed cards as an investment in 1975. Maybe a few collectors had the foresight to stock up on Brett or Yount rookie cards, but I doubt that more than a few people did. Certainly no one could anticipate a similar return today, now that every card has a value.

Plus, once rookiemania hit in the early '80s, no rookie card could be had for pennies. Here, the initial public offering analogy is valid. In 1983, collectors began stockpiling cards of baseball rookies Wade Boggs, Tony Gwynn, and Ryne Sandberg. Their cards instantly were worth more than the 1983 cards for established players such as Reggie Jackson, Pete Rose, George Brett, and Robin Yount.

When James Beckett, a former professor of statistics, came out with his first baseball card price guide in 1984, the sports collecting hobby was changed forever. From that point on, everything formally had a price. Two other magazines, *Tuff Stuff* and *Sports Cards,* now put out price guides. In addition, more up-to-date price sources are available online. But none is as followed as Beckett's monthly publications on baseball, football, basketball, and hockey cards. (See Figure 10-1.) Check out Chapter 15 for more information on these guides.

Figure 10-1: A Beckett Baseball Card Monthly from 1997 featuring Roger Clemens on the cover.

Beckett, Tuff Stuff, and Sports Cards, to varying degrees, also offer price guide information for autographs and various memorabilia — Kenner Starting Lineups, press pins, medallion coins, and a host of other oddball merchandise. But their card price guides generate the most interest.

Beckett arranges its card price guides by year and by brand. Prices for each set, along with the most prominent cards in each set, are listed in two columns, in effect producing a range of values. The LO and HI columns reflect current retail selling ranges. According to the "How to Use and Condition Guide" in each issue, the "HI column generally represents full retail selling price. The LO column generally represents the lowest price one could expect to find with extensive shopping."

Beckett also provides guidelines for pricing cards based on condition. Cards are graded according to the following categories:

Mint (MT)

Near-Mint/Mint (NRMT-MT)

Near-Mint (NRMT)

Excellent/Mint (EX-MT)

Excellent (EX)

Very Good (VG)

Good/Fair/Poor (G/F/P)

Beckett suggests a price guide percentage by grade, depending on the age of the card. Table 10-1 is the chart for baseball cards.

Table 10-1	Conditions and Values for Cards			
	Pre-1960	*1960 to 1973*	*1974 to 1985*	*1986 to present*
MT	150–200%	125–150%	100–125%	100%
NRMT-MT	100–150%	100–125%	100%	75–90%
NRMT	100%	100%	75–90%	60–75%
EX-MT	50–75%	50–75%	50–75%	40–60%
EX	30–50%	30–50%	30–50%	25–40%
VG	15–30%	15–30%	15–30%	15–25%
G/F/P	5–15%	5–15%	5–15%	5–15%

Here's how you use the Beckett guide to figure the value of your cards. Suppose that you have a 1968 Topps New York Mets rookie card featuring both Nolan Ryan and Jerry Koosman, which had a price range of $600–$900 in the March 1998 edition of *Beckett Baseball Card Monthly*. According to Table 10-1, it would be worth between $750 and $1,350 in MT condition; between $600 and $1,125 in NRMT-MT; between $600 and $900 in NRMT; between $300 and $675 in EX-MT; between $180 and $450 in EX; between $90 and $270 in VG; and between $60 and $135 in G/F/P. Adjusted by condition, the ranges represent the range of prices a collector could expect to pay.

Buy low and sell high

Many dealers base their sales price on HI Beckett and their buying price on a percentage of LO Beckett, usually not more than 50 percent. This skews things even further in the dealer's favor. Consider the example of a 1975 George Brett card. If you and the dealer agree that the card is in NRMT-MT condition, it is therefore priced between $120 and $200 according to Beckett. The dealer may be looking to sell at HI Beckett ($200) but may want to buy at 50 percent of LO Beckett ($60). If you found the Brett card lying in a drawer somewhere, you'd probably take $60. But you'd be foolish to pay $200 for a card that you'd be hard-pressed to get more than $60 for later.

Unfortunately, everyone seems to have a different interpretation of the Beckett pricing guide. Some dealers price all their cards according to the HI column. They assume that collectors want to haggle, so they start as high as possible. Others use the HI column for mint condition cards and the LO column for cards in excellent condition. Because the condition of cards that are not "slabbed" and graded by an independent service such as Professional Sports Authenticators is open to debate, there's no telling where within the range the cards will fall. (Turn to Chapter 11 for more information about slabbing and the PSA.)

The people that produce price guides, to their credit, always emphasize that their guides are just that — guides. As a collector, you should feel free to offer an amount far below even the LO Beckett price. No one should be obligated to buy or sell cards based on the prices quoted in any price guide. The prices are just there to provide a frame of reference. If you find that a dealer is unwilling to budge from HI Beckett prices, move on to another dealer. The market is too competitive to pay HI Beckett.

Price guides are written for dealers more than collectors. Most dealers rely on naive collectors to provide them with inventory. They prefer dealing with noncollectors who have stumbled upon a stash of long-forgotten cards they found in the home of a deceased relative and just want to get rid of — people who have no idea what the cards are worth. Only a few dealers can afford to buy cards by offering 50 percent of LO Beckett. After all, it may take a while for the dealer to get $120 for a card that cost $50.

How Beckett determines the prices

You may wonder how Beckett comes up with the prices. Beckett has a staff of price guide analysts, who attend card shows across the country. The magazines also have networks of dealer "regional correspondents" who provide pricing information. Obviously, some people may construe this situation as a conflict of interest. After all, what incentive does someone who makes a living by selling sports cards have to ever report on the price of a card going down?

To the credit of the magazines, they do report on downward trends, although no one ever mentions that dealers purchase cards for only a fraction of the prices listed, and then only if they need the cards. Dealers rarely purchase new cards from collectors.

Price Guides and New Cards

If you pick up a price guide and look at the prices for new cards, you will not believe your eyes. The prices for various insert and special edition cards are staggering. Freshly minted cards are routinely valued at $20, $50, and even $100.

Now, the people who publish the price guides tell you that they're merely reporting on the prices they've seen at card shows and card shops. The dealers, of course, price their cards according to the price guides. No wonder some people refer to this as chicken-or-the-egg pricing. This much is certain: Dealers rarely, if ever, buy new cards for even a fraction of the prices listed in guides. But because they're in the business of opening large quantities of new cards, they inevitably pull out some of the inserts and special edition cards that drive what's left of the new card business. They'll happily stick a $100 price tag on some 1998 limited edition, die-cut Michael Jordan insert card. But try finding a dealer who will give you even $10 for the one *you* pulled out of a pack.

If you ever find a valuable insert card in a pack, attempt to sell it right away. You'll soon realize that few dealers will have any interest. If someone does express interest, expect to receive an offer of no more than 10 percent of a price guide figure.

What makes the insert card part of the market even more ridiculous is how quickly dealers move on to the next product. That's why you should attempt to immediately sell any valuable card you pull out of a pack. Even if a price guide still has a card priced at $50 or $100 a few months later, dealers will have even less interest because the insert card hoopla will have moved on to the latest release.

All of this information may cause you to ask how a card can really be worth what the guide says if absolutely no one out there — except perhaps a few naive collectors — is willing to pay the prices listed in the guide. Although dealers who subscribe to the price guides want you to believe in those prices, a card is worth only what someone is willing to pay for it. In the sports collectibles business, that's usually only a small fraction of the price you see in a magazine. If a card manufacturer wants to create interest in a card line by producing only a limited number, that doesn't make it a true collectible with lasting value — no matter what a price guide says. You cannot manufacture rarity and true collectible value.

Next time you go to a card show, take some of your supposedly valuable cards along. Take a mix of old and new, especially if you have some of the newest insert cards. Ask each dealer what he'll give you for them. Don't allow the dealers to counter with, "Well, what do you want for them?" (This question demonstrates how dealers prey on unsuspecting sellers.) Ask dealers what their maximum offer is. You may be stunned at how few offers you receive and how low those offers are.

Conflicts of Interest in the Sports Card Business

The sports collecting hobby can be somewhat shady. Card manufacturers tout their products as limited editions but, for the most part, do not disclose the size of the press run. Dealers swear that their goods are worth a certain price, but they would never buy the same item from you at even a fraction of that price. Price guides list values that are influenced, at least in part, by the same people trying to sell the cards. To top it off, price guides are highly dependent on card manufacturer advertising and the health of those companies. The card manufacturers, of course, can thrive only if naive new collectors believe that sports collectibles are investments.

Does this mean that anything illegal or unethical is going on here? Of course not. But that doesn't mean that you should spend money chasing after supposedly valuable insert cards that really aren't worth much of anything.

If you learn nothing else from this book, remember that sports memorabilia is a terrible investment. Use price guides to get a relative gauge of the hobby and as a frame of reference if financial need compels you to sell your collection. Remember, though, that a newcomer can't possibly make money in sports memorabilia. That's fine, because the purpose of this book is to educate you, the consumer, and show you how to enjoy this hobby — without getting burned financially.

Chapter 11

The Value of Sports Memorabilia

*T*he most common question I hear from collectors is "What's it worth?" People are naturally curious about the value of sports memorabilia. They are intrigued about the strange economics of the sports memorabilia hobby and how paper, cardboard, and cloth can be so valuable. If they happen to own some memorabilia, they're even more curious about its value.

So, for many collectors, a better question than "What's it worth?" is "What can I sell it for?" The answers vary greatly. The fact is, numerous variables determine the value of a sports collectible, and I examine many of them in this chapter.

Card Condition

You're probably familiar with the real estate axiom that the three most important selling points of a house are location, location, location. A similar motto can be applied to sports cards: Collectors and dealers are obsessed with condition, condition, condition.

In the sports memorabilia field, if you say something is in very good condition, you probably mean that it's actually in pretty bad shape. If it's in good condition, it's really banged up. Very good and good conditions are not acceptable to collectors. They want items, particularly cards, to be in mint or near-mint condition, or at least excellent. Like diamond grading, the differences in the levels of condition for sports cards can be minuscule and highly debatable.

Cards generally are graded by the following categories. You might also see the corresponding abbreviations used in some price guides. (See Chapter 10 for the Beckett price guide system.)

Mint (MT)

Near-Mint (NRMT)

Excellent (EX)

Very Good (VG)

Good (G)

Fair (F)

Poor (P)

In recent years, collectors have added categories such as Near Mint-Mint (NRMT-MT). But that's really splitting hairs and making the grading even more subjective. Here's a primer on the general parameters for grading cards:

Mint (MT)

Mint indicates a flawless card. All four corners are sharp, the centering is pretty much perfect, and the edges are smooth. A mint card has its original color and gloss. The photo has transferred in perfect focus. The card has no print spots and, in the case of pre-1992 cards, no gum stains. Thus, a card can come straight out of the pack and not be in Mint condition unless it was flawlessly printed.

Near-Mint (NRMT)

Near-Mint refers to a card that, on close inspection, has one minor flaw that will lower its value: one fuzzy corner or two or more corners with slight fraying. The card may be slightly off-centered or have rough edges or minor printing spots. It should, however, still have its original color and gloss. Some collectors believe that a card made before 1980 should not be classified above Near-Mint unless it remained in an unopened pack for years, with no printing flaws or gum stains.

Excellent-Mint (EX-MT)

An Excellent-Mint card has some minor flaws. An EX-MT card may have two or three fuzzy corners and slightly poorer centering than a Near-Mint card. It should have its original gloss but could have slight color or focus imperfections.

The corners of cardstock tend to fray over time, especially with cards produced on the thicker, pre-1990s cardboard. In the case of a *fuzzy* corner, the corner still comes to a point, but has begun to fray slightly. When the fraying has increased to the point where layering of the cardstock is visible, it's said to have a *slightly rounded corner.* If the corner is extremely layered and round, it's called a *rounded corner.* Some collectors use the term *dinged* rather than *fuzzy.*

Very Good (VG)

In Memspeak, Very Good is *not* very good. A VG card shows obvious signs of handling. It has rounded corners with slight layering, some discoloration of the borders, and some loss of gloss. Even a minor crease in the card relegates a card to VG condition.

Good (G), Fair (F), Poor (P)

Cards rated Good, Fair, or Poor have taken a ride in bicycle spokes, spent some time in back pockets, or even gone through the wash. They have major creases, no gloss, and well-worn, layered corners. You wouldn't want to buy cards in these conditions; many dealers don't even try to sell them. But if someone gives you cards of superstars from the pre-1970 era, they're certainly worth holding onto. Heck, a T206 Honus Wagner in Good condition still is worth thousands.

Slabbing Cards

If you've spent any time at card shops or shows already, you've probably noticed that a lot of cards are placed in rigid plastic holders with a label classifying them between grades 1 and 10. A similar process has been used for years in the coin collecting hobby, but it's been widely used in the sports card business only since the mid-1990s. The purpose is to make card grading objective, instead of leaving it up to the biased eyes of dealers selling cards.

Minty fresh

Some people are obsessed over a card's "mintness." One prominent dealer even refers to himself as "Mr. Mint." But unless you're concerned about the investment value of a card — and hopefully you aren't because you understand that sports memorabilia is a terrible investment – you should not get hung up over condition. Nevertheless, it's important to recognize the various conditions, even if the distinctions are negligible. You wouldn't want to pay for an overgraded card, just as you want to make sure a card you were selling was graded properly.

The leader in the card-grading field is PSA (Professional Sports Authenticators) of Newport Beach, California. Just as the Gemological Institute of America (GIA) is the standard for diamond grading, PSA has become the most-followed grading system in the card business. Many dealers, conditioned to grading cards themselves, have resisted the slabbing process, but they're now realizing that slabbing will inevitably become universal in the card hobby, at least for valuable cards.

The good thing about PSA and the other companies involved in slabbing is that they have no financial stake in how a card is graded. They do not price cards; they only assign a grading number from 1 to 10. Each card is graded by three or four examiners, none of whom is aware of the card's owner. They also analyze the card to make sure that it has not been altered in any way. The card is placed in a hard plastic holder and can't be removed unless the holder is broken. This keeps unscrupulous dealers — no, that term is not redundant — from removing the graded card and inserting one of lesser value.

Having a card slabbed is not cheap. It all depends on the value of the card and how many you submit. It also helps if you submit your card to PSA through one of its official dealers. (PSA shrewdly markets its service by recruiting dealers across the country to, in effect, serve as agents. This arrangement has helped slabbing become more widely accepted.)

Here's a look at PSA's grading scale:

10 — Gem Mint

9 — Mint

8 — Near Mint-Mint

7 — Near Mint

6 — Excellent-Mint

5 — Excellent

4 — Very Good-Excellent

3 — Very Good

2 — Good

1 — Poor/Fair

To slab or not to slab, you ask. Purchasing a slabbed card is not wrong. In fact, by purchasing a slabbed card, you'll know that its condition was independently determined. If you ever decide to sell, you and the buyer won't have to debate its condition. But unless you have a high-ticket card that you're ready to sell, you don't need to submit cards for slabbing. Just keep your cards in pristine condition. To do that, you don't need your card slabbed.

Why All Players Are Not Created Equal

Calculating a player's popularity among collectors — and thus the value of his memorabilia — usually is not difficult. Popularity is often proportional to an athlete's performance and charisma. Michael Jordan is viewed as the best player in the National Basketball Association, and perhaps the best player of all-time, and appeals to everyone, which is why advertisers recruit him to pitch their products. Not surprisingly, he's the most popular player among collectors. Cal Ripken is considered the best shortstop of his generation, even though he recently moved to third base. He would not be considered the best player in baseball, at least now that he's approached the twilight of his career. But he is considered the most popular baseball player among collectors, as much for his work ethic and clean-cut image as for his play on the field. Explaining the standing of other players among collectors is more difficult. Here are some factors to consider:

The rookie factor

Even though rookiemania isn't as prevalent as it once was, sports collectors still suffer from "flavor-of-the-month" syndrome. They flock to the latest player touted as the next Jordan or next Emmitt Smith or next Barry Bonds. Like the stock of a promising new company, their memorabilia seems ridiculously overpriced, valued almost solely for a player's potential.

Of course, the landscape is littered with players who never reached that promise. Remember Harold Miner, the so-called "Baby Jordan?" Or National Basketball Association players like Pervis Ellison and Danny Manning, No.1 NBA picks who never became more than role players? How about Jose Canseco, whom everyone expected to break every record in baseball? Unless his career catches a second wind, he won't even make the Hall of Fame.

Memorabilia manufacturers know that rookies and hot young stars drive their sales. That fact doesn't mean that it should necessarily influence your collecting habits. Remember, unless you're collecting for investment — which I don't recommend — a player's potential or rookie status should not be a determining factor.

The New York factor

Conventional wisdom suggests that playing in New York makes you more popular among advertisers and collectors because you're in the media capital of the world. For years, this was true. Everyone from Babe Ruth to Joe DiMaggio to Mickey Mantle to Joe Namath became larger than life, in part because they played in New York.

Of course, they all won championships. These days, however, the New York factor doesn't seem to be that big a deal. Perhaps it's because New York's teams have not dominated sports over the last two decades. The football Giants have had their moments, but not like the Dallas Cowboys, San Francisco 49ers, or Green Bay Packers. The New York Knicks have been one of the game's elite teams for a decade, but they have not won a title during that span and their star, Patrick Ewing, hardly ranks among the most popular among collectors. The Yankees won a World Series title in 1996, but Tino Martinez and Bernie Williams, arguably their two biggest stars, have remained relatively anonymous. Even Wayne Gretzky and Mark Messier, who led the Rangers to the 1994 Stanley Cup, established themselves elsewhere.

The truth is, New York is no longer the center of the sports universe. Cable television has brought sports to everyone, and national broadcasts feature the most successful teams, regardless of where they're located. Allegiances no longer are dictated by where a sports fan lives. The Big Apple no longer has the magical pull that it did in the early 1950s, when the Yankees seemed to play the Brooklyn Dodgers or New York Giants in the World Series every year.

Still, you can't minimize the Yankees glorious history. Yankees collectibles related to Ruth, Lou Gehrig, DiMaggio, and Mantle remain among the most treasured in the hobby, a phenomenon that shows no sign of abating.

The Hall of Fame factor

As I mention in Chapter 3, a premium is attached to collectibles of Hall of Fame members, particularly in baseball. Much of the pricing of player memorabilia, even rookie memorabilia, is based on their potential for one day making a Hall of Fame.

For many years, the values for memorabilia of a player on the verge of induction into the Baseball Hall of Fame would rise the closer he got to induction. (A player must wait five years after retirement to appear on the ballot. He's elected in January and inducted late in the summer.) This increase in value had more to do with the bandwagon mentality surrounding sports memorabilia than with any true rise in value. After all, how could a player be that much better or highly-regarded five years after retirement? Players don't reach the Hall of Fame by surprise.

Maybe collectors have come to their senses, because the Hall of Fame markup does not seem to occur as much anymore, at least with cards. It does, however, affect autograph prices. Elected Hall of Famers can command much more money for their signatures at card shows than non-Hall of Famers.

The race factor

Race does not seem to be as much of a factor in the sports memorabilia business as it used to be, even 10 years ago. Just as hobbyists have shed their New York mentality, they also seem to have grown colorblind. These days, minority athletes such as Michael Jordan, Shaquille O'Neal, Kobe Bryant, Emmitt Smith, Tiger Woods, Ken Griffey Jr., and Tony Gwynn dominate any ranking of the most popular sports figures among collectors. However, black athletes from previous generations, especially in baseball, were not as popular among collectors. Consider the comparison of Mickey Mantle versus Hank Aaron or Willie Mays. By most standards, Aaron and Mays, who are African American, had better careers than Mantle. Of course, Mantle played for the New York Yankees, the most storied franchise in sports, and appeared in postseason play more often than Aaron or Mays. Still, no one will deny that race has something to do with this popularity. Mantle is far more popular among collectors, even now. Maybe Mantle remains such a favorite because most collectors who covet Mantle memorabilia come from an era that was more racially charged. Remember, too, that the vast majority of collectors are white.

Still, today's sports collectibles community might be slightly more progressive than society as a whole. The popularity of Negro League baseball memorabilia has soared in recent years. When baseball recognized the contributions of Jackie Robinson in 1997, 50 years after he broke the game's color barrier, it generated renewed interest in memorabilia related to the late Dodgers infielder. And one of the biggest favorites among collectors these days is Roberto Clemente, who as a dark-skinned Puerto Rican suffered dual racism. Now more than 25 years after his death in a plane crash, he's as popular among collectors as anyone besides Mantle.

Racism does exist in the memorabilia world. But today's collectors would generally choose Griffey over, say, Mark McGwire or Mike Piazza. And if they didn't, it probably wouldn't be because of race. Because McGwire/Piazza and Griffey represent the closest modern comparison to Aaron/Mays and Mantle, perhaps that's a sign of progress.

Regional appeal

Like the New York mentality, regional appeal isn't as big a factor as it used to be. But players on teams that have national followings will always be popular among collectors. Teams such as the Yankees, Boston Red Sox, Chicago Bulls, Dallas Cowboys, Green Bay Packers, and Boston Celtics have fans across the U.S. Plus, they've had extraordinary success. Other teams have a more unlikely following. The St. Louis Cardinals, for instance, have intensely loyal fans and throngs of supporters throughout the Midwest. The Atlanta Braves, ironically, developed a huge following when they were terrible during the 1980s because superstation WTBS broadcast their games to a national television audience. Their one bright spot from that era, slugger Dale Murphy, remains a collectors' favorite, even though he's a long shot for the Hall of Fame. Part of his popularity is due to his play and All-American image, but some of it results from his national exposure on WTBS long before the era of ESPN SportsCenter and CNN-Sports Illustrated.

The Chicago Cubs have attracted fans because of their storied Wrigley Field ballpark, their reputation as lovable losers, and their longtime broadcaster Harry Caray, now deceased. But superstation WGN is what brought Caray and the Cubs to a national audience. The popularity of team and player memorabilia reflects that national interest.

The mortality factor

Sadly, a ghoulish element affects the price of sports memorabilia, especially autographs. When a player dies, his autograph inevitably increases in value because, regrettably, he won't be signing any longer. In recent years, however, an athlete's death seems to be less of a factor in autograph values because most elderly sports stars have spent years signing on the card show circuit, so plenty of autographs are available.

Whenever celebrities die, admirers rush to snap up products related to them. For example, fans buy albums of singers and videocassettes of actors. After Princess Diana died in 1997, a cottage industry of Diana collectibles was created. For the most part, people simply are trying to show genuine appreciation for someone's life and want something to remember the person by.

Sports memorabilia can get a little out of hand, however, at least on the surface. In 1992, a promoter advertised a signing with baseball Hall of Famer Billy Herman, who was terminally ill with cancer. The ad mentioned Herman's illness and stated "this might be his last signing session." Herman died shortly after the promoter sent out flyers for the signing, and many collectors received the flyers after Herman's death. Now, in fairness to the promoter, he was only helping Herman raise money for his family. But because that fact was not explained in the flyer, the event seemed rather tasteless at the time.

The hefty prices charged for the autographs of Joe DiMaggio and Ted Williams, for instance, undoubtedly are due in large part to the market and their status as the greatest living baseball players. But the fact that they aren't getting any younger also contributes to the high prices; DiMaggio was born in 1914 and Williams in 1918.

The X factor

A player's popularity also can be affected by other intangible factors, most related to his personality. Cal Ripken is admired for his work ethic and for representing down-home values. Players such as David Robinson of the San Antonio Spurs, Steve Young of the San Francisco 49ers, Barry Sanders of the Detroit Lions, and Tony Gwynn of the San Diego Padres have earned points for being nice guys in addition to being fabulous athletes.

Other players seem more famous, and thus more popular among collectors, for cultivating a celebrity image that becomes greater than anything they've accomplished in sports. Professional basketball player Dennis Rodman is a tremendous rebounder, but he would be a relative unknown were it not for his hair-dyeing, cross-dressing, body-piercing antics. Deion Sanders has played on Super Bowl champions, but he's more famous as a sneaker pitchman and for constantly changing sports, even though he'd probably be Hall of Fame caliber in one sport or the other if he'd just focus his energies. Still, fans seem to love Rodman and Sanders more for their personalities than for their on-field accomplishments.

On the other hand, some athletes may be less popular among collectors because of their reserved, almost shy personalities. NBA stars Patrick Ewing and John Stockton and former Chicago Cubs second baseman Ryne Sandberg have shunned media attention. Even though they're among the game's all-time greats, fans know precious little about them. As a result, they've never quite been embraced by collectors, considering what they've accomplished.

Other athletes have been shunned by collectors because of the way they've treated fans. Baseball's Albert Belle has a long rap sheet of incidents of rude and boorish behavior toward fans. Hall of Famer Willie Mays has a reputation for being surly toward the public, even when he's being paid to sign autographs in person.

Don't collect a player because of market factors. If you happen to like Albert Belle or John Stockton, you're in luck. You'll probably find it easier to acquire these players' items because their stuff is relatively affordable and not as popular. Try not to jump on the bandwagon for someone like Dennis Rodman or Deion Sanders. That kind of collectible popularity usually is not sustained for long. Players who demonstrate character on and off the field usually are the ones with true collectible value.

Artificial Supply and Demand

Sometimes players create a false market for their memorabilia by limiting supply to increase demand and, of course, their own profit. Joe DiMaggio and the late Mickey Mantle started this practice by refusing to sign bats unless they received literally thousands of dollars in return. In a sense, it was as if they were already dead, at least as far as collectors of autographed bats were concerned.

Unfortunately, the behavior of DiMaggio and Mantle had a big impact on the price of a lot of sports memorabilia, with athletes everywhere refusing to sign bats, equipment, jerseys, helmets, hats, lithographs, and oversized pictures unless they were paid a premium. In fairness to the players, they figured that if collectors could sell "premium" items that they autographed for much more than, say, 8-x-10 photos, they were due a fair cut. Most collectors have no problem with that, but the prices in many instances — such as for DiMaggio and Mantle signatures on bats — were outrageous.

Other athletes, such as former baseball pitcher Steve Carlton, ex-Notre Dame and Green Bay Packers star Paul Hornung, and one-time Boston Celtics center Bill Russell, worked the market in their favor by refusing to sign at all for years. Then, not surprisingly, they were suddenly willing to sign — for exorbitant prices.

Don't let artificial supply and demand cause you to overpay for autographs. Although the principle of supply and demand dictates the collectibles market as much as it does any other market, why should you reward someone for selfishness and greed?

Too much supply

Amazingly, some players are criticized for their generous signing habits because such accessibility renders their autographs virtually worthless. Baseball Hall of Fame pitcher Bob Feller estimates that he's signed more than 1 million autographs, which inspired the popular hobby saying that a Feller item is worth more if it's *unsigned*. Although Feller is a long-time veteran of the show circuit, he's probably signed more autographs for free in person than anyone. If everyone were as generous as Feller, autographs would have little value at all. And that wouldn't be such a bad thing, would it?

Paying for Extras: Why New Cards Cost So Much

Artificial supply and demand also helps explain the market for new cards. Since sports cards became big business, manufacturers have walked a fine line between producing too many sports cards and not enough. Even though collectors usually have no idea how many cards are produced, they quickly get a feel for the market. If it seems like not many cards are out there, prices will go up. On the other hand, if it seems as if the cards have been overproduced, the prices will go down.

Of course, those prices apply to cards in the secondary market of card shops and shows. The suggested retail price is generally the same across the board. The manufacturer sells the cards at its wholesale price and does not directly benefit if the cards soar on the secondary market.

Notice that I said "directly" benefit. Manufacturers do, of course, indirectly benefit. If collectors believe that Company X's card lines are extremely limited, they'll buy up the next card product very quickly. Knowing this, Company X produces more than it did previously. Of course, it doesn't want to produce too much, knowing that collectors will abandon the company as quickly as they jumped on the bandwagon. Because the card companies never have to release production figures, no one can really tell just how many cards are circulating.

A backwards logic in the sports card business says that the more expensive a pack of cards, the more collectible and valuable the cards are. The card companies know that collectors don't buy as many cards as they used to, but they try to keep them spending the same amount by adding more bells and whistles to their cards and blaming the higher costs on the increase in printing costs.

In reality, printing costs have stayed consistent in recent years. If anything, costs have dropped a little because printing is a competitive business. Card manufacturers, for the most part, no longer own their press facilities — a significant savings in itself — and can shop around until they find the cheapest means to print their cards.

Manufacturing rarity and true collectible value is impossible. A card manufacturer may slap an expensive price tag on its cards and claim to have used revolutionary printing technologies, but those factors don't mean that the cards have any intrinsic collectible value.

Why So Many Card Sets Are Available

As recently as the early 1980s, collecting every line of sports cards was easy. Companies produced one line for each of the four major sports, or some combination of the four. They were released at logical times, a few months before the start of the season. After collectors had put together the complete set of a sport — or bought a complete set — they had to wait for the following season for a new one to come out. No longer. These days, companies make dozens of sets and subsets of all four major sports and release them all year long. They release a new hockey card line in July and football sets in April. Again, a different marketing philosophy is at work here. The manufacturers know that there are far fewer collectors now than there were ten years ago, so they focus their efforts on getting those people to spend more.

However, card manufacturers should be trying to win back the people who gave up on collecting or at least trying to earn new customers. Instead, perhaps not surprisingly, they try to wring more money out of their loyal consumers. In that sense, the card business perfectly mirrors sports itself. Instead of worrying why fewer people attend sports events, a phenomenon in all four major sports in recent years, team officials raise ticket prices and build smaller stadiums. Instead of increasing demand, they try to limit supply and make that supply pricier. The same formula is being applied to the sports card business.

Don't fall into the trap of trying to collect everything. Remember, collect new cards if you enjoy them, not because of all the false promises of investment value, insert cards, and other smoke-and-mirrors marketing. If you try to collect more than a handful of sets, you'll find yourself frustrated and in debt.

Why Card Companies Won't Discuss Production Figures

Sports memorabilia may be the only collectible field in which the size of a production run is rarely disclosed. Think about that. If you paid big money for a lithograph print, you'd expect to know how many of them were produced. After all, although you may pay a certain price for something that was one of a hundred, you wouldn't pay the same price for something that was one in a million. No one is that foolish!

And yet, that's exactly how card manufacturers treat their customers. Production runs are carefully guarded; even many employees of card companies have no idea how many cards are produced. But who can blame the manufacturers? If they can produce and sell 4 billion baseball cards, as Upper Deck did in 1991, why should they tell anyone? They'd rather try to sell 5 billion the next year. If they announce the 4 billion figure, they can't produce more the next time around because collectors would view the next product as less rare — and less collectible — than the previous card set.

In the case of insert cards, laws require companies to disclose the odds of pulling a special card out of a pack. Even then, you still don't know how many cards are produced, but you can at least figure out how relatively rare the inserts are.

Whenever you see a card or memorabilia line marketed as "limited edition," demand to know just how limited the edition is. The term "limited edition" is nothing more than shameless hype. After all, anything short of infinity is, by definition, limited edition. If a company created 10 trillion insert cards, those cards could be called a limited edition, if only because 11 trillion weren't produced.

Card manufacturers always try to apply the standards of the stock market to their own industry. If the public perceives that a shortage of their cards exists, they figure that they'll produce more the next year. In the stock market, companies can't print more shares just because the demand for the existing ones goes up. They can, but not without announcing a stock split and issuing additional shares to existing stockholders. Amazingly, no laws or regulations keep card manufacturers from going back on press and printing *more* cards. Because they never have to announce the size of the press run, no one can ever prove that additional cards were cranked out.

Card manufacturing is somewhat like the book publishing business. If a book sells well, the publisher arranges for additional printings. But the first printing is always labeled as such, and first editions of up-and-coming authors often become valuable collectors items. But with sports cards, you not only don't know how many cards were produced, but you don't necessarily even know when!

Don't accept something as rare and collectible just because a manufacturer says so or because the market seems to have it in limited quantities. Unless the size of the production run is made public, don't purchase anything hyped as limited edition.

Whatever happened to trading?

With all the talk of buying and selling in the sports memorabilia business, collectors can easily forget that the best way to build a collection is through trading. Some of the most prominent collectors rarely spend a dime on their collection. They just trade their excess for things they really want. By keeping an eye out for items that they know their trading partners may want, they maintain a constant supply of trade materials.

Before the sports card hobby exploded into a business in the early 1980s, trading was the norm. A collector who wanted to complete a set had to purchase more packs or, more likely, trade with buddies. Sports cards were even referred to as *trading* cards.

Although the buying and selling of cards seem to have killed trading, savvy collectors know that trading is the best way to add to a collection. And you don't have to be a veteran hobbyist who accumulated a vast collection before the hobby boom to do so. You can start by picking up extra collectibles in your travels. If you attend the first game of an expansion team or first game in a new stadium, pick up extra copies of programs. If you stumble upon a wacky oddball item in your grocery store featuring a superstar player, pick up several, especially if you know that the product is being released only regionally.

Most importantly, develop a network of collector friends. Get copies of their up-to-the-minute wish lists. Ask them what objects they've had difficulty finding. Make friends with dealers. It's a rare dealer who isn't a collector himself. If you find the item that he's spent years searching for, you'll be in a great position to make a fabulous deal. Make sure that you have phone numbers where trading partners can be reached at all times. That way, you can double-check before acquiring it yourself.

Some collectors become such good friends that they naturally pick up two of everything. They're constantly trading and keeping an unofficial tally to make sure that their buddy isn't getting too far ahead. Money rarely changes hands, but both collections grow. Occasionally, they'll sell an extra or unwanted big-ticket item at auction to earn "play" money to purchase something they really want. These savvy hobbyists rarely dip into their own pockets for their collections.

The people who manufacture and market memorabilia hate these folks because they rarely spend their own cash. That's okay. Remember, keeping these guys in business is not your job, and the best feeling in sports collecting comes from making significant upgrades to your collection without spending a dime.

Chapter 12

Making a Pitch for Your Collectibles

....

In This Chapter

▶ Discovering the liquidity of sports memorabilia

▶ Selling to dealers

▶ Bidding farewell to your stuff at auction

▶ Becoming a dealer

▶ Selling through advertisements and online

....

*E*ven if the idea of parting with your cherished sports memorabilia is the farthest thing from your mind right now, someday you may need to sell your collection. You may reach a point where you no longer want to keep collecting. Or maybe you need extra cash to finance a home or a child's education. Perhaps your collection has become unwieldy, and you need to pare it down. Maybe you recently got married, and your spouse has ordered you to get rid of everything. (I'm not a marriage counselor, but this could be a bad sign.) So, although you never started a sports collection for investment purposes, you may need to unload your memorabilia to pay for a major purchase. Or perhaps your collection simply no longer fits in with your current lifestyle.

Or maybe you've inherited a collection and have no idea how to liquidate it. People face this situation all the time. Families of sports memorabilia collectors often have no clue about where or how to sell the collection. Unfortunately, dealers often take advantage of these innocent folks.

I have a friend whose collection probably is worth $500,000. His wife is not from the U.S. and has little interest in sports, let alone memorabilia, even though her husband's collection takes up their entire basement and a spare bedroom. Fortunately, my friend has a colleague who also is a serious collector and a dear friend. My friend has a clause in his will that stipulates that, upon his death, his collector buddy is to sell off the collection on behalf of the family.

Why most sports memorabilia is unsellable

The market for sports memorabilia, in many respects, is a one-way street. Sure, price guides list attractive values for almost everything. But the value of an item in a price guide and the price that you'll actually receive can vary tremendously — that is, if you can even find a home for what you're trying to sell. Most collectibles produced since the mid-1970s have little true value because they've been mass-produced and hoarded. Most of these items are not rare, contrary to what dealers will tell you when they're trying to sell. (Of course, they'll be the first to admit that what *you* have to sell is commonplace and they want no part of it.)

Price guides are produced for dealers, not collectors. Many collectors make the mistake of looking at price guides the way they view a blue book for automobile prices or the business section of a newspaper for stock quotes; they figure that they'll receive a price close to the one listed. Not so with sports memorabilia. So many variables are involved. Most dealers don't want anything produced after the mid-1970s, and then they want it only if they get it at rock-bottom prices.

Also remember that the sports collectibles market is not nearly what it once was. There are fewer buyers of merchandise, and precious few buyers purchase big-ticket items. The sad reality is that if you're looking to unload your collection, it may take a while.

My friend's arrangement makes sense. What if someone offered the grieving widow $75,000 for everything? Heck, she'd take the money and run. That's a lot of cash, plus she gets her basement cleared out. But even though that sounds like a lot of money, it represents only a fraction of what the collection is worth. Unfortunately, you may not have a big-time, knowledgeable collector friend to help you unload your collection.

In this chapter, I explain how to sell your memorabilia efficiently and for the highest price.

How to Liquidate Your Collection

Many collectors make the mistake of attaching a price to their collection. They take inventory of it periodically, charting price guide values as if they were keeping track of their stock portfolio. They come to believe that they have a readily available cash reserve, "liquid" reserves.

TIP

Timing the market

Financial experts often say that timing the stock market is an impossible job. They recommend that investors make purchases over time, so that the highs and lows of the market will eventually average out. "Dollar cost averaging" is what they call it.

Timing the sports memorabilia market is also impossible. Dealers often are asked whether it's a good time to sell. What are they supposed to say? If they answer no, they have no chance of buying a nice collection. If they say yes, they'll look self-serving. The answer is, nobody knows. The market for sports memorabilia has taken a huge downturn since 1991. Many collectibles are worth far less than they were at that time.

On the other hand, some things, such as Mark McGwire's 1985 Topps rookie baseball card,

have increased in value. If you held on to them, you probably can sell for more these days. Of course, it still seems like a lot more has gone down than up in value.

The only factor in deciding when to sell should be your personal considerations. You might, however, want to consider what time of year you sell your collection. There's a school of thought that says you are better off selling baseball memorabilia, for instance, during the heart of the season from May through September, football memorabilia in the fall, and so on. That's probably less of a factor than it once was, especially with card companies producing sets for all four major sports year-round. If you want to sell, no time is better or worse than any other time.

But what if you need the cash immediately? Can you sell the collection quickly? It depends on what you have, but generally, the answer is probably no. Even if you have rare, vintage memorabilia, you may be hard-pressed to sell it quickly — unless you're willing to take a tiny fraction of its worth. Even pawn shops aren't an option, because few of them deal in sports memorabilia.

Chances are, however, that you're selling only after careful thought and not in an emergency situation. If you do not have a financial emergency, you probably can afford to hang on to your collection until you've found the highest bidder. But selling it still will take work, in some cases as much work as it took you to acquire some of those hard-to-find pieces in the first place.

The point is that *sports memorabilia is anything but liquid.* I had a friend who had what he thought was $10,000 in collectibles to sell. He had complete card sets from the 1970s and early 1980s; autographed photos, balls, and lithographs; several dozen unopened "wax" boxes purportedly worth between $100 and $200 apiece; hundreds of publications; assorted football cards from the 1960s in pristine condition; and all sorts of oddball merchandise. He consulted price guides and meticulously logged the values.

If anything, he was conservative, recognizing up front that dealers pay, at most, 50 cents on the dollar. Finally, he loaded everything into a van and took it to the biggest sports memorabilia dealer in his area. The dealer, whom my friend knew well, made a careful inventory and offered $1,800. Having already offered the collection by phone unsuccessfully to other potential buyers, my friend graciously took this offer.

Selling memorabilia has become more difficult because there are fewer collectors and dealers. Unless you have a rare, game-used uniform, it's almost impossible to find a dealer willing to spend more than $2,000 on anything submitted by a collector. The dealer who bought my friend's collection for $1,800 in 1995, for example, has since folded up his shop after nearly two decades of business.

The Dealer Sell

Dealers tell you that they frequently buy from collectors. "Always Buying" signs are posted everywhere at card shows. The fact is, most dealers are bargain hunters. They prey off uneducated consumers, waiting for some poor, unsuspecting customer to wander up to their booth or card shop with a box full of goodies that they uncovered in an attic somewhere. The dealer may offer $100, figuring that the collector won't know any better. Sadly, even in this era of price guides, many people don't. Only when collectors later find out that their box of cards from the 1960s was worth thousands do they realize that they were fleeced.

Even under the best of circumstances, dealers can afford to pay only 50 percent of book value if they hope to turn a modest profit. This pricing guideline makes sense, of course, because dealers buy at wholesale and sell at retail. Many collectors tend to forget this policy and are insulted by such offers. Don't be.

You may wonder which merchandise is easier to sell: cards, autographs, game-used equipment, or oddball merchandise. The answer is, it depends. Because cards have such a history and a universally accepted system of pricing in Beckett Publications (see Chapter 10), you'll usually have an easier time selling cards. If you have a game-used jersey that once belonged to Babe Ruth, you may have to go the auction route to find a buyer who's wealthy enough. But if you live in the Baltimore area and have a lot of Cal Ripken oddball merchandise, you'll have no trouble selling it quickly. So your chances of selling your collectibles depend on what you have and where you live.

Don't deal with friends

Many people don't engage in financial trans- actions, such as selling sports memorabilia, with family and friends. They tend to get burned. Your collector buddy may expect a great deal from you. After all, he's your friend. He'll promise to take good care of the item, unlike some cutthroat dealer who's just look- ing to sell it. You'll still be able to see it when you visit your buddy's house. Of course, your friend is willing to offer only $300 for that same $1,000 jersey, capitalizing on your friendship. Who knows? He may even turn around and sell it. My advice: Don't deal with friends. Trad- ing with like-minded collector friends is okay because it allows you to build a collection without putting forth cash. These people, how- ever, can be the most difficult to sell to be- cause they believe they deserve a friendship discount.

Selling cards

When selling cards, the bigger the dealer, the better off you're going to be. Because of the downturn in the market, only a few dealers can afford to pay big bucks for cards. You'll recognize them at the larger card shows. They're the ones peeling off freshly minted $100 bills. They have huge lists of clients who are willing to pay dearly for quality cards and merchandise. They may have already sold your cards before they've completed the deal with you. For them, the goal is to keep the money and merchandise moving at all times.

Selling miscellaneous items

If you have a diverse collection that you want to sell, you may have to turn to people other than dealers. Dealers who specialize in cards, for example, may not want to purchase all of your autographs and oddball merchandise. But if you have collector friends who have long coveted certain items in your collection, see whether they're interested. From a wholesale/retail angle, you may be better off selling to them. For example, if you have a game-used jersey with a market value of $1,000, a dealer may be willing to pay only between $400 and $500 for it; after all, he wants to turn a profit when he sells it for around $1,000. But your collector buddy may offer between $600 and $700, which is a better deal than paying the typical retail price. But before selling to friends, consider my advice in the sidebar "Don't deal with friends." And if you're indeed uncomfortable dealing with collector friends, you may want to see the sections "The Dealer Consignment" or "The Auction Route," later in this chapter.

Strategies for selling

After you've made the decision to sell, it's important to have a plan so that you get the most for your collection without spending too much time and effort. Here are a few guidelines to follow:

- ✔ **After you make a decision to sell your collection, detach yourself emotionally from it.** A buyer isn't going to pay you more simply because you really loved the stuff. If anything, he'll grow impatient with your reluctance to part with it. Act professionally and unemotionally when you're selling your collection. You may even want to say that you're selling it for a friend. Be sure to stress, however, that your friend asked for your help because of your extensive knowledge of the market.

- ✔ **Consider the time and effort factor when selling a collection.** Many collectors make the mistake of breaking up their collection, figuring that they may get more cash overall if they sell it in pieces. Although this belief is generally true, you'll spend more time tracking down buyers, and once you consider the hassle and aggravation, it may not be worth it.

- ✔ **If possible, find a dealer who will buy everything.** You may be able to get a better price if you sell piecemeal, but you may decide that the time you save by not traveling to find buyers is worth a few dollars. After you find a dealer willing to take it all, don't let him pick and choose; he's only trying to find a way to pay less. He can always find a home for anything, no matter how worthless he claims it is.

- ✔ **If possible, accept only cash.** Dealing by check takes a leap of faith on either your part or the buyer's. Either you accept a check and hope that it clears, or the buyer waits for the check to clear before receiving your memorabilia. By making the transaction in cash, neither party has to wait.

- ✔ **If you have a valuable collection, you should expect the dealers to come to you.** Some dealers may even fly in from across the country. If you're a veteran collector, you probably know which dealers will do this. But if you have inherited a collection from a deceased relative, you could look for prospective buyers in hobby magazines such as *Sports Collectors Digest* and *Tuff Stuff.*

The Dealer Consignment

Sometimes a dealer may offer to sell your collection or a piece of the collection for you, either at his store or at a card show. Usually a dealer wants only high-ticket items, such as game-used jerseys. A neighborhood card shop owner, however, may be willing to take on a whole collection for you if space allows. After all, the dealer is getting a consignment fee, which can range from 10 to 50 percent depending on your level of friendship.

TIP

When to avoid the dealer consignment

If you're trying to sell an entire collection or a large part of one, dealer consignment probably isn't the route to take. The dealer probably doesn't have the space. Besides, it doesn't make sense for you. I knew one collector who took a box of valuable cards from the 1950s in near-mint condition to a friend who was a card shop owner. The collector was appalled when his buddy offered only 35 percent of book value. Even after the dealer calmly explained the economics of the industry and said that he bought at wholesale prices and sold at retail prices, the collector still shook his head in frustration.

Finally, the dealer offered to take the cards on consignment. The collector would receive 80 percent of the sale price. Because the collector lived near the store, he could check in periodically to see if any of the cards had sold. Even though the dealer specialized in older cards and had a wealthy clientele, this process took a while because many of these cards were priced at hundreds of dollars apiece, according to *Beckett Baseball Card Monthly.*

The collector's stash probably was worth $10,000. He could have gotten $3,500 from the dealer immediately and walked away. Instead, he placed the cards up for consignment and, over time, collected about $6,800. He wouldn't get $10,000, of course, because no collector is going to pay full book price and the seller gave the dealer permission to be flexible with customers. Plus, the dealer took his 20 percent cut.

You're probably thinking that this collector did the right thing. He nearly doubled his money by going the consignment route, right? True, very true. But this process took *five years.* Had he shrewdly invested the $3,500, his proceeds might have grown to $6,800, and he wouldn't have needed to make countless visits to the card shop.

Take the example of a $1,000 jersey. Instead of paying you $400 up front and trying to sell it for $1,000, a process that could take months, or even a year or more, the dealer agrees to sell it for you, taking a $150 commission. This way, the dealer doesn't have to put up more money. Plus, you get more cash in the end, depending on the terms of the consignment.

WARNING!

Collectors who sell items on consignment often get burned when card shops and dealers go out of business. If the dealer files for bankruptcy protection, you may really have a hard time getting your consignments back. The dealer figures that you're probably not going to go through the hassle to get a lawyer and fight for an item that's probably worth less than a few hours of legal fees.

Dealing . . . with the IRS

The dirty little secret of many people who deal in sports collectibles is their flagrant income tax evasion. Card shop owners, of course, are held to a higher standard as retail outlets. But the people who deal privately and at card shows conduct transactions almost exclusively in cash. Even auction houses that sell items worth thousands of dollars on consignment leave it up to the consignors to report it to the Internal Revenue Service. Now, I'm guessing that only a small percentage of people do report their sales, and I can't imagine that the IRS spends much time auditing this kind of stuff. But I still have to warn you about it. An auditor probably will have little mercy on someone who makes thousands of dollars from sports memorabilia and doesn't report it.

It's very easy to fall into a false sense of friendship with a dealer, especially one who operates a local card shop. These shops often become neighborhood hangouts, and you become as chummy with the dealer as you do with your friendly bartender. Keep things in perspective. A fine line exists between friendship and business. Don't forget which side of that line the dealer operates in.

The Auction Route

Like card shows, card shops, and the cards themselves, auctions also have become watered down in recent years. There might be more of them, but quantity does not mean more quality merchandise. Sports auctions used to refer only to the massive, multimillion dollar sales held by huge houses like Leland's, Sotheby's, Christie's, and the now-defunct Richard Wolffers. These days, everyone has jumped on the auction bandwagon. (For more information about auctions, turn to Chapter 8.)

Flip through an issue of *Sports Collectors Digest,* and you'll see numerous ads for telephone and in-person auctions. Even small dealers find that they can make some nice cash by taking items on consignment, advertising the auction to their regular customers, and then renting a hotel ballroom for the sale. Almost everything, it seems, ends up selling.

Why sports memorabilia sells at auctions

Something about the psychology of an auction makes it a very effective way to sell sports memorabilia. An item that's been sitting in a card shop for months without generating any interest may sell instantly in an auction, often for more than the shop's asking price. In fact, some dealers routinely put stuff aside for an auction instead of displaying it in their store. They don't want to risk selling it for less.

When people participate in an auction, it's not just about buying stuff. An element of gamesmanship is involved. People get so involved in the competition for an item that they misjudge their true level of interest. For some people, the thrill of the competition means more than the item itself. People are willing to pay some outrageous prices when they get caught up in all the excitement.

People also buy into the notion that if something's in an auction, it must be valuable. Auctioneers prey on this mentality. They'll ask for a ridiculously high opening bid and then lower the initial price to the point where it sounds extremely affordable. In reality, the item may still be way overpriced, but it sounds reasonable compared to the initial price the auctioneer threw out. After an initial bid is made, the competitive juices start flowing. Before you know it, someone has grossly overpaid.

How you profit — or lose — from an auction

The fan factor is a crucial element of sports memorabilia auctions. If two bidders are competing for, say, a Michael Jordan jersey, it almost becomes a contest to see who is the more serious Jordan collector or the bigger Jordan fan. In a weird sort of way, the fact that they're overbidding for the item further proves the greatness of their hero — at least to them.

Ridiculous? Of course it is. Fortunately, you can be the one profiting if it's your item in the auction. Some risk is involved, however. Even though you get to place a minimum bid requirement on the object, if it doesn't receive a bid, you'll have to pay the dealer/auctioneer a handling fee. Plus, you may be disappointed if it receives only the minimum bid.

Carefully consider your minimum bid. If the fee for items that don't sell is insignificant, you may be better off with a higher asking price. Of course, if you're just trying to get rid of something — especially because you had trouble selling it through other channels — the amount of the opening bid shouldn't matter to you. If you submitted something to an auction through the mail and it goes unsold, you may be responsible for return postage and insurance. You should decide up front who's responsible for those charges.

Don't be surprised if the auction house takes its cut out of your share of the sale. These days, only the larger auction houses charge a "buyer's premium," a 15 percent commission tacked on to the sale price. This way, the auction makes bigger headlines. For example, if a game-used jersey sells for $100,000, the house can issue a press release saying that it sold for $115,000. There's nothing misleading here. In fact, it's the norm. For high-ticket sales, wealthy bidders don't seem to have a problem with a buyer's premium.

For smaller sales, where most items fall in the $50 to $150 range, a seller's premium is more effective. Dealers who operate these auctions won't be making headlines, and these auctions attract collectors of more modest means. A buyer's premium may stop some potential buyers from bidding at certain points. Ideally, the auctioneer will split the commission between the buyer and the seller. But that rarely happens because of the calculations and paperwork involved.

You as a Dealer

You always have the option of becoming a dealer yourself, taking out space at a card show, and sitting on the other side of the table. The advantage here is that you can sell your merchandise at retail price — at least in theory — and have a steady parade of customers coming by.

In reality, however, working as a dealer can be very frustrating. If you ever want to truly gauge the state of the sports memorabilia market, take out a table at a card show. For starters, you have to pay $75 to $100 for a table at a reasonably-sized show of 50 to 100 tables. Don't waste your time at one of the 30-table events at a budget hotel where everyone has the same recently minted cards.

In order to cover your table fee, you have to make $75 to $100 just to break even. Don't underestimate how long breaking even can take. Amazingly, people who have full-time jobs during the week set up at card shows on weekends and often struggle to break even. Although some of the part-timers make a lucrative side income, I can't imagine why the rest of the "weekend warriors" waste their time.

Countless people will try to sell dealers cards from the 1990s, cards they believe are worth hundreds of dollars because Beckett says so. Some collectors will have vintage cards that you won't be able to afford. (Of course, you've probably taken out a table because you're trying to unload your collection, not augment it.)

Unless you're really lucky, you're probably going to sell only a fraction of your collection. You're out the table fee, and you waste a good chunk of your weekend. Is this really how you want to spend your free time? Think about whether you wouldn't rather sell your cards directly to a dealer instead of at a card show. You may make less money, but you'd have more time.

Before becoming a dealer, consider, above all else, whether you really want to be identified as a sports memorabilia dealer. That title could ruin your good reputation!

Becoming a dealer, even for a day, is not a cost-effective means of selling a collection.

Advertising and Online Sources

Of course, you can always take the traditional route and sell your collectibles by taking out an ad in a local newspaper or hobby publication or even online. These ads may locate your target audience more quickly, although they also will attract scores of bargain hunters who figure that you're a naive seller and not an educated collector.

The local newspaper strategy

If you've ever placed an ad in a newspaper, your phone probably rang off the hook. There's probably no better way to sell a car, appliance, or piece of furniture. But is it an effective way to sell a sports memorabilia collection? It depends.

I had a friend whose collection consisted mostly of hundreds of 1969 Topps baseball cards in near-mint condition. He didn't have a complete set but had many of the major stars. Although he had never been a serious collector, he knew the value of the collection and was looking for a way to make a down payment on a new home. He did not have the time to rent a table at a card show and didn't want to take the 30 percent or 35 percent of book value that a dealer would offer.

So he took out an ad in the paper. Sure enough, he received numerous calls from people hoping that he would take $100 for them. Finally, he got a call from a collector who wanted to complete a 1969 Topps set. My friend invited the collector over and sold the cards for about 60 to 70 percent of book value. It was a very cheap investment of time and money — about $30 for the ad.

Does this method work in every instance? Probably not. The seller really only had one item to offer, 1969 Topps baseball cards. He didn't have a diverse collection that he would have had to sell bit by bit. If he had been selling a diverse collection worth more than $10,000, he probably would have been better off finding a major dealer willing to purchase everything.

Many people dislike selling things through the newspaper. They shudder at the thought of welcoming strangers into their home. These are the same people who would rather trade in an automobile for less money than sell it on their own. Personal safety is an important concern in this situation. Always be careful when you sell through newspapers.

The hobby magazine strategy

Sports memorabilia publications probably are the best way to reach your target audience. The most prominent publications, which I discuss in more detail in Chapter 15, are *Sports Collectors Digest* and *Tuff Stuff*.

Sports Collectors Digest, or *SCD*, is produced by Krause Publications of Iola, Wisconsin. Krause also publishes *Sports Cards Magazine*. *SCD* contains some editorial content, but it's mostly advertising. Much of the advertising comes from big-time dealers, some of whom take out eight- to ten-page spreads. The content includes a large classified section for collectors, with categories such as game-used memorabilia, individual player collections, publications, cards, autographs, and so on.

Tuff Stuff has more editorial content than *SCD*, but it does have a small classified advertising area in the back of the publication. Some collectors also take out small display ads.

Beckett Publications accepts advertising from card manufacturers and dealers. The Beckett magazines contain hardly anything from individual collectors, however, so this isn't really an option if you're looking to sell your collection.

Although you're likely to reach the most prospective buyers by advertising in the hobby publications, that sales approach has its disadvantages. Any communication is likely to be through expensive long-distance phone calls. You have to spend a lot of time fielding calls from people simply looking for a huge bargain. You'll also get calls from people who simply want to hear about your collection, which gets annoying when all you want to do is sell.

You may have to send pictures of your collection out to prospective buyers, another time and money expenditure. And, at some point, unless you live within driving distance, either you or the buyer is going to have to make a leap of faith. Either the buyer is going to have to give you a check up front, or you'll have to send the collection first. Obviously, from your standpoint, it's preferable to send the collection *after* you've received payment.

Shipping collectibles

No matter how you send sports memorabilia, whether through the U.S. mail, United Parcel Service, or Federal Express, be sure to pack thoroughly. Use plenty of bubble wrap, Styrofoam peanuts, or newspaper. It's impossible to overprotect sports memorabilia. Make sure that your shipment is properly insured.

Dealers and collectors seem to prefer UPS because it offers the best insurance. Federal Express has limits on the declared value of contents and how much it's responsible for in terms of loss. Be sure to carefully read the company's fine print on "service conditions, declared value, and limit of liability."

From a cost-effectiveness standpoint, selling through advertising probably is not the preferred way to sell a large collection. Hobby ads are a great way to sell individual items, meet like-minded collectors, and locate something you've had difficulty finding. But unless you want to spend months on the phone, pay postage costs, and face the possibility of getting ripped off, you probably want to look to other alternatives for unloading a large collection.

Online ads

The Internet has revolutionized all areas of shopping, and sports memorabilia is no exception. Countless Web sites are dedicated to sports collectibles, which I discuss in Chapter 17.

Because of the vast scope of the World Wide Web, you can easily find like-minded collectors who may be interested in what you have to sell. But, as is the case with hobby ads, the Internet's best value may be in helping you locate hard-to-find items and sell small collections or individual items. To sell a large collection, you're better off finding a local buyer or a dealer willing to come to you. Of course, you may discover that person online.

The Internet is a fabulous tool, but you can meet a lot of scoundrels out there. People can easily remain anonymous online, so always check references and research anyone you deal with via the computer. Buying sports memorabilia online is an effective way to build your collection, but it's probably not an advisable way to make a big-ticket purchase.

Part IV
Frauds, Scams, and Other Dangers

The 5th Wave   By Rich Tennant

"It's a more expensive photo of Honus Wagner because it's signed by both Honus aaand Xena who's shaking his hand."

In this part . . .

These chapters provide a glimpse into the dark side of the sports memorabilia hobby, where card counterfeiters and scam artists thrive. I show you how to recognize cards that have been trimmed, repaired, or otherwise altered, and I illustrate how some shrewd marketers prey on naive collectors. If you ever get ripped off, don't say I didn't warn you.

Chapter 13

Counterfeit Cards, Smoke, and Mirrors

● ●

In This Chapter

▶ Avoiding counterfeit cards

▶ Knowing about reprints

▶ Recognizing altered cards

▶ Understanding pack tampering

● ●

I touch upon forgeries and frauds in Chapters 3 and 4, at least as they pertain to autographs, uniforms, and game-used equipment. Unfortunately, those problems are not the end of a collector's worries. When you're collecting cards, particularly vintage editions, you have to deal with a Pandora's box of trouble.

Many collectors argue that counterfeit cards are not a problem anymore. After all, when Upper Deck came along with its counterfeit-proof cards in 1989, the other manufacturers eventually followed suit. These days, with all of the foil stamping, holograms, and glossy finishes printed on cards, duplicating the newer cards is virtually impossible — or at least cost prohibitive.

Unfortunately, people tend to forget the 100 years before Upper Deck. Those cards were produced by using more elementary printing techniques and are easily counterfeited. And as technology continues to improve, cranking out good fakes of early sports cards becomes easier all the time. In this chapter, I explain what to look for when buying cards in the secondary market and how to recognize the telltale signs of counterfeiting.

I also explain the dangers of buying unopened cards and how some dealers tamper with wax packs and clear, shrink-wrapped "rack" packs, ensuring that the naive buyer will be left with a handful of Rafael Belliards and Dave Magadans.

Counterfeit Cards

In a hobby where autograph forgeries and fraudulent game-used merchandise are everywhere, I'm amazed that more card counterfeiting doesn't occur, especially with cards produced prior to the anticounterfeit technologies first employed in 1989. Counterfeiting is fairly easy, and its practitioners take only a modest risk compared to, say, money counterfeiters. Someone who starts printing $20 bills is likely to land in far hotter water than someone printing copies of a card worth $100. Go figure.

The card manufacturers, of course, do not approve of counterfeiting, because they've paid licensing fees to produce cards. The card companies also are concerned about the issue of quality control; fakes usually are not up to their standards. Plus, the card companies don't want someone reproducing their cards for profit. But they don't become too incensed about these violations. In a sense, a counterfeiter who sells a card for $100 isn't that much different from a dealer who sells a legitimate one for the same price. Either way, the card company has received only pennies as part of the wholesale price it charged for the pack of cards in the first place. So why should card companies get too bent out of shape over counterfeits? What are they going to do? Spend money to chase these guys down? Tracking down counterfeiters is often not worth a card company's time and trouble. Although the card manufacturers pursue counterfeiters, they don't spend vast resources to do so at a time when they're struggling to stay afloat financially.

The professional sports leagues and players associations also pay a lot of lip service to punishing counterfeiters. In reality, the problem is low on their list of priorities. They spend far more resources chasing down people who are selling unlicensed T-shirts and souvenirs at major sporting events. Heck, given the greed of the folks running pro sports, they'd probably endorse counterfeiting if they could find a way to get a cut of it!

Law enforcement officials don't dedicate much energy to fighting sports memorabilia fraud either. They have more pressing problems. Plus, many police officials still fail to recognize that the hobby became a big business two decades ago. Where do you suppose a report of card counterfeiting ranks on their priority list?

None of this lack of concern about counterfeiting is meant to encourage card counterfeiting, of course. But counterfeiting may be a bigger problem than people realize because counterfeiters know that no one is particularly concerned about this offense, so they feel free to continue to break the law. In the book *Sportscard Counterfeit Detector* (Krause Publications, 3rd Edition), authors Bob Lemke and Sally Grace identify more than 200 cards that have been widely counterfeited. With each edition of the book, the list grows longer. And those cards are just the ones that have been recognized.

The infamous Pete Rose and Don Mattingly fakes

The first major case of card counterfeiting occurred in 1982, when a quantity of 1963 Pete Rose rookie cards began surfacing in southern California. The cards were printed on a thinner cardstock than Topps used and displayed some obvious printing variations. But because counterfeiting had never been a problem, the fakes initially went unnoticed.

Eventually the culprits confessed and got off with slaps on the wrists, setting a tone for how law enforcement agencies would deal with subsequent counterfeiters. After the Rose cards were stamped "original counterfeit," the lawyers for one of the counterfeiters filed a motion to get the cards back. Amazingly, it was granted, and the counterfeiters were free to sell them, which they did. Even today, the counterfeit Rose cards occasionally appear on the market, identified as such. They're usually priced around $25, based on their novelty value if nothing else.

In 1986, counterfeits of Don Mattingly's 1984 Donruss rookie card began surfacing. Unlike the Rose card, the counterfeit Mattingly card was difficult to distinguish from the genuine card without a microscope. (The inspiration for Upper Deck came from a card dealer who unwittingly purchased some fakes and a printing company executive who, upon being presented with a fake Mattingly and a real Mattingly by the dealer, could easily tell them apart.)

Not surprisingly, you can find examples of numerous counterfeits. The more expensive the card, the more likely it is to be reproduced. Just as a money counterfeiter concentrates his efforts on $20, $50, and $100 bills, a card counterfeiter is more inclined to roll the dice with more-valuable cards.

Guarding against counterfeiting

Unfortunately, guarding against counterfeiting isn't easy. Some scales can determine whether a cardstock that weighs less than the real thing was used, but I've yet to meet a collector who carts such a scale to shows or card shops. Many printing discrepancies can be seen through a microscope, but who wants to carry one of those around? Compounding the problem is that some printing variances, especially with older cards, are legitimate.

For the most part, dealers do not knowingly sell counterfeit cards any more than merchants give counterfeit bills as change. But dealers can be fooled, and unfortunately, even some of the most honest ones sometimes knowingly sell fakes rather than absorb the financial loss and destroy the cards.

Card counterfeiting is not as rampant as autograph forgeries and bogus game-used merchandise. Perhaps printing cards is more difficult. Perhaps card counterfeiting is not as profitable. Nonetheless, you should always keep your guard up when buying expensive sports cards. But, counterfeiting aside, you may want to think long and hard before dropping big money on cards on the secondary market under any circumstances. After all, you probably already know that sports collectibles make for terrible investments. Why take the risk?

What to consider when buying cards

In Chapters 3 and 4, I provide long checklists of things to consider when purchasing an autograph or game-used item. Though card counterfeiting is not as big a concern as autograph forgeries or bogus uniforms, you still should take some precautions when purchasing sports cards produced before 1989, when card companies began using printing technologies that made card counterfeiting close to impossible. Here's a list of questions you should ask:

- ✔ **Did you purchase the cards from a private collector, estate sale, or yard sale?** Did they come from a friend or neighbor who was cleaning house and found some old cards? You're probably okay because these cards were most likely purchased as packs and saved for years. Plus, a seller who is a personal acquaintance probably isn't trying to dupe you.

- ✔ **Did you purchase the cards from a dealer?** Most dealers recognize counterfeits and take active steps to avoid knowingly selling fakes. People who are going to sell counterfeits will most likely take them to a dealer, which means that dealers are more likely to have counterfeits.

- ✔ **Were the cards produced in the 1990s?** Because of advanced printing technologies, card companies have pretty much eliminated counterfeiting.

- ✔ **Are the cards in question among the most commonly counterfeited?** You may want to consult *Sportscard Counterfeit Detector*. If a card is not included in that book, you're not necessarily off the hook. And, conversely, if a card is listed in the book, you shouldn't be automatically worried. But a listing in the book should give you some idea whether counterfeiting of the card in question is within the realm of possibility.

- ✔ **How valuable is the card?** Counterfeiters aren't likely to waste their time unless the card is particularly valuable.

Reprints, Broders, and Fantasy Cards

The only difference between counterfeits and reprints is intent. The counterfeiter produces cards with the intent of passing them off as the real thing. The reprinter wants to avoid this intentional deceit and usually marks the cards prominently as reprints or makes them easily distinguishable. A *reprint set* is an intentional reproduction to be marketed and represented as something different from the original set, even though it may look almost identical. Topps, for instance, has issued reprint editions of several of its sets from the early 1950s. But unlike the pre-1957 Topps cards, which measured $2^5/_8$ x $3^3/_4$ inches, the reprints were the same size as modern cards, $2^1/_2$ x $3^1/_2$ inches.

Unfortunately, not all reprints are as easy to identify. Many reprints have little notation to begin with, but others can be easily altered and marketed as the real thing. Another trick is to age the reprint card to make it look older. Even if it's still marked as a reprint, on the back perhaps, some collectors and dealers won't think to look there because the card looks genuine from the front.

A cousin of the reprint/counterfeit is the *Broder,* named for the man who created the cards in the early 1980s. A Broder is an original sports card produced without the consent of the athlete, his league, or his players association. These cards have little collectible value because they're not widely available. Producing a Broder would be no different than if you shot a roll of film at a ball game and had the photos made into cards. Probably no one would be interested in buying them, even if you did manage to distribute them. Plus, you'd incur the wrath of the players and the leagues.

Another variation is the *fantasy card,* produced with the same design as a regular series of cards, but not by the original card manufacturer and often of a player who was not active at the time the original cards were produced. After Michael Jordan took batting practice with the Chicago White Sox in 1990, four years before he spent a year playing baseball full time, a fantasy card in the design of the 1986 Donruss card was produced without the consent of Donruss. Until the mid-1990s, some hobby publications included a nine-card insert sheet of fantasy cards. Among their designs was a sheet of current baseball players in the design of 1969 Topps cards. Although the concept was not meant to be a moneymaker, other than to improve circulation of the magazines, the leagues and players associations objected, so the hobby publications stopped including cards.

Trimmed or Repaired Cards

Card collectors have to watch out for more than counterfeits. They also have to deal with trimmed or repaired cards. Unlike counterfeits, these are genuine cards. But because they've been altered, most collectors have little use for them. The problem, of course, comes in identifying them. You're more likely to see trimmed and restored cards from before 1980 because they're likely to be more valuable and in lesser condition.

Identifying a trimmed card

A *trimmed card* has at least one of the edges of the card shaved in order to make the corners sharper or to make the picture on the card appear more centered. The shaving can be done rather easily with a razor blade or Exacto knife, and a cut of $1/16$ inch is usually sufficient. Of course, $1/16$ inch is significant when dealing with cards that measure only $2^1/2$ x $3^1/2$ inches, which is the size of cards produced since 1957. (Topps and Bowman cards produced from 1952 to 1956 measured $2\,5/8$ x $3^3/4$ inches.) The cut is even more significant on tobacco cards, which are much smaller.

Amazingly, few collectors think to measure cards before buying, especially if the card is encased in a Lucite holder. (One good thing about the Professional Sports Authenticators grading system is that it measures cards to make sure that they have not been trimmed.) Maybe collectors don't want to offend the dealer, which is ridiculous if you think about it. Would you buy a used car without taking it for a test drive or examining underneath the hood? Of course not. So why should cards be any different?

Many dealers will appreciate your attention to detail. They even may have measuring devices available, or you can purchase your own for a nominal fee. They're well worth the investment. A standard ruler also does the job.

No reputable dealer objects to having his cards measured. Remember, too, that few dealers knowingly sell trimmed cards. But because checking every card is too time-consuming, inevitably a few slip through. Make sure that they don't slip through to you.

Identifying a repaired card

A *repaired* or *restored card* is one that someone has improved. Usually, someone "improves" the condition of a card by bolstering the corners by using cardboard from other cards. But unlike stadium seats or game-used bats, which often are repaired, repairing sports cards is not acceptable, and collectors and dealers do not view repaired cards as genuine collectibles. At one time, many collectors believed that they were okay as long as the cards were somehow marked accordingly, but you can see that the potential for abuse is here. In many cases, someone who restored a card would place a subtle dot somewhere that signaled that the card is a restoration. But after it's sold or traded a few times, someone eventually forgets to mention that the card has been repaired.

One good way to check for restoration is to hold a card up to light. Chances are, you can see the restoration work at the corners, which will appear translucent.

Has your T206 been trimmed?

The T206 Honus Wagner tobacco card (shown in Chapter 2) is more prone to trimming than many other baseball cards because, if you take a random grouping of T206s, you'll see that they are not consistently cut to a uniform size. They are generally 1½ x 2⅝ inches, but frequently an additional length on top or bottom can be trimmed off within the standard tolerance — leaving a pair of razor-sharp corners. Because the white border has a flat finish, a careful trim can upgrade a VG card with rounded corners to Ex+ — a big jump in value. A veteran collector can see the difference with magnification; the novice might not.

Pack Tampering

The most despicable practice in the sports collecting hobby is opening packs of cards, replacing stars with lesser players, and then resealing the packs and selling them as if they were never opened. This offense goes on far more often than anyone wants to admit. Why? Unopened packs are particularly valuable because of the potential for hidden riches inside. Unfortunately, some dealers remove those riches and reseal the packs.

How packs can be tampered with

Tampering is not much of a problem with cards produced since about 1992. After Upper Deck released its 1989 cards in tamper-resistant foil packaging, other card companies gradually followed suit. By 1992, all packaging was done in foil packaging. Prior to 1989, companies used *wax* packaging that could be opened and resealed. (See Figure 13-1.) Even from 1989 to 1992, some companies continued to use wax packaging. The problem occurs with the cards packaged in wax. New collectors may be surprised to learn that some warehouses contain unopened boxes of cards from as far back as the 1950s. Several dealers specialize in unopened packs, which are very popular among collectors. After all, few things are more exciting for collectors than opening a pack of cards that's 20 or 30 years old and knowing that they just may pull out a valuable card.

But some dealers try to have the best of both worlds. By taking wax packs and carefully opening them, they can *cherry pick* through the packs, taking out the star players and replacing them with lesser cards. The packs can be easily resealed with an iron or clear glue and resold as unopened.

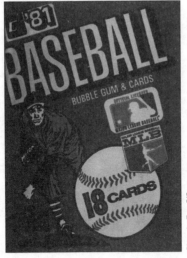

Figure 13-1:
A 1981
Donruss
wax pack.

For many years, card manufacturers also packaged their cards in shrink wrap or cellophane. Collectors could see the top and bottom cards of these *cello* packs (see Figure 13-2) or *rack* packs (three-cellos, as shown in Figure 13-3), which were sealed more thoroughly than wax packs. They were not tamperproof, however, and anyone skilled with a scalpel or razor blade could alter a pack. People tended to put more valuable cards into cello or rack packs because the value of an unopened cello or rack generally is two times the price of the visible cards.

When buying expensive, vintage, unopened packs, insist that they're "guaranteed unopened." This guarantee really doesn't mean anything more than a certificate of authenticity, but it does force the dealer to put his good name behind the goods. Of course, you're still not guaranteed that the dealer wouldn't unknowingly sell you tampered goods. After all, dealers can get burned with unopened cards just as easily as they can with fake autographs, counterfeit cards, and bogus game-used uniforms. The older the unopened pack, the more suspicious you should be.

The success of random sequencing

Another revolutionary idea that Upper Deck implemented was the notion of *random sequencing* — packing cards in a different order in each pack. For years, cards had been packaged in a consistent sequence each year. The card of a certain lesser player would always appear in front of a certain star. So a collector who saw a rack or cello pack with the lesser player on top knew to buy that pack because it would also include the star.

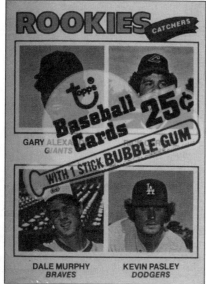

Figure 13-2:
A 1977
Topps cello
pack.

Figure 13-3:
A 1978
Topps rack
pack.

Nothing is unethical about this practice, but it can cause problems. A collector who opens enough packs to memorize the sequences can go through additional boxes of cello or rack packs at a card shop, show, or toy store and pick out the ones that contain the desirable cards. Collectors who come along later thus would have less of a chance of getting the good cards.

This cherry-picking process also can be used for vintage material packaged in rack packs or cello packs produced before 1989. In 1975, the cards of rookie baseball players George Brett and Robin Yount were packaged close in sequence. This card order meant little in 1975, which was before the card market exploded and everyone became obsessed with rookies. But by the mid-'80s, when collectors realized that Brett and Yount were headed to the Hall of Fame, collectors began learning the sequences and cherry-picking through boxes of cello and rack packs left over from 1975.

Can something be too cheap?

People in the sports collecting hobby often look disdainfully at an item and remark, "That can't be authentic. It's priced way too low." A certain backwards logic here implies that if the collectible were genuine, the seller would be trying to get market value for it. Because it's marked down, something must be wrong with the collectible.

It's a natural response. When you go shopping for anything from clothes to automobiles to homes and see something that seems under-priced, your natural instinct is to believe that it's too good to be true. You look for a defect in the car. You search for holes or missing buttons in the garment. And you ask about termites or bad plumbing in the house. After all, why would anyone want to unload stuff at a discounted rate?

Many people sell sports memorabilia at a discount because they need to dispose of the items quickly. They're not professional dealers, just people looking to liquidate. Chances are, they obtained their collection for pennies. Maybe they saved the cards from their childhood. Maybe they accumulated a collection of autographs when players still signed for free through the mail or for only a few bucks at card shows. Maybe they just put a couple boxes of unopened cards in a closet each year and forgot about them.

Whatever the reason, some collectors just want to sell and move on. Because they had little invested up front, they'll make a huge profit even if they don't get full market value.

People tend to get very paranoid when they see autographs priced affordably. They expect to see high prices because of the staggering inflation that's taken place. For instance, if you want Joe DiMaggio or Ted Williams to sign a photo, you may have to pay between $150 and $200 at a card show. So if you see an autographed photo for $100, does that mean the item isn't authentic? Not necessarily. Because both players have signed thousands of autographs through the years, either free in public or for $5 or $10 apiece at card shows, lots of autographed photos are out there. Maybe a dealer bought a collection of two dozen signed Williams photos from the estate of a collector. With so much inventory, the dealer may just want to sell them for whatever price he can get.

The "too cheap" argument also implies that the seller wants to unload an item quickly, before a knowledgeable dealer questions the item's legitimacy. The fact is, few memorabilia experts will ever question anything out of fear of litigation.

Does this mean that you shouldn't worry if something is surprisingly low priced? Of course not. You should bring a healthy dose of skepticism to any sports memorabilia purchase, regardless of price.

Does this mean that you'll never be able to obtain valuable cards in vintage rack and cello packs? Not at all. The star cards could be visible. But the packs will be priced accordingly, with dealers following the standard practice of pricing the pack for twice the value of the visible cards. But you still could pull the pack out of a box if the dealer guarantees that it's been unsearched. Just as you can insist on a guarantee that packs are unopened, you also can demand that a box be guaranteed unsearched. Again, this guarantee may mean little, but at least a dealer has to put his reputation on the line.

Chapter 14

Field of Schemes

● ●

In This Chapter

▶ Avoiding common scams

▶ Finding out what you should never buy

▶ Discovering how to avoid mail order fraud

● ●

*A*s a sports memorabilia collector, you probably derive much satisfaction from your hobby. But you'll enjoy it even more if you understand and avoid the scams that give the sports memorabilia business a bad name.

This business is chock-full of scams that you need to be aware of. They may result in only modest losses on your part, but that doesn't make them any less frustrating. In fact, these scams may seem more troublesome because the scoundrels who pull them off prey on the fact that you won't risk going after them. They figure that you already feel foolish and won't want to admit your gullibility to others. Plus, because you didn't lose thousands of dollars (hopefully), they know that it's not worth your while to haul them into court.

The best way to avoid these hassles is to know how to recognize these scams, most of which, unfortunately, are legal. In this chapter, I show you how to avoid becoming a victim.

The Grab Bag Full of Junk

Selling grab bags full of worthless cards is a favorite trick of dealers at card shows and card shops. They literally make up grab bags full of cards, charging $1 or $5 for the unseen contents of a brown paper bag that's been stapled closed. They guarantee that at least one valuable card is included in the group, although a collector never knows that unless he buys all the bags. Even then, dealers can claim that they already sold a few bags and that the valuable card must have been in one of them.

These cards inevitably are worthless. You usually get an assortment of cards from the early 1990s, when manufacturers produced cards in such huge volume that they'll never be worth anything. Don't get excited if you pull a big-name player out of a bag. Just pull out your Beckett price guides to see how little these cards are worth. (See Chapter 10 for more information on the Beckett price guides.)

Some people may argue that selling grab bags is no different than what card manufacturers do with insert cards. (See Chapter 2.) After all, an unopened pack of cards is a grab bag itself. The difference is that the same laws that require the folks who run lotteries and other contests to make odds public also, for the most part, apply to card companies. The companies, too, must run the odds of winning certain cards.

But the dealer who sells grab bags is not held to such a standard. Fortunately, many show promoters prohibit this practice, although many card shop owners still use grab bags as a way to get rid of worthless inventory. Grocery stores also sometimes have a variation of the grab bag, with gumball machines dispensing baseball cards instead of gum. (Ironically, this gimmick is the closest connection that the cards have to gum these days.) Rarely do you get cards worth the 25 or 50 cents you put in the machine.

Sports memorabilia is not only a bad investment; it's almost always a bad bet. The packs of cards cost so much because manufacturers have fooled collectors into believing that these insert cards have lasting collectible value. They know that you'll pay $5 for a pack of cards for the chance to get something worth $20, at least according to the price guides — even though you'll never, ever find someone to pay that price.

Games of Chance

For the most part, card show promoters have prohibited games of chance, along with grab bags. In games of chance, a dealer sells chances to spin a wheel. Wherever the needle stops, the collector receives the prize pegged to that portion of the wheel. This game is not such a bad thing if the prizes are identified, and they often are. Sometimes, however, you get only a grab bag.

If you're looking for the thrill of gambling, games of chance are not the way to go. I suppose that spending a couple bucks on a game of chance is fairly harmless. The games become risky, however, when new collectors buy into the myth that the prizes — often freshly minted insert cards — really have lasting collectible value. Believing this myth influences their entire mind-set, leading them to obsess over price guides and insert cards and to collect not because they're genuinely interested but because they buy into the false notion that this stuff is really worth something.

Maybe you believe that there's nothing wrong with obsessing over the money to be made off sports collecting. Indeed, how popular would sports itself be were it not for gambling, office pools, and fantasy leagues? But when you struggle to find a buyer for those insert cards that you obtained by buying countless expensive packs, don't say I didn't warn you.

The 100-Cards-for-$19.95 Scam

Many respected national magazines run ads offering 100 cards for $19.95, or something similar. Companies who run this scam prey on the uneducated customer. I'm sure that you've seen some version of the ad, which usually appears in big, bold type.

> **WAREHOUSE CLEARANCE!! $79 WORTH OF OUT-OF-PRINT BASE-BALL CARDS . . . FOR ONLY $16.95. . . . YES, ONLY WHILE SUPPLIES LAST. ALL ORIGINAL TOPPS, FLEER, UPPER DECK, PINNACLE, AND DONRUSS GENUINE MINT CARDS!! AT LEAST 100 PER BOX! NOT SOLD IN ANY STORES!**

The ads typically include a collage of cards, all of star players. Of course, they picture cards from sets that any serious collector knows are virtually worthless, such as 1990 Donruss, 1991 Topps, 1992 Upper Deck, and 1992 Fleer. (Isn't it amazing how almost all cards from the 1990s have almost no value whatsoever after a few years have passed?) Of course, the unsuspecting buyer does not know that these cards are worthless.

The ad continues, in slightly smaller print:

> DON'T MISS THIS AMAZING OPPORTUNITY TO PURCHASE $79 WORTH OF BASE-BALL CARDS FOR THE FABULOUSLY LOW PRICE OF JUST $16.95. IN ORDER TO MAKE ROOM FOR CARDS FOR THE UPCOMING SEASON, WE'RE OFFERING OUR EXCESS INVENTORY AT INCREDIBLE PRICES. EVERYTHING MUST GO!! WE ABSO-LUTELY GUARANTEE THAT EVERY PLAYER YOU'LL RECEIVE IS ONE OF THE GAME'S LEADING PLAYERS.

> WE CAN ONLY OFFER THESE IN VERY LIMITED QUANTITIES, SO DON'T DELAY. ONCE THEY'RE GONE, THEY'RE GONE FOR GOOD. REMEMBER, AT CARD SHOWS, YOU MIGHT EXPECT TO PAY ALMOST $3 FOR A SINGLE CARD. BUT WE'LL GIVE YOU AT LEAST 100 CARDS FOR ONLY $16.95. YOU MIGHT WANT TO BUY TWO, ONE FOR YOURSELF AND ONE FOR A FRIEND. WE KNOW YOU WON'T BE DISAPPOINTED.

> YOU'RE GUARANTEED TO RECEIVE THESE TOP STARS: BARRY BONDS, KEN GRIFFEY JR., TONY GWYNN, OZZIE SMITH, FRANK THOMAS, WADE BOGGS, AND MANY MORE. (SORRY, BUT NO DEALERS, PLEASE)

Companies can get away with this scam because nothing is totally false about any of these statements. But here's how they bend the truth at the expense of the customer. (The preceding example was compiled from actual ads.)

- ✔ **"Warehouse clearance."** The company leads you to believe that it has a huge warehouse of cards somewhere and is just waiting for the new cards. In reality, the company doesn't do business in new cards. It buys huge quantities of star players from lesser sets that are completely worthless. Dealers all but give them away to these *repackagers,* who take worthless cards and present them for re-sale.

- ✔ **"All original . . . genuine mint cards."** All original? This statement makes it sound as if card companies make reproductions of recently printed cards. Genuine mint? Wouldn't you hope that a bunch of cards from the last decade would still be in genuine mint condition?

- ✔ **"Out of print."** If you didn't collect cards, you'd think that this was a big deal, like if a book was out of print. Of course, you'll be able to find large volumes of these cards at shows and shops forever.

- ✔ **"Not sold in any stores."** Yeah, but readily available from other sources everywhere.

- ✔ **"Incredible prices."** I guess that you could call this price incredible considering that you probably can purchase the same lot of cards at a card show for pennies.

- ✔ **"One of the game's leading players."** Hmm, that's ambiguous enough to include almost anyone. Most veteran players have been around long enough to have been considered one of the game's leading players at some point. Baseball players such as Will Clark, Brian McRae, Kenny Rogers, Ken Hill, Dennis Martinez, Wally Joyner, Gary Gaetti, Travis Fryman, and Cecil Fielder could qualify as leading players. Does that make them future Hall of Famers or even current stars? Probably not.

- ✔ **"In limited quantities."** Yeah, limited to how many suckers are willing to send in $16.95.

- ✔ **"In order to make room."** This sounds like an automobile sales pitch, and you know how honest those are. Here, the company is hoping that naive buyers will think that they're getting a bargain because it's a year-end closeout. As if the company really needs to clear room for new inventory. It probably just wants to bring in more of this leftover garbage to sell.

- ✔ **"Once they're gone, they're gone for good."** We should be so lucky. Card sets such as 1990 Donruss are so plentiful, I'm guessing that they'll still be worth $10 a set in the year 2090.

Variations on a scam

An advertisement in one airline catalog promises "five decades of baseball cards for only $49.95." The cards, dating from the 1950s to the 1990s, even include Babe Ruth and Ty Cobb. Now, if you know your baseball, you know that neither of these guys played in the 1950s. But they appeared in many "all-time greats" sets produced long after their deaths. These later cards have little value, but inevitably some people will think that they're getting valuable Ruth and Cobb cards. Instead, they get a few cards of all-time greats, along with the usual early late '80s and early '90s hodgepodge of worthless cards of star players.

Another offer in the same catalog offers 100 unopened wax packs of baseball cards for "only" $79.95. The packs are stacked one on top of the other and it would be impossible for a novice collector to tell which packs are represented. But if you know your wax, you'll recognize that the virtually worthless 1988 Topps, 1988 Donruss, and 1990 Donruss packs make up the majority of the stack.

If you go to a card show, any dealer will sell you a box of 36 packs from any of those card lines for $5. That's 108 packs right there for $15. Or you could send $79.95 to the airline magazine. I don't recommend that you do either, but you can see how this offer is really a rip-off. Amazingly, the ad mentions that a pack of 1952 Topps baseball cards may contain a Mickey Mantle card worth thousands of dollars. True, but the offer also stresses that your 100 packs will come straight from the 1980s and 1990s.

Many cards from the 1950s soared in value by 1980; don't assume, however, that today's cards will be worth anything 30 years from now. Back then, nobody looked at cards as collectibles, they weren't produced in the huge quantities of today, and nobody kept them — let alone in pristine condition. Of course, the ad doesn't mention any of those facts to the readers. Isn't the scope of sports memorabilia scams amazing? Even people traveling 30,000 feet above the earth can get ripped off!

✔ **"You might expect to pay $3 a card."** Heck, if you go to a card show, you might expect to pay $100,000 if a T206 Honus Wagner is available. Why draw the line at three bucks?

✔ **"You're guaranteed to receive these top stars."** Okay, this is where they really grab the suckers who figure that the deal can't be that bad if it at least includes these guys. Think again. Consider these prices that *Beckett Baseball Card Monthly* places on the following cards: 1990 Donruss Barry Bonds, 8 cents; 1990 Score Ozzie Smith, 8 cents; and 1991 Fleer Wade Boggs, 7 cents. Get the picture?

So if you get 100 of these cards, they may be worth $7 or $8. Are they worth $16.95 as touted? Well, technically, they are if you go by the HI column in the Beckett price guide. But because there's such a huge

> supply and a low demand, they're priced below the Beckett LO value at card shows. At a card show, you may pay only $3 for all of them. Of course, because you probably have no interest in recently minted cards with no collectible value, my advice is to avoid them altogether.
>
> ✔ **"Sorry, but no dealers please."** Hey, you're not a dealer. You can get in on this while seasoned professionals are shut out. Of course, dealers want nothing to do with this stuff. After all, where do you think this repackager got this flotsam and jetsam?

The Starter Kit Scam

An ad promises, for example, 100 cards from any one year between 1965 and 1975 for *only* $99.95! The ad tries to convince you that you'll have a head start on putting together a set.

Like the scams listed in the earlier sections in this chapter, this one touts the deal with such language as "out of print" and "all original." Unlike the 100-cards-for-$19.95 scam, these cards at least have some true value, so there's little chance you'll get any big-name stars. You will, however, get plenty of commons. Remember, even common baseball cards from the early 1970s are valued between 40 cents and several dollars apiece, according to *Beckett Baseball Card Monthly*.

Now, I can hear you doing the calculations based on the preceding information. If you get 100 cards worth, say, an average of $1.50 apiece, aren't you getting a decent deal? Not necessarily. Dealers always discount common cards. They realize that their bread and butter comes from selling star cards. They know that few people are trying to complete sets, and they want to be helpful, if only because people rarely have any interest in commons and such customers should be carefully cultivated. So you should always expect a significant discount when buying commons.

The bigger problem is with the starter kit notion itself. Rarely does anyone decide to start collecting a vintage set from scratch. Such an approach is cost prohibitive. If you assemble a set card by card, you'll probably end up paying three to four times more than if you just buy the entire set. Many people who collect sets begin with a sizable chunk of cards. Maybe they had started to collect a set as a kid. Maybe they inherited most of a set or bought it for a huge bargain at an auction, estate sale, or flea market. For them, buying the remaining cards is very cost-effective, especially if they plan to sell the complete set.

Does this mean that you should never buy a starter kit? Not necessarily. In fact, sometimes you can get good deals at auctions. Maybe someone has half a set, including most of the major stars. Instead of buying the rest, they simply place it in an auction. Like anything else, you never know what might sell at auction for only a fraction of its worth. But I've yet to see a starter kit advertised that wasn't a rip-off.

Even if you do get a bargain by purchasing a starter kit, you still have to consider how much the kit helps you get a start on completing the set. A few hundred commons don't help much, because you still can buy the complete set for less than the cost of all the star cards purchased individually.

Information Scams

Everyone claims to have the secret to making millions. This observation seems especially true in the sports memorabilia business. Countless ads in magazines tout the secrets to financial success through sports collectibles. If you spend any time online, you've probably received some of these junk mail ads there, too. Ignore all of them. Because sports memorabilia is a terrible investment, you probably won't make any money, and even if you do, it won't be worth your time.

Recognizing these sales pitches is easy. They're very seductive, promising untold riches. They usually insist on cash, sent to post office boxes. If you actually receive anything in return, it's usually a form letter with a list of "hot rookies" or card products. You may receive a packet of information touting collectibles for sale. Some of these scoundrels are so brash that they've been known to send postcards that say things like "The secret to making money through sports collectibles is to invest your money else-where" or "Don't send cash through the mail." These scams take place all the time. I'm not making them up.

Don't fall prey to information scams. Remember, nothing substitutes for research and education when collecting sports memorabilia. (I talk more about research in Chapters 15 and 16.)

Mail Fraud

Sometimes collectors send away for something and never receive it, even though their check is cashed. This problem isn't confined to the sports collecting hobby, of course, although it does seem to occur quite frequently here.

Your best defense is to research the company beforehand. Call the Better Business Bureau to check the company's reputation. Find other collectors who have dealt with the firm. If the company advertises in a hobby publication, you can generally feel comfortable about its legitimacy. Still, sometimes the magazines do not thoroughly check new advertisers. It might be worthwhile to call the magazine to make sure that the advertiser is legitimate, especially if there's no phone number listed, only a post office box. If you've already gotten burned, make sure to call the magazine and let it know.

Never buy something sight unseen or from an unfamiliar source. And if something sounds too good to be true, it probably is.

The Dealer Franchise Ploy

The dealer franchise ploy rarely pops up anymore, but it's still important to be aware of it. Here's an example of how this scam works: In the early 1990s, several dealers tried to franchise their card stores. Like any franchiser, they demanded a hefty licensing fee. The franchisee also needed plenty of start-up capital.

Two of the dealers were particularly effective in their pitches. They had flamboyant personalities, took out page after page of advertising in hobby publications, and claimed to be making millions. They each had a packet of press clips testifying to their success. (Because each dealer operated privately held companies, how could reporters have known that they were not nearly as successful as they claimed?) By 1994, however, both dealers were bankrupt, and the few poor franchisees were left on their own.

Now, as we approach the twenty-first century, sports memorabilia is probably one of the worst businesses to get into. Most card shops have closed their doors since the early 1990s. No one with any knowledge of how this market has plummeted in recent years would consider opening a new store or buying an existing one. But even if someone did, why would a person pay for franchise rights? Buying sports memorabilia franchises is not like buying a McDonald's or Subway franchise, where franchisees are paying for huge brand recognition. No card shop has a national reputation or a formula for success.

Some collectors, feeling they have a good knowledge of the industry, have made the mistake of opening card stores only to realize that they didn't have the business sense necessary to make such an operation work. Remember, very few people seem able to make even a modest profit anymore selling sports memorabilia.

Unlicensed Memorabilia

Unlicensed memorabilia isn't really a scam, although the major sports leagues and their players associations would like you to consider it one. *Unlicensed memorabilia* refers to anything created without the consent of either the player or a sports league. If you take a picture of a player at a game, blow it up into a poster, and begin selling copies, that's an example of unlicensed memorabilia. You'd incur the wrath of the player and the league and probably end up in court. You'll know something is not officially licensed if it is not stamped or tagged with the appropriate sports league, NCAA, and/or players association logos.

Is unlicensed memorabilia any less collectible than licensed merchandise? Hardly. In fact, if a producer is forced to stop selling unlicensed memorabilia, some of the merchandise is already in collectors' hands, making it more valuable. And if the memorabilia is, for example, a poster of someone very popular, like Michael Jordan or Cal Ripken, then you'd have something even more collectible, at least in theory.

Surprisingly, you don't see many unlicensed collectibles for sale anywhere. Beckett Publications doesn't list unlicensed cards in its price guides, and if a card line is not included in Beckett, collectors and dealers act as if it doesn't exist. Plus, many card show promoters do not allow dealers to sell unlicensed products, in part because of the close relationships among the leagues, card manufacturers, and promoters/dealers.

Don't bother with unlicensed collectibles. There's little market for them. The general feeling is that something must be readily available through official channels, with the blessing of the players depicted, in order for it to be viewed as collectible. Otherwise, you could manufacture your own collection.

Part V

How to Become Your Own Best Expert

The 5th Wave By Rich Tennant

@RICHTENNANT

SPORTS CARDS

"Sure it's mint. Taste it."

In this part . . .

1f you want a short course on how to become an expert on sports memorabilia, you've come to the right place. The first 14 chapters of this book can be of great assistance, but other sources are available to help you become an even more educated consumer. Although dealers and experts in the sports collecting hobby may tout their decades of experience, you can become an authority yourself more quickly than you may think.

This part guides you through the maze of hobby magazines and books showing you how to separate the useful information from the shameless hype. I also suggest some helpful additions for your collectibles library and where to find useful information online. Perhaps most importantly, I explain what to believe and what not to believe from the so-called experts. By the time you're done, hopefully, you'll be a lean, mean collecting machine who will know how to locate the best memorabilia at the best prices.

Chapter 15

Researching and Finding Information on Sports Memorabilia

In This Chapter

▶ Following the trends in sports memorabilia

▶ Knowing what sports memorabilia books and magazines to believe

▶ Questioning authority

*R*esearch is probably not a word that you want to see in a chapter title. When you hear the word *research,* you probably think of term papers and all-nighters. But collecting is a hobby, so it shouldn't involve work, right? Relax. Sports collectibles research is *fun.* In fact, if you're a sports fan at any level, you've probably been informally researching for years without even realizing it.

Still, keeping up with the sports collecting hobby takes a little effort. Even if you have no intention of collecting new cards and memorabilia and trying to keep up with the dizzying number of sets and products released, you probably still want to keep abreast of the market and what's available. In that sense, sports memorabilia is no different than, say, real estate or stocks. Even if you have no plans to buy or sell, you may still want to know what's going on.

Unfortunately, a lot of misinformation exists about sports memorabilia. Sports memorabilia no longer is a great investment, as it was briefly in the 1980s, but you'd never know it from reading much of the hobby press. If the stock market were to crash tomorrow, *The Wall Street Journal* and *Money* magazine would not be touting stocks. But people in the sports collectibles field approach their business differently. Manufacturers, dealers, and even the hobby media like to perpetuate the myth of sports collectibles investment, using marketing and public relations to convince collectors that everything out there is a Grade A, no-risk, blue-chip investment.

After you cut through the corporate schlock and insider hobby babble, however, you can find a lot of useful information. You may even want to be aware of the rumors and innuendo because, in this business, the perception of reality often is as significant as the reality itself. For example, if everyone believes that a product is rare, the product does become rare, at least for a while.

Your biggest weapon as a sports memorabilia collector is a healthy dose of skepticism about authenticity and prices. In this chapter, I show you how and why you should question the so-called experts. More importantly, I show you the tools that can help you become your own best expert.

Sports Books

After you decide on a specific niche of collecting, you may want more specialized information than even this book can provide. Fortunately, you can find plenty of resources to help. In Chapter 4, I recommend books that illustrate what baseball uniforms looked like through the years and which numbers players wore on their uniforms. For jersey collectors, such information is invaluable.

No matter which sport you collect, you need a definitive reference tool.

- ✔ For baseball, you can choose between *The Baseball Encyclopedia* (Macmillan) and *Total Baseball* (ed. John Thorn et al., Viking). Both are chock-full of alphabetized information on every man who's played the game, along with all-time lists of record holders and year-by-year statistical leaders. You'll be surprised how often you consult these books for hobby purposes or just to win arguments. (If nothing else, at eight pounds each, they serve as useful doorstops.)

- ✔ For football, check out *The Pro Football Encyclopedia* (by Tod Maher and Bob Gill, Macmillan) and *Total Football* (by Bob Carroll, Harper Collins).

- ✔ For hockey, try the *Complete Encyclopedia of Hockey* (by Zander Hollander, Gale Research).

- ✔ For basketball, try *The Official NBA Basketball Encyclopedia* (by Alex Sachare, Villard).

Find out as much as you can about players, especially when collecting vintage cards and memorabilia. When buying a uniform, find out whether a player actually was with the team the year the jersey claims to represent. Maybe he only played briefly for the team that season. The jersey could be legitimate, but it may have been barely worn. (See Chapter 4 for more information on researching game-used uniforms and equipment.)

Krause

One great source for hobby-related books is Krause Publications of Iola, Wisconsin. Krause produces books and magazines on hobbies ranging from ceramics to firearms to stamps to toys. But it's perhaps best known for its sports collecting titles. Krause's annual *Sports Collectors Almanac* lists every modern card set and value for the four major sports, along with motor sports. Two other books, the *Standard Catalog of Baseball Cards* and the *Standard Catalog of Football, Basketball, and Hockey Cards,* list every major card set, breaking them down by stars and offering a little background on each card set.

Other helpful Krause titles include the *Sportscard Counterfeit Detector* (mentioned in Chapter 14), the *Sports Equipment Price Guide,* and the *All-Sport Autograph Guide.* Krause also has specialized titles covering everything from NASCAR memorabilia to Green Bay Packers collectibles. Don't get too hung up on the prices listed. The values may be inaccurate because they're not updated more than once a year. Besides, because you're not in this hobby to make money, the books are more valuable in helping you recognize relative worth. My personal favorite of the Krause books is *The Sports Card Explosion,* which is a compilation of noteworthy articles in *Sports Collectors Digest* that chronicle the growth of the hobby.

Through the years, Krause has published its share of books with titles such as *101 Sports Card Investments.* Again, unless you're still not convinced that sports memorabilia is a terrible investment, stay away from such hoopla. You may want to flip through some investment books — including those not produced by Krause — just to chuckle at some of the investment picks from the past. (Actual baseball card investment suggestions from a non-Krause book published in 1990: Bob Hamelin, Will Clark, Dale Murphy, Jim Abbott, Delino DeShields, Tim Raines, and Gregg Jefferies.) You can find Krause titles in the hobby/collectibles section of most bookstores or at its Web site at www.krause.com (shown in Figure 15-1).

Topps

Another fabulous reference tool is *Topps Baseball Cards: The Complete Picture Collection, a 40-Year History, 1951-90,* by Frank Slocum and Red Foley. This massive book pictures every Topps card sorted by year and number, with an introduction before each set. In many ways, owning this book is as good as having every Topps card, although you see only the front of the cards. This oversized hardcover book is out of print and hard to find, but it occasionally pops up in used bookstores.

Figure 15-1:
Krause
Publications
on the Web.

Fortunately, Slocum also produced *Baseball Cards of the Fifties: The Complete Topps Cards* and *Baseball Cards of the Sixties.* Because these books were produced in 1994, you still can find them on discount tables at bookstores. Books also are available about Topps cards from individual teams up until 1989, when the books were printed. These affordable books frequently are sold at card shows and used bookstores. Besides being good reference tools, they make a nice addition to any team-related collection.

Beckett

James Beckett made a name for himself with his price guide magazines, so it's not surprising that most of Beckett's books are price guides. Beckett publishes an annual price guide book for each of the four major sports, along with auto racing. In addition, Beckett has a series of alphabetical checklist books that list all of the cards ever produced by player and a *Beckett Almanac of Baseball Cards and Collectibles.* (For more on James Beckett and his price guides, see Chapters 10 and 11.)

In part because of the decline of the sports card market, Beckett has become more of a mainstream sports book publisher in recent years. The shift began in the early 1990s when the company released a line of Beckett

Tribute magazines. Although the initial magazines paid homage to veteran and recently retired athletes such as football player Joe Montana and baseball star Nolan Ryan, they soon included tributes to "youngsters" such as basketball player Shaquille O'Neal and Frank Thomas. When those were well received, the company began producing the magazines in hardcover book form, which led to more traditional books, such as a recent coffee-table book on golfer Tiger Woods.

Team and Related Sources

Professional sports teams sometimes can be a big help to collectors, especially in building a reference library. Media guides, in addition to being collectible, also are handy reference tools. Not only are they chock-full of information on the team, but in the case of baseball, they also have biographies and lists of almost every player in the organization. Yearbooks and programs also can serve as reference sources and are collectible.

However, don't expect to get much other collectible-related information from a professional sports franchise, other than perhaps a schedule of games where team mementos will be given away. Public relations staffs are grossly overworked and underpaid, and the last thing they want is to deal with collectors, who rank just below fantasy leaguers on their list of priorities. Still, you should always take advantage of opportunities to get to know team employees. You never know when they may be able to provide helpful material for your collection.

Hobby Magazines: What to Believe and What Not to Believe

In the early 1990s, sports memorabilia magazines were almost as common as sports card sets. But as the memorabilia market softened, many publications went out of business. Today, only three hobby publishers are left:

- Krause Publications, which puts out _Sports Collectors Digest_ and _Sports Cards_
- Beckett Publications, the price guide experts
- _Tuff Stuff,_ perhaps the best single source for articles and commentary on the industry

All three publishers offer solid information, along with price guide offerings. The only drawback is that because they're so dependent on card company advertising, a lot of editorial space is wasted on "stories" that are essentially press releases about new cards from the manufacturers. Another drawback, particularly in the case of Krause and *Tuff Stuff,* is that some articles are written by and for memorabilia dealers. Most collectors don't want to read a question-and-answer piece featuring some card manufacturer talking about "product," "the marketplace," or "distribution channels." And most readers probably aren't interested in some dealer rambling on about what has or hasn't been selling in his store.

If your only source of hobby information is these publications, you may think that the industry is flourishing and that thousands of collectors are scrambling to pick up the next hot investment. Fortunately, beneath the shameless hype, you may find much useful information.

Krause publications

Krause's signature magazine is *Sports Collectors Digest (SCD).* Tabloid-sized and published weekly on thin newsprint, it's dominated by advertising. In fact, it's more valuable as a vehicle for collectors and dealers to buy, sell, and trade than as a news source. If you can't find the memorabilia that you're looking for in *SCD,* it probably doesn't exist. *SCD* does include a page of news briefs, a handful of columns, and some interesting where-are-they-now profiles, but many collectors actually turn to the index of advertisers first. *SCD* does have some insightful writers. Keith Olbermann, for instance, wrote for *SCD* in the early 1980s before his television career blossomed as an ESPN anchor and MSNBC talk show host.

Krause's other main hobby publication is *Sports Cards,* which began as *Baseball Cards* in the early 1980s. It has far more editorial content than *Sports Collectors Digest* and features a price guide. Krause also puts out two publications geared mostly to card company executives and dealers: *Trade Fax,* a twice-weekly newsletter, and *Card Trade,* a monthly publication covering card marketing and distribution. Most collectors will not find this corporate insider talk very helpful.

Tuff Stuff

Yes, the name *Tuff Stuff* may be corny, but the publication does stand out. In fact, back when many publications had "Sports Card" or "Trading Card" in their titles, the name was quite helpful from a marketing standpoint.

Tuff Stuff, based in Richmond, Virginia, is a good all-in-one reference tool. Of all the hobby publications, it does the best job of providing mainstream sports articles and investigative pieces, some written by prominent sports writers from *The New York Times, Chicago Tribune,* and the *Philadelphia Daily News. Tuff Stuff* is guilty of employing a few hobby dealers who write columns that only hobby dealer types will care about, but overall, you definitely get your $4.99 worth of information. *Tuff Stuff* has an easy-to-use price guide for cards, autographs, and Starting Lineup figures. (See Figure 15-2.)

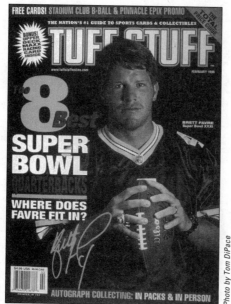

Figure 15-2: Brett Favre featured on *Tuff Stuff.*

Beckett Publications

The longtime price-guide leader, Beckett has individual magazines for baseball, football, basketball, hockey, and motor sports, along with a "Future Stars" publication. (Figures 15-3 and 15-4 show some Beckett publications.) All these publications may be a bit much for you; if you want all your card information in one source, *Sports Cards* or *Tuff Stuff* may be a better buy. Then again, if you collect only one sport, you may prefer one of Beckett's single-sport publications.

Figure 15-3:
A Beckett
Hockey
Card
Monthly
featuring
Eric Lindros
and John
LeClair on
the cover.

Photo by Tom DiPace

Figure 15-4:
Rusty
Wallace
adorns an
issue of
Beckett
Racing &
Motorsports
Marketplace.

Photo by Tom DiPace

The price is right . . . or is it?

Most collectors are tempted to flip right to the price guide as soon as they pick up a new hobby magazine. In theory, collectors are no different than investors who turn to the business section of the newspaper each morning to check the progress of their stock portfolios.

Remember, though, that price guides are just that — guides. They're produced for dealers, and the prices, to a large extent, reflect the opinions of dealers. They also reflect retail values. You, the collector, should not expect to receive retail value, because, presumably, you'll be selling to a dealer who will pay, at most, 50 percent of book value. Even if you want to rent a table at a card show and become a dealer yourself, you'll have a hard time finding collectors who are willing to pay full book value for anything.

So don't take the prices listed literally. If you read them long enough, you'll notice a pattern. A new card set comes out and soars in value, especially if it includes insert cards and subsets, which nearly all new card lines do these days. The inserts will be priced at ridiculous levels, some for hundreds of dollars. (Of course, the only people who pay these prices are naive collectors. Dealers rarely buy insert cards. Card manufacturers and dealers don't want you to know this, of course. If people realized that insert cards were virtually worthless, the card companies would go out of business. And so, presumably, would many dealers. Then the world might be a better place.)

After a few months pass and dealers have turned their attention to new sets, the "old" cards start to come down in price. Cards that were worth hundreds of dollars suddenly are worth much less. Why is that? Are they any less rare? Could it be, just possibly, that the hoopla surrounding these hundred-dollar cards was over in a matter of . . . months? Could it be that a true collectible market never existed for these cards in the first place?

Absolutely. Back when the card market was driven by investors, the card manufacturers shot themselves in the foot by touting every set as a limited-edition, blue-chip investment. Now that most of the investors have left, the only thing keeping the companies afloat is this false notion of insert cards as something akin to the golden tickets in the movie *Willy Wonka and the Chocolate Factory*.

Does this mean that the price guides aren't being truthful? Of course not. If a few dealers manage to find a few suckers to spend big bucks on certain insert cards, well, they must be worth that much. They can report it to the price guide people, who in turn publish it. With pre-1990 cards, fortunately, the prices have stabilized and don't fluctuate much. These prices are more reflective of the market. For new cards, however, don't believe the hype.

Beckett's editorial content has improved over the years, and it now includes timely articles about sports and collecting. Its main focus, of course, remains the price guide. So if you're not concerned with the month-to-month fluctuations in card values, you may not get much out of Beckett. If you are, you'll probably have a hard time waiting for the next issue.

Like *Tuff Stuff,* Beckett finally recognized the need for a magazine dedicated to older material. Beckett *Sports Vintage* is probably the best Beckett magazine in terms of articles and information. It does, of course, include a price guide.

Questioning the So-Called Experts

As you do your research, you may find yourself questioning the so-called experts in the field. There's nothing wrong with doing so. After all, how do you become an expert in the sports memorabilia field? It's one of those questions without an answer, sort of like asking when does a model become a supermodel?

The reality is that anyone can become an expert. Just tout yourself as one, and people will believe you. You don't need any training. You don't need a license or certification. No one gets a degree in sports memorabilia. All you have to do is announce yourself as an expert. Have some business cards made. You are now an expert. Congratulations.

Now, would you trust you for advice on sports collecting? Of course not. So why would you trust some bozo dealer without checking his credentials? He probably has no more experience or expertise than you do. Even if you do believe that he's an expert, you should still question the authenticity of autographs, insist on documentation for game-used uniforms, and measure cards to make sure that they weren't trimmed. A dealer may indeed be a top expert, to the point where he thinks that he can pull a fast one on you, the naive collector.

You don't have to be rude, but you don't need to blindly accept everything the dealer says either. Indeed, no matter what you were taught as a kid or, perhaps, in the military, when dealing with sports collectibles, you must learn to question authority. Do this in a polite manner, of course, and never publicly question the legitimacy of an item. If you do, you're risking a lawsuit.

Even if you're not a confrontational person by nature, you'll automatically raise an eyebrow about prices and items as you discover more about the hobby. After you begin to feel like an expert yourself, you'll be insulted that certain things are priced so high or others are passed off with so little documentation.

Questioning Authority 101

Whenever I see a game-used jersey for sale at a card show, I always ask about its origins. Here's an example of a typical exchange.

Me: Hey, how you doing? I was wondering where you got that jersey.

Dealer: It came from a really good source.

Me: Oh, you mean like the player himself? Or maybe the team?

Dealer: I can't say. I can tell you it's a good jersey. Look here. See, it's got all the right tags. It shows good game use.

Me: Yeah, it sure does. But I could buy a jersey just like this from the manufacturer and wear it to play softball. I'm not saying this isn't real, but how can I prove it? I mean, if I'm going to give you $1,200, I need to know for sure.

Dealer (getting agitated): Look, all I can tell you is that it came from a source with the team.

Me: Great, that helps a lot. Do you have a letter from the club on team stationery that you could give me with this?

Dealer: Look, if you don't want the jersey, it makes no difference to me.

Me: No, I really want the jersey. But what if I'm short of cash next year and need to sell it? How would I be able to prove to a buyer that it was legitimate?

Dealer: I'll be happy to give you a letter of authenticity with my name on it, with a lifetime guarantee. If you ever find that it's no good, I'll give you the money back.

Me: Hmmm. That's good enough for me, but it may not be for the guy I sell it to. What about the source? Can we get a letter from him or her?

Dealer: I'm afraid not.

Me: Okay. So what you're telling me is that you can't tell me where this came from, other than to say it came from a team source. But you can offer me one of your own letters of authenticity with a lifetime guarantee. That sounds pretty good. By the way, how would I ever know if it wasn't legitimate?

Dealer: It's good. I trust the source.

Now, would you buy a jersey in this situation? I hope not. Could it be real? Of course. Maybe the dealer got it directly from the player and doesn't want the player to know that he's selling it. Maybe he's selling it on behalf of the player who doesn't want anyone to know that he's selling his uniforms. Perhaps the jersey came from a clubhouse attendant who didn't want to be identified. Maybe it was stolen. Maybe the dealer bought it from another dealer who gave him the same "source" story. Maybe it's just a replica that he's trying to pass off as real. Maybe he hopes it's real but thinks that it's probably not and knows deep down that he was probably sold a bill of goods from someone else.

Maybe you're suspicious for other reasons. Maybe the jersey is lacking the two inches of "extra length" that the player always requests when he orders jerseys. Maybe you've read an article in a hobby magazine in which the player said that he keeps all of his uniforms in a locked, temperature-controlled room with his wife's fur coats. Maybe the jersey had 1991 tags, but you know that the player was traded right before the 1991 season and wouldn't have worn the uniform. Maybe the jersey was signed, but the autograph looks nothing like the ones you've received from the player in person. Maybe you know of another dealer who for years has had an exclusive arrangement to buy the team's entire run of jerseys at the end of each season.

Maybe you know all this not only because you've followed the advice in this book but because you've gone out and done further research. You didn't do formal research, of course, but you've picked things up by reading and paying attention to developments in the hobby. Without even realizing it, you've become more educated than the so-called experts.

Chapter 16

Being a Good Consumer

The more you research sports memorabilia, the more you'll get to know the market. In a short time, you'll find yourself going to card shops and shows and shaking your head at some of the prices you see, knowing full well that you could obtain the same collectibles elsewhere for a fraction of the cost. This awareness can come in particularly handy when you want to approach the dealers who have the overpriced goods and see how far you can talk them down.

Because of the downturn in the sports memorabilia industry, it's a buyer's market. You don't have to pay market price for most items, no matter how much the dealer talks about their rarity and value. Chances are, you can always look elsewhere. Any dealer unwilling to haggle will not remain in this business for long.

You may always fear, of course, that you'll never see a particular item again. That's a legitimate concern. But the more you understand the market, the more you will begin to recognize what's rare and what is not. If you've collected the memorabilia of an individual player for some time, for instance, you'll know when you need to grab an item that you've never seen before.

But, for the most part, you'll realize that patience is your biggest asset. Remember that you're not buying one of the necessities of life. You have the luxury of taking your time. In this chapter, I show you how to make the most of that time.

Shop Around

Patience is not a trait associated with the collector mentality. As a collector, you're used to immediate fulfillment. You're constantly on the prowl for things to add to your collection. Your basic instinct is to find and acquire as quickly as possible. The idea of going to a show or auction without buying something strikes you as a waste of time.

Now, in some instances, that approach can work to your advantage. For example, many collectors like to be the first ones through the door at a card show or the first to make a preemptive bid at an auction. They believe that they'll find the undervalued goods first at a card show. By bidding high early at auction, they hope to scare off potential buyers who may not be as savvy. In some cases, this strategy is effective.

But being patient is not the same as being passive. If you see something that you want, by all means go for it. Just be willing to walk away if the deal is not to your liking. Try to avoid convincing yourself that you must have it; this attitude gives leverage to the seller or the person you're trading with. Instead, settle on a price beforehand that you're willing to pay in cash or trade, and stick to it. That way, you stick to your budget — a budget based on your intimate knowledge of the market.

Someone else almost always is trying to sell the same item that you're afraid to pass up:

- ✔ Have you checked the ads in *Sports Collectors Digest?*
- ✔ Have you looked at a list of upcoming auctions?
- ✔ Can you obtain the item through your network of fellow collectors, some of whom may be willing to trade?
- ✔ Can you locate it online?
- ✔ Is the item common enough that you'll see it again at a card show or shop?

Even if you and the seller disagree on price and fail to make a transaction, don't give up. If you're at a show, check back at the end. The seller may not want to haul the merchandise home, especially if it's a large item. Or maybe the seller had a poor show and wants to recoup some of his losses. Remember, dealers don't want to leave without making as much of a profit as possible.

Don't (Always) Buy Sight Unseen

Unfortunately, sports memorabilia is not always what it's purported to be. That game-used jersey that sounded so authentic based on its catalog or advertised description may have several obvious authenticity flaws after you get a firsthand look at it. Even sports cards that look like they're in near-mint or excellent condition in photos may look worse when viewed in person.

Of course, if you pursue all possible channels in building your collection, you're going to be dealing with out-of-town dealers and fellow collectors. Sooner or later, you may have to take a risk and send away for something you haven't seen beforehand with payment. That's fine, so long as you have a money-back guarantee. In instances where you're sending money first or you're buying sight unseen, it's important to know your dealer. If the dealer advertises in a hobby publication, call the magazine's advertising department to make sure that he's legitimate.

Fortunately, most auction houses include photos in their auction catalogs with almost every item or *lot* in the sale. Generally speaking, the bigger the expenditure, the more cautious you should be in purchasing an item sight unseen. Of course, if you develop a network of collectors and dealers with whom you deal frequently, you'll feel more comfortable about buying and trading long distance.

Demand a Lifetime Guarantee

When dealing in sports memorabilia, warranties and guarantees sometimes don't mean much. Anyone who would try to pass off a counterfeit signature or fake piece of memorabilia would think nothing of writing a bogus guarantee to accompany it. Such documentation, however, is valuable in some instances.

Sometimes, a dealer unknowingly sells a forged autograph or bogus item. Maybe a big-time con man is caught and admits to passing off a large quantity of false merchandise. Even some of the most experienced dealers get burned. But just because a dealer was swindled doesn't mean you should also be a victim. A dealer should be willing to refund your money if you ever discover that an item is illegitimate. A dealer who's confident in his merchandise shouldn't object to giving refunds when he knows that he's wrong.

A guarantee doesn't mean that a collectible is authentic, but it does mean that you will get your money back if it's proven not to be.

Reputations mean everything in the sports memorabilia business. Those who make the effort to guarantee their goods and remedy bad situations are the ones whose reputations will remain golden. You should deal with these folks whenever possible.

Chapter 17

Sports Collecting Online

*T*he Internet has revolutionized many aspects of society, and sports memorabilia collecting is no exception. If you want to buy, sell, or trade, you can find numerous opportunities by surfing the Web. If you're looking for information, rumors, and chat room discussions, you can discover plenty of sites to meet your needs. And if you're a collector who still believes in the myth of sports card investment, some sites bring you up-to-the-moment price guide information.

I'm assuming that if you're reading this chapter, you already know how to get around online. If not, plenty of books can show you how, including *Internet For Dummies,* 5th Edition, by John R. Levine, Carol Baroudi, and Margaret Levine Young, as well as *World Wide Web Searching For Dummies,* 2nd Edition, by Brad Hill (both from IDG Books Worldwide, Inc.). The great thing about surfing the Web is that you're always finding cool new sites. If you're experienced in this area, you probably know of some good sites, which may not be listed here. It's not my intention to offer a definitive list of helpful collecting Web sites here, even if it were possible.

But I hope that you find this chapter useful as a starting point to collecting online. The great thing about people who work in the sports memorabilia business is that they generally cooperate. By visiting one site, you're likely to find links to dozens of others.

Searching for Sites

You won't have trouble finding sports memorabilia sites. A search for sports memorabilia at www.yahoo.com (shown in Figure 17-1), one of the Internet's best directories, turns up hundreds of sites relating to sports collectibles

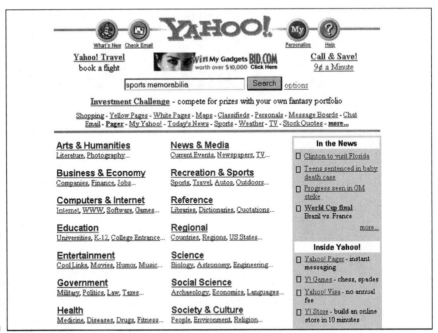

Figure 17-1:
Yahoo! lets
you search
its entire
directory.

and sports memorabilia. Many of these sites belong to dealers, but you also find sites for auction houses, individual collectors, card companies, and card publications. Most sites can be divided into two categories: informational and commercial.

Informational sites

Informational sites ultimately are trying to sell you something, but you can also find a wealth of information at no charge. Card company Web sites, for instance, typically have a listing of upcoming products, along with corporate information and, perhaps, a way to e-mail the company's customer service department. (Figures 17-2 and 17-3 show some sample sites.)

Here's a list of the card companies that have Web sites:

- ✔ **Fleer:** www.fleerskybox.com
- ✔ **Donruss/Leaf:** www.donruss.com
- ✔ **Topps:** www.topps.com

Figure 17-2:
The trading card page of Topps on the Web.

Figure 17-3:
The Web presence of Upper Deck.

✔ **Upper Deck:** www.upperdeck.com

✔ **Pacific:** www.pacific-trading-cards.com

✔ **Pinnacle Brands:** www.pinnacle-brands.com

Each of the hobby publications has a Web site, including Beckett (www.beckett.com), *Tuff Stuff* (www.tuffstuffonline.com), and Krause Publications (www.krause.com). These sites typically offer hobby news and information, price guides, and other links. Because they don't want to undercut sales of their magazines, the sites aren't a substitute for the publications, but they often offer information that the magazines don't.

Many amateurs publish sports memorabilia information on the Web, so don't believe everything you read, especially in a business fueled by rumor, half-truths, and misinformation. Despite that warning, you still may find some of the best information from less-traditional and well-known sources.

You can also enter chat rooms to talk about your hobby. You may find yourself stumbling upon like-minded collectors and striking up deals. If nothing else, you'll probably discover a few things that you didn't know before.

Of all the informational Web sites, my personal favorite is Beckett. (See Figure 17-4.) I remember getting my first look at this site during Major League Baseball's All-Star FanFest in Dallas in 1995, and I'm still impressed. Beckett does a good job of keeping the site up-to-date. In addition to the requisite features — price guide, buy/sell areas, and news sections — it features links to individual collector's pages, a list of upcoming card shows, and, of course, a place to buy the numerous new books and publications that Beckett regularly cranks out.

Buy/sell sites

Classified ads are in plentiful supply in cyberspace, where collectors and dealers can post notices for items that they want to buy, sell, or trade. You can even participate in auctions at Teletrade (www.teletrade.com) and e-Bay (www.ebay.com). The sports card and memorabilia page of Teletrade is shown in Figure 17-5, and the home page of e-Bay appears in Figure 17-6.

Some people have reservations about buying online — and with good reason. Because of the relatively unregulated nature of Internet commerce, scam artists abound. Combine those unsavory types with all of the unscrupulous behavior that takes place in the sports collectibles business, and you may find yourself unwilling to make a transaction online under any circumstances. But if you follow the buying guidelines that I discuss throughout the

Figure 17-4:
Beckett
does the
Web.

Figure 17-5:
Teletrade
highlights
items from
its next
Web
auction.

Figure 17-6:
e-Bay has various categories of auctions.

book, you should have few problems. Keep your purchases small; you wouldn't make a huge buy via the mail, so don't do so online either. Research the dealer — or site owner, in this case — and ask for references. Ask the seller to e-mail you a scanned photo of any item that you're considering buying.

Fortunately, much of the Internet is self-policing. If someone runs off with your money or collectible, you can report the person to the party that operates the Web site and inform your fellow collectors. There's even a Web site devoted to reporting bad dealers and collectors: `www.localnet.com/~theedge/badtrade.html`. You can't necessarily check out a dealer there beforehand, but by seeing a list of the bad apples, you can see whether the one you're dealing with is listed.

Making new friends online is very easy. You'll quickly discover things for your collection that you may have never found otherwise. But don't let your guard down. All the rules of being a smart, naturally suspicious sports memorabilia collector apply online — perhaps even more so.

I've intentionally refrained from suggesting too many sites in this section. One of the joys — and one of the frustrations — of the Internet is the search for new sites and information. Because the number of Web sites is expanding so rapidly, you're likely to find better sites than any I could list here. Good luck and happy surfing!

Part VI
The Part of Tens

The 5th Wave   By Rich Tennant

"Let's make sure I have your ad right. It reads, 'Single male, very good condition, handled, not abused; slightly rounded corners, some gloss lost from surfaces but no scuffing; seeks same in female companion.'"

In this part . . .

This part presents some fun information to consider about sports memorabilia. I recap the most important themes of this book in the chapter entitled "The Ten Commandments of Sports Collecting" and then introduce you to my "Ten Most Collectible Players," both active and all-time. Just as it's fun to argue over the greatest-ever players in any sport, you'll find yourself debating the most collectible players as you become more involved in the hobby. Finally, I list some of the top auction sales ever, including some sales of memorabilia relating to the king of sports collectibles, Mickey Mantle.

Chapter 18

The Ten Commandments of Sports Collecting

Maybe you recognize the difference between oddball and game-used memorabilia. You know how to avoid the scams. You're smart enough to steer clear of junk and recently produced memorabilia with little collectible value. Still, sometime you'll be hesitant to buy an object, and you'll need some reassurance. Thus, before you make that big purchase or trade, be sure to obey the following commandments.

Thou Shalt Focus, Focus, Focus

The first rule of collecting: Have a theme. Do not wander aimlessly through the collectibles world. Shady dealers will prey on you. If you don't focus your energy, you'll end up with a hodgepodge collection that's unwieldy, difficult to display, and impossible to unload should your financial situation require it. Collect what you like, not what you think is popular or may be worth something down the road.

Thou Shalt Not "Invest" in Sports Memorabilia

Sports memorabilia is a terrible investment. No matter what anyone tells you, you will not make a huge profit by buying and selling collectibles. You can throw your money away in far better places. Sports collectors must buy at retail but sell at wholesale, so your "investment" must double in value just for you to get your money back. You're better off playing the slot machines or the lottery. Look instead for unique memorabilia with true collectible value, not mass-produced, gimmick merchandise.

Thou Shalt Not Collect Manufactured Memorabilia

Although the term "manufactured memorabilia" sounds redundant, and is, it represents a healthy chunk of the current collectibles market. Memorabilia companies like to manufacture rarity, marketing their products as limited-edition, can't-beat-it-with-a-stick, act-now-before-it's-gone, one-of-a-kind merchandise. But the things that become true collectibles over time often are the things you'd least expect. Before you buy that signed replica jersey, remember that the shirt has not been anywhere near a sporting event and the autograph is grossly overpriced because it's on the jersey. If you're a sports bar owner, go for it. If you're a collector, go elsewhere.

Thou Shalt Not Buy a Secondhand Autograph of a Living Sports Figure

Why buy a secondhand autograph and take a chance that a signature is a forgery? You can obtain autographs either free in person or for a fee at a card show. Pay for the autograph ticket; it's worth the peace of mind. Sure, you may have to travel to get it or wait until the player hits the card show circuit in your town. Have patience. Yes, you can remove much of the doubt surrounding the authenticity of secondhand signatures by considering the source, the player involved, the possibility of forgery, and so on. And, yes, if the player is deceased, you have no other option but to buy a secondhand autograph. But why buy something that you have even a kernel of doubt about? Would you pay to have your car repaired if it only *might* run? Play it safe and get the autograph yourself.

Thou Shalt Not Buy Sight Unseen

Do not buy a sports collectible without examining it first yourself. Good photographs usually are an acceptable way to preview the merchandise, but viewing the item in person is a better idea. That old advice that "if something's too good to be true, it probably is" is particularly true in this hobby. Do not fall prey to ads in hobby publications that promise the world. Although the magazines do a good job of screening advertisers, some bad apples always slip through. If possible, obtain the item in the mail before you make your decision. This approach works if you have a relationship with the dealer already. He'll feel comfortable about sending the collectible to you, and you'll have a degree of confidence in the item because you've worked with the dealer before. Remember that you probably would buy very few things in life sight unseen. Sports collectibles should not fall into that category.

Thou Shalt Research, Research, Research

If you do your homework, you'll not only avoid getting burned by forgeries and other scams, but you'll also discover buried treasure that others have overlooked because they weren't willing to do the research. Build a strong sports library. Learn about the players, when they played, and for which teams. Make sure that you know the number a player wore during a given season. Become familiar with uniform styles from different eras and what specifications — size, model, brand, and so on — players might have used for their uniforms and equipment. Acquaint yourself with the look of signatures. Familiarize yourself with price guides, not for an item's "investment value" (remember the second commandment) but to avoid overpaying and to develop an understanding of the market.

Thou Shalt Consider Condition, Condition, Condition

Sports memorabilia collecting is a condition-driven hobby. Even though you are not supposed to be concerned about an item's investment value, you do want to put together a unique collection that has true value if you ever do need to sell it. Toward that end, always be sure to consider an item's condition. Buying something in lesser condition is okay, as long as you pay only a fraction of the price listed in a price guide. Sometimes such an item is more desirable than a brand-new item. For example, uniforms, stadium seats, and pieces of equipment should show wear and tear. After all, people collect such items because they have a direct tie to the game. If you collect cards, do not get hung up on slabbing and grading. (See Chapter 11 for details.) Look for cards in excellent condition or better and worry about slabbing only if you have a valuable card and wish to sell it.

Thou Shalt Question Authority

Would you take everything a lawyer said at face value? How about a used car salesman? A television evangelist, perhaps? Of course not. Sports memorabilia dealers, unfortunately, are in this group, too. Always approach dealers with a healthy degree of skepticism. If they claim that a superstar jersey is game-used, ask them to prove it. What's their source? What kind of paperwork do they have for it? Do they know the player personally? If they're peddling autographs, ask how they obtained them. Is there a paper trail? Were the autographs acquired firsthand or from another dealer? How can you be sure of the item's authenticity? Just because a dealer says he's been in the business forever doesn't mean that he hasn't gotten burned a few times. Even the most knowledgeable dealers end up with bad merchandise that people have come to believe is legitimate once it's passed through enough hands. Research is your best friend.

Thou Shalt Shop Around and Demand a Lifetime Guarantee of Authenticity

You have no excuse to overpay for sports memorabilia. You shouldn't even pay book value, for that matter. This is a buyer's market. Memorabilia manufacturers and dealers are competing for the dollars of a dwindling number of collectors. Everything is negotiable. If a dealer won't budge from his price, move on. Dealers who won't be flexible in their pricing won't be around much longer. Finally, no matter how much research you've done and how comfortable you feel with the authenticity of an item and its source, always demand a lifetime guarantee of authenticity when buying autographs and game-used items. What if an athlete suddenly announces that he's never autographed a football helmet in his life? If you have one, there's no way it could be real. You want to know that the person you acquired the helmet from will refund your money. Of course, in the fly-by-night world of sports collecting, tracing the source may be hard, especially after a period of years. The competitive market claims more victims all the time. In the end, the guarantee is just a piece of paper. But having a guarantee at least requires the dealer to state his reputation in writing.

Thou Shalt Have the Collector Mentality

Think about collecting at all times. If you're at the movies and see a stand-up cardboard figure or movie poster for a sports film, ask the manager for it. Pick up a team schedule when you stop at the gas station. Keep a few official baseballs in your car, especially if you live in an area where you may run into athletes casually. Let your friends and relatives know about your interest. They'll be on the lookout for you. Visit yard sales, estate sales, and auctions. Keep in mind that the things no one ever thinks to save often end up being cult collectibles. Above all else, have fun. Money, greed, and unethical behavior have corrupted this hobby, just like sports itself. But if you approach sports memorabilia as an educated consumer hoping to assemble a collection that complements your love of sports, you'll have a blast.

Chapter 19

The Ten Most Collectible Active Players

• •

In This Chapter

▶ Ken Griffey Jr. (baseball)

▶ Shaquille O'Neal (basketball)

▶ Dale Earnhardt (auto racing)

▶ Tony Gwynn (baseball)

▶ Emmitt Smith (football)

▶ Tiger Woods (golf)

▶ Jeff Gordon (auto racing)

▶ Alex Rodriguez (baseball)

▶ John Elway (football)

▶ Mark McGwire (baseball)

• •

*I*n a hobby fueled by rookies and the latest sensations, the list of the ten most collectible players who are still active is always subject to change. Indeed, as recently as January 1996, this ranking would have looked much different. Tiger Woods was still an amateur golfer at Stanford University. Alex Rodriguez had not yet played his first full season in the major leagues. John Elway had not yet won a Super Bowl, and Mark McGwire looked like a man who never would reach his potential because of injuries.

You may wonder why Michael Jordan, Cal Ripken, and Wayne Gretzky are not on this list. They've transcended the ranks of active players and can be found in Chapter 20 in the list of the ten most collectible players of all time. They certainly would rank 1-2-3 if included in the list in this chapter. As of the late '90s, the following ten players had most captured the attention of sports collectors and stood the best chance of one day breaking into the all-time list.

Don't think that you should be collecting the players in this list. In fact, you may be better off if your favorite player is not among the Top Ten. Finding memorabilia of a player of a lesser stature may be much easier because you'll have fewer people to compete with as you build a collection.

Incidentally, the following list is ranking of popularity and not necessarily of collectible value.

Ken Griffey Jr.

(Seattle Mariners, 1989 to present)

All you really need to know about Ken Griffey's popularity among collectors is that Pacific Trading Cards created a best-selling candy bar in his name not long after he reached the majors in 1989. Card manufacturer Upper Deck made a smashing debut that year in part because it made Griffey its No.1 card. Along with Cal Ripken, Griffey is perhaps the only player in baseball who has corporate America clamoring for his endorsement. From the time he broke into the majors at 19, he's had strong appeal among kids. Nearly a decade later, he remains popular among collectors and advertisers because of his infectious grin and breathtaking talent. If he plays another decade, he could break Hank Aaron's all-time home run mark. His collectibles are the most sought after of any baseball player besides Ripken.

Shaquille O'Neal

(Orlando Magic, 1992 to 1996; Los Angeles Lakers, 1996 to present)

Before he played a game in the National Basketball Association, Shaquille O'Neal was the second most popular player, after Michael Jordan, among collectors. O'Neal's rookie season immediately followed the success of the 1992 Olympic Dream Team, and interest in the league had never been higher. Although many NBA observers believe that he's an underachiever who's more interested in cutting rap albums, making movies, and filming commercials, that opinion hasn't hurt him in the minds of collectors. He single-handedly carried the sports card industry from 1992 to 1994, especially when the baseball strike hit in 1994. (See Figure 19-1.)

Figure 19-1:
1996–97
Shaquille
O'Neal
warm-ups.

Photo courtesy Leland's Auctions

Dale Earnhardt

(NASCAR, 1979 to present)

Seven-time NASCAR national champion Dale Earnhardt supposedly makes more money licensing his name and image to collectible companies than any other athlete, including Michael Jordan. I should put an asterisk by that claim, however. Because just as the line between sport and advertising is blurred in auto racing, so too is it hard to tell the difference between licensed collectibles and licensed products. Would you consider Earnhardt T-shirts, plaques, or model race cars emblazoned with his familiar No. 3 from his racing car memorabilia? Probably not, but millions of NASCAR fans would. Though it's possible to acquire an Earnhardt helmet, racing suit, or even a piece of an automobile, most NASCAR enthusiasts seem less concerned with "game-used" memorabilia and more interested in kitschy merchandise that you see at truck stops and at Winston Cup events. For a long time, rooting for Earnhardt was like supporting the New York Yankees or Dallas Cowboys, but his lack of success at the Daytona 500 made him an underdog, at least until he finally won in 1998.

Tony Gwynn

(San Diego Padres, 1982 to present)

The only reason that Tony Gwynn isn't more popular is because he's played his entire career in the relative obscurity of San Diego. Arguably the second best hitter ever, behind Ted Williams, Gwynn is always gregarious and approachable. He's a willing signer in public, and even when he appears at card shows, he often charges a low fee that goes to charity. That means his signature remains affordable. He only seems to get better with age, winning his eighth batting title and enjoying his best season ever in 1997 at age 37. Gwynn collectors would like to keep their hero a secret, but that will be difficult as he approaches the 3,000-hit plateau. Figure 19-2 shows the Louisville Slugger Silver Bat award that Gwynn received in 1996. The award is presented annually to the winner of the Batting Crown in each league.

Figure 19-2: Tony Gwynn's 1996 silver bat.

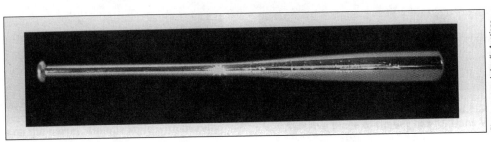

Photo courtesy Leland's Auctions

Emmitt Smith

(Dallas Cowboys, 1990 to present)

The best player on the National Football League's team of the '90s, Dallas Cowboys tailback Emmitt Smith is as popular for his down-to-earth attitude as for his running skills. Running backs and quarterbacks generate the most interest among collectors, and Smith, along with Barry Sanders of the Detroit Lions, almost certainly will go down as the best rusher of the '90s. Through the 1997 season, Smith had three Super Bowl rings (1992, 1993, and 1996), winning the game's Most Valuable Player award in 1993. (See Figure 19-3.)

Tiger Woods

(PGA Tour, 1996 to present)

Tiger Woods has helped put golf on the map. Thanks to Tiger, a sport that's often viewed as lily-white became more popular among minorities and other sports fans who have never followed the game. He also generated interest in golf collectibles — and not just those relating to his own young career. Before Tiger, interest in golf memorabilia suffered, in part because it was rather unwieldy. Signing a golf ball is hard, and attractively displaying a

Figure 19-3:
Emmitt
Smith 1995
signed
game-used
cleats.

Photo courtesy Leland's Auctions

signed flag takes some creativity. Nonetheless, by raising the game's profile, the 1997 Masters champion has increased interest in golf collectibles, including balls, flags, signed photos, and lithographs. (See Figure 19-4.)

Figure 19-4:
The Tiger
Woods
trophy from
his early
years
(1982).

Photo courtesy Leland's Auctions

Jeff Gordon

(NASCAR, 1993 to present)

Jeff Gordon came along just as his sport was getting ready to explode. The 1993 NASCAR Rookie of the Year and 1995 Winston Cup champion, Gordon became the youngest winner of the Daytona 500 in 1997 at the age of 25. His youth, good looks, and self-deprecating demeanor also contribute to his popularity among collectors. Like Dale Earnhardt, Gordon has made a small fortune by marketing his image and his race car. Because he came along just as the sport was getting big, you'll have a hard time finding anything rare and unusual related to his career. Take heart, though. You'll face a challenge just trying to collect everything that's out there.

Alex Rodriguez

(Seattle Mariners, 1995 to present)

Alex Rodriguez is on the verge of unseating Ken Griffey Jr. as the most popular baseball player in Seattle. That prediction alone speaks volumes about this player's meteoric rise. Rodriguez has modeled his play and his demeanor after Cal Ripken, and every indication is that he could be just as popular as Ripken among collectors, and possibly a better player. Bilingual, with GQ looks, Rodriguez has broad collector appeal. Kids love him. Don't look for a Topps baseball card of Rodriguez, however, before 1998. Because Rodriguez refused to sign over his image rights during a Topps-sponsored amateur tournament, the company did not allow him to play in the tournament. Rodriguez did not forgive the company until 1998, when he allowed Topps to use his image on baseball cards.

John Elway

(Denver Broncos, 1983 to present)

By finally winning a Super Bowl in 1998, John Elway seems to have moved ahead of Dan Marino, at least in the minds of collectors. Interest in Elway collectibles soared after he led his team to that Super Bowl victory. Famous for his last-minute drives, Elway and the Broncos had lost during three previous visits to the Super Bowl. He owes much of his popularity among collectors to playing in Denver, where fans support their teams like no other city in the U.S. And collectors like nothing more than a lovable loser who finally comes out on top. (See Figure 19-5.)

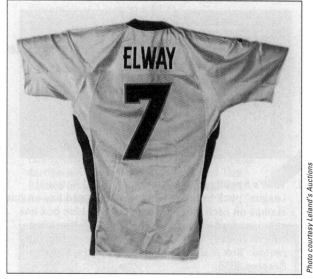

Figure 19-5:
A John
Elway 1997
Denver
Broncos
game-worn
jersey.

Mark McGwire

(Oakland Athletics, 1986 to 1997; St. Louis Cardinals, 1997 to present)

As recently as 1994, Mark McGwire was viewed as an example of unfulfilled potential. Chronic back and foot injuries threatened his career. But after hitting 52 home runs in 1996 and 58 home runs the following year, McGwire now looks like a cinch to join the exclusive 500 home run club and may break Roger Maris's single-season home run mark (61) along the way. Considering that Mickey Mantle and Babe Ruth rank among the most popular players of all time among collectors, it's no wonder that hobbyists have recently been scrambling for McGwire memorabilia; McGwire is one of few players who can rival Mantle and Ruth for prodigious home runs. When he joins the 500 home run club, he should rank among the top collectible players of all time.

Chapter 20

The Ten Most Collectible Players of All Time

In This Chapter

▶ Mickey Mantle (baseball)

▶ Roberto Clemente (baseball)

▶ Joe DiMaggio (baseball)

▶ Ted Williams (baseball)

▶ Babe Ruth (baseball)

▶ Michael Jordan (basketball)

▶ Cal Ripken (baseball)

▶ Nolan Ryan (baseball)

▶ Joe Montana (football)

▶ Wayne Gretzky (hockey)

*A*ll the names in this chapter are familiar to even casual sports fans. These players are not necessarily the ten best athletes of all time, although you could make a compelling argument for any of them. These players, however, have captured the hearts of collectors more than other players. Is Michael Jordan a better player than, say, Magic Johnson or Wilt Chamberlain was? Maybe, but some fans might argue for Magic or Wilt. Still, Jordan is king among hoops collectors. Was Mantle even the best center fielder of his generation who played in New York? A strong case could be made for Willie Mays. But Mays doesn't have half the popularity of Mantle among collectors.

To reach this status among collectors, a player must not just be a champion on the field; he also must have a larger-than-life persona as an American hero. If you opt to focus your collection on any of these players, you'll find plenty of company. That can be a good thing because you'll have plenty of people to trade with and numerous resources when you're looking for that tough-to-find item. On the other hand, plenty of fellow collectors will be competing for that item.

Only three non-baseball players appear on this list, which again demonstrates the overwhelming popularity of baseball collectibles over football, basketball, and hockey memorabilia. In this chapter, I examine the popularity of the Top Ten collectible players of all time.

Mickey Mantle

(New York Yankees, 1951 to 1968)

No one can argue with the fact that Mickey Mantle is the most popular player among collectors, period. His 1952 Topps rookie card is the most treasured of the post–World War II era. His autograph was so sought after that, at the time of his death in 1995, he was making more than $3 million annually by signing autographs.

To understand the Mantle mystique, remember that a generation of young boys grew up with Mantle as their hero. That group is now middle-aged, with plenty of income to spend on Mantle collectibles. For many collectors, Mantle represents a more innocent time when baseball really was America's pastime, before it became corrupted by greed. Mantle also is a remarkable story, a strong country boy who managed to avoid his family's history of health problems and become a superstar, blessed with breathtaking power and speed. Yet he's seen as a tragic hero, a player who may have been even better were it not for knee injuries and hard drinking. (See Figure 20-1.)

Figure 20-1: A white china mug from a Mantle restaurant that's now closed.

Photo courtesy Leland's Auctions

Roberto Clemente

(Pittsburgh Pirates, 1955 to 1972)

Roberto Clemente's legend has grown after his death, especially among collectors. His career was tragically cut short when he died on New Year's Eve 1972, when a plane he boarded that was carrying relief supplies to earthquake victims in Nicaragua crashed in the Atlantic Ocean. A Puerto Rican who suffered dual racism for being both Hispanic and dark-skinned, Clemente was known for more than his spectacular play; he also was famous for his charitable endeavors and for being outspoken on racial issues. Clemente played in 11 All-Star games and won 4 batting titles, 12 Gold Gloves, and a National League Most Valuable Player award. Because of racism, his cards and collectibles (see Figure 20-2) were not as widely collected as those of Mantle and others, making them much more valuable now.

Among his collector admirers is James Beckett, who put Clemente's 1965 Topps card on the cover of the first issue of his *Beckett Baseball Card Price Guide*.

Figure 20-2: A Roberto Clemente signed photo.

ROBERTO CLEMENTE

Photo courtesy Leland's Auctions

Joe DiMaggio

(New York Yankees, 1936 to 1942; 1945 to 1951 / coach Oakland Athletics, 1968 to 1969)

Joe DiMaggio has never been as popular as Mickey Mantle among collectors. Most of DiMaggio's contemporaries are deceased, he has a reputation for being aloof, and his memorabilia (see Figure 20-3) is priced beyond the reach of most collectors. When he does appear at card shows, his autograph costs a whopping $175. Still, there's something magical about DiMaggio. He was married to Marilyn Monroe, was immortalized in song by Simon and Garfunkel, and seems to play the part of "living legend" perfectly. He likes to be introduced at public events as "the greatest living ballplayer," which irks some Ted Williams fans.

Figure 20-3: A 1940s Joe DiMaggio stadium pennant.

Photo courtesy Leland's Auctions

Ted Williams

(Boston Red Sox, 1939 to 1942; 1946 to 1960 / manager, Washington Senators, 1969 to 1971; Texas Rangers, 1972)

As a player, Ted Williams had a love-hate relationship with Red Sox fans, but that's been long forgotten, at least among collectors who prefer to concentrate on his extraordinary life. Universally regarded as the greatest hitter in baseball history, Williams compiled a .344 lifetime batting average and hit 521 home runs despite missing nearly five seasons while serving in World War II and Korea.

Always outspoken and feisty, even after two strokes, Williams has marketed himself well in recent years. For a while, Williams fell prey to con men and bad business deals, but his son, John Henry, now operates the sales and distribution of his father's autographs and memorabilia. (See Figure 20-4.)

Figure 20-4:
A dozen Ted Williams signed baseballs.

Photo courtesy Leland's Auctions

Babe Ruth

(Boston Red Sox, 1914 to 1919; New York Yankees, 1920 to 1934; Boston Braves, 1935 / coach, Brooklyn Dodgers, 1938)

Although he died in 1948, Babe Ruth remains popular among collectors, even if most of them cannot afford cards, let alone memorabilia, from his prodigious career. How famous is Ruth? Even people who have no knowledge of baseball have heard of his legendary exploits on the field and his tremendous appetites off the field. He's even become part of the American vernacular. (See Figure 20-5.) A huge feat is said to be a "Ruthian" accomplishment.

Ruth was a prolific autograph signer, and films from his day often show him signing dozens of baseballs at a time. These days the balls are relatively affordable at $5,000.

Michael Jordan

(Chicago Bulls, 1984 to 1993, 1995 to present)

After the pope, Michael Jordan is perhaps the most recognizable man in the world. Jordan is the rare athlete who has ascended to the level of cultural icon. Many non-sports fans know him for his Air Jordan sneakers, his *Space Jam* movie role, or his commercials for everything from McDonald's to Gatorade. Even nonathletic types can relate to him; Jordan did not make his high school varsity team until his junior year. Since then, his only failure came in 1994, when he retired from basketball and tried to make a run at Major League Baseball.

Figure 20-5:
A 1930s
Babe Ruth
Old Gold
cigarettes
advertising
sign.

Photo courtesy Leland's Auctions

Unfortunately, his autograph is rampantly forged, and numerous dealers have tried to pass off replica Jordan jerseys as game-worn. He's had a long-standing deal with Upper Deck Authenticated, which markets autographed replica jerseys, photos, and magazine covers.

Cal Ripken

(Baltimore Orioles, 1981 to present)

At a time when fans are increasingly distanced from professional athletes, Cal Ripken is a throwback to more innocent times. He's the living embodiment of the work ethic: He hasn't missed a game since 1982. He's a clean-cut, All-American guy whose many endorsements include milk and hot dogs. He's been known to sign autographs for hours after games. Along with Tony Gwynn of the San Diego Padres, Ripken probably represents the last of the baseball superstars who will play their entire careers with one team.

Because he's a contemporary player, countless Ripken products (see Figure 20-6) are available, most of them affordable. A dealer/collector named Don Harrison of Hampton, Virginia, has tried to keep up with Ripken memorabilia by publishing a Cal Ripken memorabilia checklist. With each edition, the paperback checklist gets thicker. Harrison, the owner of The Tenth Inning card shop, can be reached at 757-827-1667.

Figure 20-6:
A 1990 Cal Ripken game-used jersey.

Photo courtesy Leland's Auctions

Nolan Ryan

(New York Mets, 1966 to 1971; California Angels, 1972 to 1979; Houston Astros, 1980 to 1988; Texas Rangers, 1989 to 1993)

Nolan Ryan's appeal with fans and collectors is due as much to his clean living, work ethic, and remarkable longevity as it is to his athletic ability. During his last big league season, in 1993 at the age of 46, Ryan still was throwing 95 mile-per-hour fastballs.

Considered only an above average pitcher for much of his career, Ryan seemed to get better with age. He finished as the all-time leader in strikeouts (5,714) and no-hitters (7) while recording 324 wins. He inspired numerous collectibles, particularly in the latter years of his career. He even appeared on a box of Kellogg's Corn Flakes. (Figure 20-7 shows a signed and dated ball used in one of his no-hitters with the Astros in 1981.)

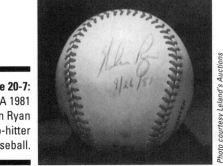

Figure 20-7:
A 1981
Nolan Ryan
no-hitter
baseball.

Photo courtesy Leland's Auctions

Joe Montana

(San Francisco 49ers, 1979 to 1993; Kansas City Chiefs, 1993 to 1994)

In a sport of giants, Joe Montana represented the common man. Rising from the bottom of Notre Dame's quarterback depth chart, he became one of the top quarterbacks in college history and perhaps the best-ever quarterback in the National Football League. Collectors love a winner, and few athletes were victorious more often than Montana, who led the 49ers to four Super Bowl titles, winning the MVP award three times. Montana's memorabilia popularity also is fueled by the huge groups of collectors who follow Notre Dame and the 49ers.

Autograph collectors often are disappointed by Montana's signature; it's little more than his initials and two horizontal lines. Montana has provided autographs for Upper Deck Authenticated for years.

Wayne Gretzky

(Edmonton Oilers, 1979 to 1988; Los Angeles Kings, 1988 to 1996; St. Louis Blues, 1996; New York Rangers, 1996 to present)

The Great One, as Wayne Gretzky is known, is a collector himself and probably has a few items from some of his colleagues on this list. The National Hockey League's all-time leader in points, goals, and assists, Gretzky helped fuel the sport's growth in the '90s after his 1988 trade from the Edmonton Oilers to the Los Angeles Kings. He's been tops among hockey collectors for years. (See Figure 20-8.)

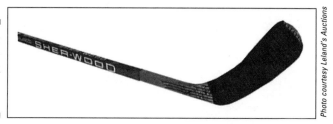

Photo courtesy Leland's Auctions

Figure 20-8:
A game-
used stick
from Wayne
Gretzky.

Just when it seemed that his popularity might be slipping, he signed with
the New York Rangers as a free agent in 1996, keeping himself front and
center in the minds of collectors. He's been affiliated with Upper Deck
Authenticated for years.

Chapter 21

The Ten Biggest Sports Memorabilia Auction Sales Ever (Unofficially)

● ●

In This Chapter

▶ Eye-popping auction sales

▶ A million dollars in jersey sales

▶ Mickey Mantle collectibles

● ●

*Y*ou probably will never spend $100,000 or more on a sports memorabilia item. But in case you have unlimited financial resources, this list of top sales should give you a ballpark idea of what you could expect to pay. Incidentally, some might consider the $772,500 someone paid for President John F. Kennedy's golf clubs at a Sotheby's auction in 1996 to be the highest price paid for "sports" memorabilia. I consider this more "Presidential" memorabilia, so I've not included it in this chapter.

Honus Wagner Baseball Card ($640,500)

In 1996, dealer Robert Lifson bought a T206 Honus Wagner baseball card at a Christie's auction. The card was purchased by Treat Entertainment from hockey star Wayne Gretzky, who along with former Los Angeles Kings owner Bruce McNall had paid $451,000 for it at a Sotheby's auction in 1991. Treat made the card the focal point of a Wal-Mart sweepstakes. The winner, Patricia Gibbs, a postal worker from Hollywood, Florida, consigned it to Christie's.

Eddie Murray's 500th Home Run Ball ($500,000)

In 1996, Baltimore businessman Michael Lasky made headlines when he offered a staggering $500,000 to Danny Jones, who had caught Eddie Murray's 500th home run ball at Oriole Park at Camden Yards. Although many experts placed a value of roughly $10,000 on the item, Lasky, the owner of the Psychic Friends Network and an infomercial company, paid Jones an annuity worth $25,000 annually for 20 years.

Honus Wagner Baseball Card ($451,000)

Wayne Gretzky and Bruce McNall paid $451,000 for the T206 Honus Wagner at Sotheby's in 1991. The sale grabbed headlines, and not just because of the staggering price paid for the card. McNall had earned a reputation as a rare coin and art collector even before he purchased the Los Angeles hockey team.

A.J. Foyt's 1977 Indianapolis 500 Car ($410,000)

Although this item did not generate the biggest sale of all time, it's the biggest sports artifact — at least in terms of size — to go for a six-figure price. In 1992, Indianapolis Motor Speedway president Tony George spent $410,000 for the car that A.J. Foyt drove in 1977 to capture his record fourth Indianapolis 500 victory. The car was one of 28 vehicles sold as part of a sale that raised more than $1.6 million.

1927 Lou Gehrig Road Jersey ($363,000)*

On September 9, 1992, a 1927 Lou Gehrig road jersey sold for $363,000 at a Richard Wolffers "Treasures of the Diamond" auction in San Francisco. Although the jersey has often been touted as the highest priced jersey ever sold at an auction, many people place an asterisk by the sales figure to clarify that the payment was a combination of cash and collectibles. The jersey was particularly sought after because it was from the 1927 Yankees, considered by many experts as the best baseball team ever.

__Note:__ Some people in the sports collecting hobby view some of the prices reported by the now-defunct Richard Wolffers auction house with skepticism. In several instances, the price paid was not in cash but rather a combination of cash and sports memorabilia. Collectors do not place much stock in the prices paid as indicative of the market because they were not always cash transactions.

Lou Gehrig Farewell Uniform ($306,130)

Lou Gehrig's popularity with collectors has continued in recent years. In 1997, five collectors pooled resources to buy the uniform worn by Lou Gehrig during his tearful farewell speech at Yankee Stadium on July 4, 1939. He died two years later from amyotrophic lateral sclerosis, which is now more commonly known as "Lou Gehrig's disease." The collectors purchased the uniform from a Robert Edward Auction in Hoboken, New Jersey.

1938 Lou Gehrig Road Uniform ($220,000)

In 1991, collector Mark Friedland purchased a 1938 Lou Gehrig road uniform at a Richard Wolffers auction in San Francisco. At the time, the sale represented the second-highest price paid for a sports item, following the $451,000 paid for the Honus Wagner card by Wayne Gretzky and Bruce McNall earlier in the year. Friedland, of Aspen, Colorado, had been the runner-up in the bidding for the Wagner card.

Babe Ruth Coaching Uniform ($176,000)

At the Richard Wolffers "Treasures of the Diamond" sale in September 1992, a collector paid $176,000 for Babe Ruth's 1938 Brooklyn Dodgers road uniform from his stint as a coach. Ruth had expressed interest in managing after his career, but coaching was as close as he came. Ironically, this former Yankee player coached for a rival New York franchise.

1924 Ty Cobb Uniform ($176,000)

Ty Cobb's 1924 Detroit Tigers uniform sold for $176,000 at a Leland's auction in August 1992. This uniform came with a letter of authenticity from Cobb himself.

1954 Mickey Mantle Home Jersey ($165,000)

Mickey Mantle, perhaps the most popular sports figure among collectors, cracked the Top 10 when his 1954 home jersey sold for $165,000 at a Richard Wolffers auction in San Francisco in 1992.

Ten for a Million ($1.145 million, actually)

These sales don't quite make the Top Ten all-time, but they still represent some big money. If you had $1.145 million, you could have purchased the items in the following list.

1. $137,500 — 1968 Nolan Ryan home jersey, Richard Wolffers auction, 1992

2. $132,000 — 1939 Joe DiMaggio home jersey, Richard Wolffers auction, 1993

3. $132,000 — 1961 Roger Maris home jersey, Sotheby's auction, 1992

4. $132,000 — 1929 Babe Ruth road jersey, Leland's auction, 1993

5. $115,500 — 1900 Honus Wagner road jersey, Richard Wolffers auction, 1993

6. $111,000 — 1960 Mickey Mantle home jersey, Leland's auction, 1992

7. $110,000 — 1931 Lou Gehrig red-white-and-blue pinstriped jersey worn when he and several other players toured Japan after the season, Leland's auction, 1993

8. $99,000 — 1941 Joe DiMaggio uniform, Sotheby's auction, 1992

9. $93,500 — 1955 Ted Williams road jersey, Richard Wolffers auction, 1993

10. $82,500 — 1921 Ty Cobb home jersey, Sotheby's auction, 1992

Ten Non-Uniform Mickey Mantle Collectibles Sold at Auction

Mickey Mantle ranks as the most popular athletic figure among sports memorabilia collectors. Numerous items from Mantle's life have been placed up for grabs since his death in 1995. Here's a look at some of the more unique ones.

1. $121,000 — The 3-x-5-inch painting of "The Mick" that was used for his 1953 Topps baseball card was purchased by Marriott Hotels and Resorts at a Guernsey's auction in 1989.

2. $60,500 — In 1994, Mantle's boyhood home, located just off Route 66 in Commerce, Oklahoma, became one of the most unusual auction items when it was consigned to Leland's. (See Figure 21-1.)

*3. $24,150 — A copy of Mantle's last public speech, delivered at the Baylor University medical center.

*4. $23,000 — A collection of 260 signed business cards from the Manhattan restaurant bearing Mantle's name.

*5. $13,800 — A tuxedo that Mantle wore at former teammate Billy Martin's wedding.

*6. $9,200 — Mantle's passport.

7. $7,700 — A Mantle bat, used between 1965 and 1968, sold at a Leland's auction in 1995.

*8. $7,175 — Mantle's American Express platinum card.

*9. $6,900 — A lock of Mantle's hair.

10. $900 — Mantle's high school graduation photo, matted, sold at a Robert Edward auction in 1995.

*These items were part of a Leland's auction in November 1997. The lots came from Greer Johnson, Mantle's longtime business manager and companion. The entire sale raised $541,880, a portion of which went to charity.

Figure 21-1:
The Mantle
boyhood
home.

Photo courtesy Leland's Auctions

Part VII
Appendixes

The 5th Wave   By Rich Tennant

"I think it's going a bit far to call what the team's bulldog mascot did to your shoe an 'autograph'."

In this part . . .

Throughout this part, I help you build your sports memorabilia vocabulary so that you can impress your friends and become a swaggering, wheeling-and-dealing sports memorabilia collector who gets the most for your money. I also provide you with helpful addresses for teams from the four major sports leagues, sports card manufacturers, leading auction houses, and sports memorabilia show promoters. You also can find a listing of the members of the Baseball and Football Halls of Fame as a quick reference.

Appendix A
Sports Memorabilia Terms

Airbrushing

The touching up of card photos, usually when a player has changed teams. Done rather crudely by hand through the 1970s, airbrushing is now done via computer.

All-Star card

A card specifically designating a player as All-Star or All-Pro. All-Star cards are different from the player's standard card and are almost always worth less.

Archival mounting

Museum term referring to the process of framing an item without altering its form with tape, glue, dry mounting, and so on.

Autographed card

A sports card that has been signed. Autographed cards are often worth more than an unsigned card, but some collectors view autographed cards as signed photos, not cards.

Autopen

Mechanical device used to quickly produce signatures. Equivalent of a stamp, although more difficult to recognize as an inauthentic signature.

Base brand

Basic set of sports cards produced by a company, and also the lowest priced.

Beckett

The most-followed line of card price guides in the sports collecting field. Founded by James Beckett and headquartered in Dallas, Texas, Beckett Publications produces numerous collectibles-related magazines.

Bid board

An area at a card shop where customers can place memorabilia, usually cards, up for auction. The card store owner receives a percentage of the sale price.

Blank back

A card with no printing on the back, either intentionally or because of a printing error.

Bobbin' head dolls

Also known as bobbers, or nodders. Cartoonish dolls made of papier mâché or plastic in the 1960s. Sports Accessories and Memorabilia (SAM) resurrected the product in 1992 and continues to make ceramic bobbers.

Book price

The full-retail price of a card that appears in a price guide.

Bowman

A top competitor to Topps that produced baseball cards from 1948 to 1955, football cards from 1948 to 1955, and basketball cards in 1948. Topps purchased Bowman in 1956, effectively putting it out of business. In 1989, Topps began producing cards under the Bowman brand.

Broders

Unlicensed cards not available through normal distribution channels. Named for the man who created many of them in the 1980s, they're not regarded as collectible.

Case

A sealed case of boxed cards that card companies sell to dealers and retail outlets.

Cello packaging

Also called cellophane packaging. Widely used in the 1970s and 1980s for the sale of individual packs of 15 or so cards. Top and bottom cards are visible. A cello box often contains 24 packs.

Centering

Refers to the positioning of a photo on a card. The better the centering, the more valuable the card.

Chase cards

Also known as inserts. Special cards randomly inserted in packs.

Checklist

A list of every card in a particular set or portion of a set, along with a box next to each name. Checklists that have been checked are effectively defaced.

Cherry-picking

Practice of memorizing the card sequencing of cellophane-wrapped packs and picking out the packs that include valuable cards.

Commons

Term used to refer to cards and memorabilia of non-star players.

Condition

One of the most important factors in determining the value of cards and memorabilia. The better the condition, the higher the value.

Convention

Also called a show. A gathering of collectors and dealers at a hotel, gymnasium, or civic facility who buy, sell, and trade sports memorabilia.

Counterfeit

A card or collectible made to look like the real item. Counterfeits have no collectible value.

Cut

Or "cut signature." An autograph cut out of a document.

Dealer

A person who buys, sells, and trades sports memorabilia for a profit. A dealer may work full time or part time and can run his business out of a store, through mail order, at card shows, or through some combination of these outlets.

Distributor

A middleman between card and memorabilia manufacturers and retail outlets and dealers. Distributors sometimes have exclusive access to certain products.

Donruss

Producer of baseball cards since 1981. Formerly based in Illinois, it's now part of Pinnacle Brands in Grand Prairie, Texas.

Double print (DP)

A card produced twice as frequently as the rest of the set or series.

Doubles

Also known as duplicates or dupes. Extra cards or memorabilia items that can be traded or sold.

800-count box

The standard for storing card sets. Only boxes with side flaps should be used.

Equipment

Any item used in a sporting event, including uniforms, hats, balls, pucks, sticks, bats, clubs, yard markers, golf flags, and so on.

Error (ERR)

A misprinted or misspelled card. Not usually more valuable than an error-free card unless a corrected version was printed.

Excellent-Mint (EX-MT)

A condition of a card with some minor flaws.

Extended set

A late-season set that includes rookies who emerged during the season and traded players in their new uniforms. Also known as update or traded sets.

Extra length

Uniform jersey term that refers to the practice of ordering slightly longer shirts so that they won't come untucked.

Facsimile

A reproduction of a person's signature.

Factory set

A complete set of cards packaged and collated by the card company and marketed as a set. Often shrink-wrapped or otherwise sealed, factory sets are generally worth more than hand-collated sets.

Fantasy card

A card of a player that did not actually appear in a set but that is produced in the same design of a past card set.

F.D.C. (First Day Cover)

An envelope bearing a painting or portrait of a sports image and postmark canceled on the first day that it was available for public sale.

Fixtures

Any non-seat items that came out of a stadium, such as turnstiles, aisle signs, restroom signs, press box signs, and so on.

Flannel

General term used to refer to the heavier, predominately wool blend fabrics used for many baseball uniforms before the 1970s.

Fleer

A New Jersey-based card manufacturer of baseball, football, and basketball cards. Parent company is Marvel Entertainment.

Fuzzy corner

Term used in card grading to refer to a card that still comes to a point but has begun to fray slightly.

Foil pack

Tamperproof card packaging widely used since 1989.

Foil stamping

A metallic image printed on a card.

Food set

A card line produced and distributed as an insert or premium in food packages, such as cereal and snack cakes.

Gamer

Term used by baseball players to refer to a game-used glove, bat, or jersey.

Game-Used/Game-Worn

Terms referring to uniforms and equipment that have been used in a professional sports event.

Hartland

Line of plastic figurines, produced between 1958 and 1963 of 18 top baseball players. An anniversary edition was produced in 1988.

Hobby

Folksy term used by some veteran collectors to refer to the sports collectibles business/industry, as in "the hobby."

Hobby only

A sports card line that is available only through card shops and dealers, not in retail stores and bulk shopping clubs.

HOF

Hall of Fame.

HOF plaque postcards

Popular, glossy, yellow postcard reproductions of the plaques at the Baseball Hall of Fame in Cooperstown, New York. Very popular for autographs.

Hologram

The silver, white-light projection stamp on Upper Deck cards. Technology is similar to credit card holograms, to prevent counterfeiting.

Inscribed

A note or personalization accompanying an autograph.

Insert

See *chase cards.*

Kellogg's

Cereal company that produced three-dimensional baseball cards included in boxes of cereal in the 1970s and early 1980s.

Knits

The modern, polyester-based fabrics used for modern sports uniforms.

Layering

Term used in card grading that refers to the separation of card stock layers at the corner of the card.

Leaf

Parent company of Donruss. Donruss issued cards in Canada under the leaf name from 1985 to 1988 and has produced cards for U.S. distribution since 1990. Leaf and Donruss now are part of Pinnacle Brands.

Leland's

New York sports memorabilia auction house. Name comes from its chairman, Joshua Leland Evans.

Limited edition

In theory, one of a finite number. In the sports memorabilia business, however, some manufacturers tout items as limited editions but don't disclose the number of items produced.

Lithograph

A high-quality art print. Typically a limited number of lithographs are produced from an original portrait or painting and are sometimes signed by the artist and/or the subject.

LOA (Letter of Authenticity)

Also known as Certificate of Authenticity. Usually accompanies an autograph or game-used item. More a warranty than a guarantee, an LOA is a statement by the seller backing the genuineness of the article.

Manufacturer's tag

A tag sewn or attached into a jersey identifying it as from a particular company, such as Russell or Rawlings.

Memorabilia

Usually used to refer to sports collectibles other than cards, although some consider cards to be memorabilia.

Mini

A smaller edition of a standard issue card set, the most famous of which is the 1975 Topps "mini" baseball series.

Mint (MT)

The condition of a flawless card.

MSA

Mike Schechter and Associates. Tampa licensing firm that produced many of the cards included in food products during the 1970s, 1980s, and early 1990s.

Multiplayer card

A card picturing more than one player, usually a rookie or league leader card.

MVP

Most Valuable Player.

Mylar

Type of plastic from which many card holders, plastic sheets, and other card protection devices are made.

Nameplate

The strip containing a player's name on the back of a jersey.

National

Refers to the annual National Sports Collectors Convention, the sports collecting hobby's premier event. Also refers to the National Sports Daily, a short-lived newspaper produced from 1990 to 1991. Although few copies were saved, some collectors stockpile the paper for its colorful covers featuring big-name stars.

Near-Mint

Condition that describes a card that on close inspection has one minor flaw that lowers its value.

Nine-pocket sheet

Standard-sized plastic sheet. Roughly the size of notebook paper and designed to fit into a three-ring binder, it holds nine standard-sized cards, or 18 if placed back-to-back.

NOB (Name on Back)

A term used to describe jerseys.

Oddball

Catchall category of sports collectibles other than cards, autographs, and game-worn uniforms. Examples of oddball sports collectibles include advertising pieces, ticket stubs, publications, figurines, beer cans, and Coca-Cola memorabilia.

Off-center

A card printed with uneven borders.

O-Pee-Chee

Longtime Canadian licensee of Topps that produced bilingual (French/English) baseball and hockey cards.

Pacific Trading Cards

A Lynnwood, Washington, producer of baseball and football cards.

Panel

An uncut strip of two or more cards.

Parkhurst

A Canadian manufacturer of hockey cards in the 1950s and 1960s. In recent years, the name has been licensed to major manufacturers.

Perez-Steele

Popular line of Hall of Famer postcards produced by artist Dick Perez and business partner Frank Steele. Ideal for autographs.

Phantom

A ticket or press pin produced in anticipation of a team's making the play-offs, but not used when the team failed to make it.

Pinnacle Brands

Dallas-based card manufacturer that produces card brands Pinnacle, Score, Action Packed, Leaf, and Donruss.

Police set

A card set licensed to police or fire departments. These cards picture a player on the front and a crime prevention tip or other advice to children on the back.

Polyethylene

A flexible plastic used to make nine-pocket sheets and other card protection devices. Polyethylene is safer than PVC for card storage.

Premium

Mid-range brand of sports cards. It has more bells and whistles and costs more than base brands but is not as elaborate or expensive as super premium. Also refers to the cost of an autograph at a card show. A ticket for a premium item, such as a bat or jersey, costs more than a flat item.

Press pins

Small metal trinkets handed out to members of the baseball media covering the Super Bowl, World Series, Major League Baseball All-Star Game, and Baseball Hall of Fame induction ceremonies.

Price guide

A book or magazine that lists and places values on sports cards and memorabilia.

Private signing

An event at which a player signs autographs in private for a dealer, who often accepts non-autographed items from collectors to have signed for a fee. Not as preferable as getting something signed at a card show.

Promo

A promotional sports card distributed at a special event and/or to dealers and media as a sample of an upcoming card set.

PSA (Professional Sports Authenticator)

Card grading service out of Newport Beach, California. Company grades cards on a scale of 1 to 10. The sports card equivalent of the Gemological Institute of America.

PVC (Polyvinyl chloride)

Material used to make many of the early plastic sheets for photos and trading cards. Collectors should not use it because it causes the plastic to melt onto the memorabilia.

Rack pack

Also known as Rak pack. A package of three decks of 15 or so cards wrapped tightly in cellophane so that the top and bottom cards are visible. Widely sold in the 1970s and 1980s.

Repaired

A bat that has been restored to its original condition.

Redemption certificate

Found in packs of cards, these documents can be exchanged for valuable cards and memorabilia as part of promotions.

Regional set

A card set distributed in one geographic area of the country. Often limited to cards depicting one team.

Restored

A card or memorabilia item whose condition has been improved. Restored bats and stadium seats are often still valuable collectibles. But restored cards fall into the same category as automobiles whose odometers have been rolled back.

Reverse negative

A sports card printed with the image flip-flopped, creating a mirrored effect. Usually regarded as an error card, but not often corrected.

Rookie

Any sports memorabilia related to a player's first season.

Rookiemania

1980s phenomenon that placed a huge emphasis on rookie cards and memorabilia.

ROY

Rookie of the Year.

Salesman's sample

An example of a jersey or championship ring produced by companies for players and team officials to preview. Not as collectible as, but often mistaken for, the real thing.

SAM (Sports Accessories and Memorabilia)

A California firm that has produced bobbin' head dolls since the early 1990s.

SASE

Self-addressed, stamped envelope. Should always be sent when requesting autographs by mail.

SCD

Sports Collectors Digest, a popular hobby publication produced by Krause Publications of Iola, Wisconsin. Published weekly, *SCD* offers industry news and commentary along with hundreds of ads.

Score

Originally Optigraphics, Score issued its first baseball cards in 1988. The company later became Pinnacle Brands, which still issues cards under the Score brand.

The Score Board

A Cherry Hill, New Jersey, company that specializes in autographed sports memorabilia.

Secondary market

Refers to the secondhand, resale market for sports memorabilia.

Sepia

A brownish tone, not quite color and not quite black and white. Often seen in vintage photos, cards, and prints.

Series

A group of cards printed and distributed at the same time. Until 1974, Topps issued its sets in series form over the course of the baseball season.

Sharpie

Versatile felt-tip marker that writes on virtually everything. Perfect for all autographs except for those on baseballs.

Shoe box

A corrugated cardboard box sold in the shape of a shoe box, but with a divider down the middle. Good for storing cards upright.

Short print (SP)

As opposed to double print, a card printed in lesser quantity than the others in the set. SP also is a brand of Upper Deck sports cards.

Sked

Short for "schedule." Refers to a calendar of a team's games.

SkyBox

Manufacturer of football and basketball cards.

Slabbing

Process of independent, professional grading and placing cards in plastic casing by companies such as PSA. Cards cannot be removed without damaging the cases.

Snap-it

A hard plastic container for individual cards that snaps and unsnaps easily.

Standard size

A card measuring $2^{1}/_{2}$ x $3^{1}/_{2}$ inches, the industry standard since Topps produced its baseball cards that size in 1957.

Star

Cards or memorabilia of premier players. Some collectors also make a distinction between superstars, stars, and minor stars.

Starter set

An incomplete set of cards meant to give collectors a head start at completing the set.

Starting Lineup

Small plastic figures featuring player images produced by Kenner since 1988.

Stub

A portion of a ticket left over from a game. Not as valuable as an untorn ticket, but still collectible.

Super premium

High end brand of sports cards. Usually produced in smaller quantities using the most-advanced printing technology. Can cost three to five times more than premium cards.

Sweet spot

Preferred spot to have a baseball autographed by just one person. Refers to the straight, narrow area between the seams opposite the stamped league logo and team president signature.

Tails cut

Refers to the practice of some players who shorten the tails of their jerseys for a smoother "no panty-line look."

TC

Team card. A card picturing an entire team or at least featuring a team checklist.

Team set

A set of players either produced or collated together.

Tobacco cards

Baseball cards packaged with tobacco products in the late 1800s and early 1900s.

Topps

The oldest existing sports card manufacturer. Based in New York, Topps has produced baseball cards continuously since 1951 and has also produced football, basketball, and hockey cards.

Trimmed card

A card that has been carefully cut to make its edges and corners appear sharper. Unethical process that renders the card worthless.

T206

Set of tobacco cards produced by American Tobacco between 1909 and 1911. Includes fabled Honus Wagner card.

Tuff Stuff

Popular monthly publication headquartered in Richmond, Virginia.

UDA

Upper Deck Authenticated of Carlsbad, California. Sister company of Upper Deck. Markets signed memorabilia with holographic authentication process.

UER

Uncorrected error card. A card that was misprinted or misspelled but never corrected.

Uncut sheet

A full press sheet of cards that was never cut and collated into individual cards.

Upper Deck

A Carlsbad, California, manufacturer of baseball, football, basketball, and hockey cards.

UV

A glossy coating applied to sports cards.

Variation

A card printed in more than one manner, usually to correct an error or printing mistake.

Very Good (VG)

A condition assigned to a card that shows obvious signs of handling.

Want list

A collector's wish list of items to buy in order to complete a set or augment a collection. The list is often sent to dealers and fellow collectors.

Wax

Type of card packaging (for example, wax pack) widely used until the late 1980s. Wax-sealed wrappers could be easily removed and the contents tampered with.

Weekend warrior

A part-time sports memorabilia dealer who does not own a shop but sets up a booth at weekend card shows.

Wrong backs

A card printed with a picture of one player on the front and the statistics of another player on the back.

Appendix B
Team Addresses

Major League Baseball

American League

Anaheim Angels
P.O. Box 2000
Anaheim, CA 92803

Baltimore Orioles
Oriole Park at Camden Yards
333 W. Camden St.
Baltimore, MD 21201

Boston Red Sox
Fenway Park
4 Yawkey Way
Boston, MA 02215-3496

Chicago White Sox
Comiskey Park
333 W. 35th St.
Chicago, IL 60616

Cleveland Indians
Jacobs Field
2401 Ontario St.
Cleveland, OH 44115

Detroit Tigers
Tiger Stadium
2121 Trumbull Ave.
Detroit, MI 48216

Kansas City Royals
P.O. Box 419969
Kansas City, MO 64141-6969

Minnesota Twins
34 Kirby Puckett Place
Minneapolis, MN 55415

New York Yankees
Yankee Stadium
Bronx, NY 10451

Oakland Athletics
Oakland Coliseum
Oakland, CA 94621

Seattle Mariners
P.O. Box 4100
Seattle, WA 98104

Tampa Bay Devil Rays
One Tropicana Dr.
St. Petersburg, FL 33705

Texas Rangers
P.O. Box 90111
Arlington, TX 76004

Toronto Blue Jays
SkyDome
1 Blue Jays Way
Suite 3200
Toronto, Ontario, Canada
M5V 1J1

National League

Arizona Diamondbacks
P.O. Box 2095
Phoenix, AZ 85001

Atlanta Braves
P.O. Box 4064
Atlanta, GA 30302

Chicago Cubs
1060 W. Addison St.
Chicago, IL 60613-4397

Cincinnati Reds
100 Cinergy Field
Cincinnati, OH 45202

Colorado Rockies
Coors Field
2001 Blake St.
Denver, CO 80205-2000

Florida Marlins
2267 NW 199th St.
Miami, FL 33056

Houston Astros
P.O. Box 288
Houston, TX 77001-0288

Los Angeles Dodgers
1000 Elysian Park Ave.
Los Angeles, CA 90012-1199

Milwaukee Brewers
P.O. Box 3099
Milwaukee, WI 53201-3099

Montreal Expos
P.O. Box 500, Station M
Montreal, Quebec, Canada
H1V 3P2

New York Mets
Shea Stadium
123-01 Roosevelt Ave.
Flushing, NY 11368

Philadelphia Phillies
P.O. Box 7575
Philadelphia, PA 19101

Pittsburgh Pirates
P.O. Box 7000
Pittsburgh, PA 15212

St. Louis Cardinals
Busch Stadium
250 Stadium Place
St. Louis, MO 63102

San Diego Padres
P.O. Box 2000
San Diego, CA 92112-2000

San Francisco Giants
3Com Park at Candlestick
   Point
San Francisco, CA 94124

National Football League

American Football Conference

Baltimore Ravens
11001 Owings Mills Blvd.
Owings Mills, MD 21117

Buffalo Bills
One Bills Dr.
Orchard Park, NY 14127

Cincinnati Bengals
200 Cinergy Field
Cincinnati, OH 45202

Denver Broncos
13655 Broncos Pkwy.
Englewood, CO 80112

Indianapolis Colts
7001 W. 56th St.
Indianapolis, IN 46224-0100

Jacksonville Jaguars
One Stadium Place
Jacksonville, FL 32202

Kansas City Chiefs
One Arrowhead Dr.
Kansas City, MO 64129

Miami Dolphins
Pro Player Stadium
2269 NW 199th St.
Miami, FL 33056

New England Patriots
Foxboro Stadium
Route 1
Foxboro, MA 02035

New York Jets
1000 Fulton Ave.
Hempstead, NY 11550

Oakland Raiders
1220 Harborbay Pkwy.
Alameda, CA 94502

Pittsburgh Steelers
300 Stadium Circle
Pittsburgh, PA 15212

San Diego Chargers
P.O. Box 609609
San Diego, CA 92160

Seattle Seahawks
11220 NE 53rd St.
Kirkland, WA 98033

Tennessee Oilers
P.O. Box 198497
Nashville, TN 37219

National Football Conference

Arizona Cardinals
P.O. Box 888
Tempe, AZ 85001

Atlanta Falcons
One Falcon Place
Suwanee, GA 30024

Carolina Panthers
800 S. Mint St.
Charlotte, NC 28202

Chicago Bears
Halas Hall
250 N. Washington Rd.
Lake Forest, IL 60045

Dallas Cowboys
Cowboys Center
One Cowboys Pkwy.
Irving, TX 75063-4727

Detroit Lions
1200 Featherstone Rd.
Pontiac, MI 48342

Green Bay Packers
1265 Lombardi Ave.
Green Bay, WI 54304

Minnesota Vikings
9520 Viking Dr.
Eden Prairie, MN 55344

New Orleans Saints
5800 Airline Highway
Metairie, LA 70003

New York Giants
Giants Stadium
East Rutherford, NJ 07073

Philadelphia Eagles
Veterans Stadium
Broad Street & Pattison Ave.
Philadelphia, PA 19148

San Francisco 49ers
4949 Centennial Blvd.
Santa Clara, CA 95954-1229

St. Louis Rams
One Rams Way
St. Louis, MO 63045

Tampa Bay Buccaneers
One Buccaneer Place
Tampa, FL 33607

Washington Redskins
Redskin Park
P.O. Box 17247
Washington, DC 20041

National Basketball Association

Eastern Conference

Atlanta Hawks
South Tower
Suite 405
One CNN Center
Atlanta, GA 30303

Boston Celtics
4th Floor
151 Merrimac St.
Boston, MA 02114

Charlotte Hornets
100 Hive Dr.
Charlotte, NC 28217

Chicago Bulls
United Center
1901 W. Madison St.
Chicago, IL 60612

Cleveland Cavaliers
One Center Ct.
Cleveland, OH 44115-4001

Detroit Pistons
The Palace of Auburn Hills
Two Championship Dr.
Auburn Hills, MI 48326

Indiana Pacers
300 E. Market St.
Indianapolis, IN 46204

Miami Heat
Sun Trust International Center
One SE 3rd Ave., Suite 2300
Miami, FL 33131

Milwaukee Bucks
Bradley Center
1001 N. Fourth St.
Milwaukee, WI 53203-1312

New Jersey Nets
Meadowlands Arena
405 Murray Hill Pkwy.
East Rutherford, NJ 07073

New York Knicks
Madison Square Garden
Two Pennsylvania Plaza
New York, NY 10121

Orlando Magic
One Magic Place
Orlando Avenue
Orlando, FL 32801-1114

Philadelphia 76ers
CoreStates Center
Broad Street & Pattison Ave.
Philadelphia, PA 19148

Toronto Raptors
Suite 1702
20 Bay St.
Toronto, Ontario, Canada
M5J 2N8

Washington Wizards
MCI Center
601 F St. NW
Washington, DC 20001

Western Conference

Dallas Mavericks
Reunion Arena
777 Sports St.
Dallas, TX 75207

Denver Nuggets
McNichols Sports Arena
1635 Clay St.
Denver, CO 80204-1799

Golden State Warriors
550 10th St.
Oakland, CA 94612

Houston Rockets
The Summit
Two Greenway Plaza
Houston, TX 77046-3865

Los Angeles Clippers
L.A. Memorial Sports Arena
3939 S. Figueroa St.
Los Angeles, CA 90037

Los Angeles Lakers
Great Western Forum
3900 West Manchester Blvd.
P.O. Box 10
Los Angeles, CA 90306

Minnesota Timberwolves
Target Center
600 First Avenue North
Minneapolis, MN 55403

Phoenix Suns
201 E. Jefferson St.
Phoenix, AZ 85004

Portland Trailblazers
One Center Court
Suite 200
Portland, OR 97227

Sacramento Kings
One Sports Pkwy.
Sacramento, CA 95834

San Antonio Spurs
Alamodome
100 Montana St.
San Antonio, TX 78203-1031

Seattle SuperSonics
Suite 200
190 Queen Anne Ave. North
Seattle, WA 98109-9711

Utah Jazz
Delta Center
301 West South Temple
Salt Lake City, UT 84101

Vancouver Grizzlies
General Motors Place
800 Griffiths Way
Vancouver, BC, Canada
V6B 6G1

National Hockey League

Eastern Conference

Boston Bruins
One Fleet Center
Suite 250
Boston, MA 02114-1303

Buffalo Sabres
Marine Midland Arena
One Seymour H. Knox III Plaza
Buffalo, NY 14203

Carolina Hurricanes
5000 Aerial Center Pkwy.
Suite 1000
Morrisville, NC 27560

Florida Panthers
100 NE 3rd Ave.
2nd Floor
Ft. Lauderdale, FL 33301

Montreal Canadiens
Molson Centre
1260 Rue de la Gauchetiere W.
Montreal, Quebec, Canada
H3B 5E8

New Jersey Devils
Continental Airlines Arena
50 Route 120 North
P.O. Box 504
East Rutherford, NJ 07073

New York Islanders
Nassau Coliseum
Uniondale, NY 11553

New York Rangers
Madison Square Garden
Two Pennsylvania Place
New York, NY 10001

Ottawa Senators
1000 Palladium Dr.
Kanata, Ontario, Canada
K2V IA5

Philadelphia Flyers
1 CoreStates Complex
Philadelphia, PA 19148

Pittsburgh Penguins
Civic Arena
66 Mario Lemieux Place
Pittsburgh, PA 15219

Tampa Bay Lightning
401 Channelside Dr.
Tampa, FL 33602

Washington Capitals
MCI Center
601 F Street North
Washington, DC 20001

Western Conference

Mighty Ducks of Anaheim
2965 E. Katella Ave.
P.O. Box 61077
Anaheim, CA 92803

Calgary Flames
Canadian Airlines Saddledome
P.O. Box 1540, Station M
Calgary, Alberta, Canada
T2P 3B9

Chicago Blackhawks
United Center
1901 W. Madison St.
Chicago, IL 60612

Colorado Avalanche
McNichols Arena
1635 Clay St.
Denver, CO 80204-1799

Dallas Stars
StarCenter
211 Cowboys Pkwy.
Irving, TX 75063

Detroit Red Wings
Joe Louis Arena
600 Civic Center
Detroit, MI 48226

Edmonton Oilers
Northlands Coliseum
7424-118 Ave.
Edmonton, Alberta, Canada
T5B 4M9

Los Angeles Kings
The Great Western Forum
3900 W. Manchester Blvd.
P.O. Box 17013
Inglewood, CA 90308

Phoenix Coyotes
1 Renaissance Square
2 N. Central, Suite 1930
Phoenix, AZ 85004

St. Louis Blues
Kiel Center
1401 Clark Ave.
St. Louis, MO 63013

San Jose Sharks
San Jose Arena
525 W. Santa Clara St.
San Jose, CA 95113

Toronto Maple Leafs
Maple Leaf Gardens
60 Carlton St.
Toronto, Ontario, Canada
M5B 1L1

Vancouver Canucks
General Motors Place
800 Griffiths Way
Vancouver, British Columbia,
Canada V5K 3N7

Hall of Fame Members

• •

*A*s far as sports memorabilia goes, not all Halls of Fame are created equal. Collectors seem to place a greater premium on memorabilia from baseball and football Halls of Fame.

The basketball and hockey Halls each have hundreds of members, but the HOF distinction does not seem to matter as much to basketball and hockey collectors. Here are the complete lists of the baseball and football Halls of Fame.

Baseball Hall of Fame

Established: 1935

Address: P.O. Box 590, Cooperstown, NY 13326

Eligibility: Nominated players must have played at least 10 seasons in the major leagues and be retired for at least five years but no more than 20 years. Voting is conducted by the Baseball Writers' Association of America.

Some nominated players not elected by the writers can become eligible through the Veterans Committee 23 years after retirement.

Phone: 607-547-7200

*Deceased

Members of the Baseball Hall of Fame

Member	Year Inducted	Member	Year Inducted
Hank Aaron	1982	Rod Carew	1991
Grover Alexander*	1938	Max Carey*	1961
Walter Alston*	1983	Steve Carlton	1994
Cap Anson*	1939	Alex Cartwright*	1938
Luis Aparicio	1984	Henry Chadwick*	1938
Luke Appling*	1964	Frank Chance*	1946
Richie Ashburn*	1995	Happy Chandler*	1982
Earl Averill*	1983	Oscar Charleston*	1976
Frank Baker*	1955	Jack Chesbro*	1946
Dave Bancroft*	1971	Fred Clarke*	1945
Ernie Banks	1977	John Clarkson*	1963
Al Barlick*	1989	Roberto Clemente*	1973
Ed Barrow*	1953	Ty Cobb*	1936
Jack Beckley*	1971	Mickey Cochrane*	1947
Cool Papa Bell*	1974	Eddie Collins*	1939
Johnny Bench	1989	Jimmy Collins*	1945
Chief Bender*	1954	Earle Combs*	1970
Yogi Berra	1972	Charles Comiskey*	1939
Jim Bottomley*	1974	Jocko Conlan*	1974
Lou Boudreau	1970	Tom Connolly*	1953
Roger Bresnahan*	1945	Roger Connor*	1976
Lou Brock	1985	Stan Coveleski*	1969
Dan Brouthers*	1945	Sam Crawford*	1957
Mordecai Brown*	1949	Joe Cronin*	1956
Morgan Bulkeley*	1937	Candy Cummings*	1939
Jim Bunning	1996	Kiki Cuyler*	1968
Jesse Burkett*	1946	Ray Dandridge*	1987
Roy Campanella*	1969	George Davis*	1998

Member	Year Inducted	Member	Year Inducted
Leon Day*	1995	Josh Gibson*	1972
Dizzy Dean*	1953	Warren Giles*	1979
Ed Delahanty*	1945	Lefty Gomez*	1972
Bill Dickey*	1954	Goose Goslin*	1968
Martin DiHigo*	1977	Hank Greenberg*	1956
Joe DiMaggio	1955	Clark Griffith*	1946
Larry Doby	1998	Burleigh Grimes*	1964
Bobby Doerr	1986	Lefty Grove*	1947
Don Drysdale*	1984	Chick Hafey*	1971
Hugh Duffy*	1945	Jesse Haines*	1970
Leo Durocher*	1994	Billy Hamilton*	1961
Billy Evans*	1973	Ned Hanlon*	1996
Johnny Evers*	1946	Will Harridge*	1972
Buck Ewing*	1939	Bucky Harris*	1975
Red Faber*	1964	Gabby Hartnett*	1955
Bob Feller	1962	Harry Heilmann*	1952
Rick Ferrell*	1984	Billy Herman*	1975
Rollie Fingers	1992	Harry Hooper*	1971
Elmer Flick*	1963	Rogers Hornsby*	1942
Whitey Ford	1974	Waite Hoyt*	1969
Bill Foster*	1996	Cal Hubbard*	1976
Rube Foster*	1981	Carl Hubbell*	1947
Nellie Fox*	1997	Miller Huggins*	1964
Jimmie Foxx*	1951	William Hulbert*	1995
Ford Frick*	1970	Catfish Hunter	1987
Frank Frisch*	1947	Monte Irvin	1973
Pud Galvin*	1965	Reggie Jackson	1993
Lou Gehrig*	1939	Travis Jackson*	1982
Charlie Gehringer*	1949	Ferguson Jenkins	1991
Bob Gibson	1981	Hugh Jennings*	1945

Member	Year Inducted	Member	Year Inducted
Ban Johnson*	1937	Mickey Mantle*	1974
Judy Johnson*	1975	Heinie Manush*	1964
Walter Johnson*	1936	Rabbit Maranville*	1954
Addie Joss*	1978	Juan Marichal	1983
Al Kaline	1980	Rube Marquard*	1971
Tim Keefe*	1964	Eddie Mathews	1978
Willie Keeler*	1939	Christy Mathewson*	1936
George Kell	1983	Willie Mays	1979
Joe Kelley*	1971	Joe McCarthy*	1957
George Kelly*	1973	Tom McCarthy*	1946
King Kelly*	1945	Willie McCovey	1986
Harmon Killebrew	1984	Joe McGinnity*	1946
Ralph Kiner	1975	Bill McGowan*	1992
Chuck Klein*	1980	John McGraw*	1937
Bill Klem*	1953	Bill McKechnie*	1962
Sandy Koufax	1972	Joe Medwick*	1968
Nap Lajoie*	1937	Johnny Mize*	1981
Kenesaw Landis*	1944	Joe Morgan	1990
Tom Lasorda	1997	Stan Musial	1969
Tony Lazzeri*	1991	Hal Newhouser	1992
Bob Lemon	1976	Kid Nichols*	1949
Buck Leonard*	1972	Phil Niekro	1997
Fred Lindstrom*	1976	Jim O'Rourke*	1945
John Lloyd*	1977	Mel Ott*	1951
Ernie Lombardi*	1986	Satchel Paige*	1971
Al Lopez	1977	Jim Palmer	1990
Ted Lyons*	1955	Herb Pennock*	1948
Connie Mack*	1937	Gaylord Perry	1991
Larry MacPhail*	1978	Edward Plank*	1946
Lee MacPhail	1998	Charles Radbourne*	1939

Member	Year Inducted
Pee Wee Reese	1984
Sam Rice*	1963
Branch Rickey*	1967
Eppa Rixey*	1963
Phil Rizzuto	1994
Robin Roberts	1976
Brooks Robinson	1983
Frank Robinson	1982
Jackie Robinson*	1962
Wilbert Robinson*	1945
Joe Rogan*	1998
Edd Roush*	1962
Red Ruffing*	1967
Amos Rusie*	1977
Babe Ruth*	1936
Ray Schalk*	1955
Mike Schmidt	1995
Red Schoendienst	1989
Tom Seaver	1992
Joe Sewell*	1977
Al Simmons*	1953
George Sisler*	1939
Enos Slaughter	1985
Duke Snider	1980
Warren Spahn	1973
Albert Spalding*	1939
Tris Speaker*	1937
Willie Stargell	1988
Casey Stengel*	1966
Don Sutton	1998
Bill Terry*	1954

Member	Year Inducted
Sam Thompson*	1974
Joe Tinker*	1946
Pie Traynor*	1948
Dazzy Vance*	1955
Arky Vaughn*	1985
Bill Veeck*	1991
Rube Waddell*	1946
Honus Wagner*	1936
Bobby Wallace*	1953
Ed Walsh*	1946
Lloyd Waner*	1967
Paul Waner*	1952
Monte Ward*	1964
Earl Weaver	1996
George Weiss*	1971
Mickey Welch*	1973
Willie Wells*	1997
Zack Wheat*	1959
Hoyt Wilhelm	1985
Billy Williams	1987
Ted Williams	1966
Vic Willis*	1995
Hack Wilson*	1979
George Wright*	1937
Harry Wright*	1953
Early Wynn	1972
Carl Yastrzemski	1989
Tom Yawkey*	1980
Cy Young*	1937
Ross Youngs*	1972

Football Hall of Fame

Established: 1963

Address: 2121 George Halas Drive NW, Canton, OH 44708

Phone: 330-456-8207

Eligibility: Nominated players must be retired five years, coaches must be retired, and contributors can still be active. Voting is done by a 36-member panel made of up media representatives from all 30 National Football League cities, one Pro Football Writers Association representative, and five at-large voters.

*Deceased

Members of the Football Hall of Fame

Member	Year Inducted	Member	Year Inducted
Herb Adderly	1980	Paul Brown*	1967
Lance Alworth	1978	Roosevelt Brown	1975
Doug Atkins	1982	Willie Brown	1984
Red Badgro	1981	Buck Buchanan*	1990
Lem Barney	1992	Dick Butkus	1979
Cliff Battles*	1968	Earl Campbell	1991
Sammy Baugh	1963	Tony Canadeo	1974
Chuck Bednarik	1967	Joe Carr*	1963
Bert Bell*	1963	Guy Chamberlin*	1965
Bobby Bell	1983	Jack Christiansen*	1970
Raymond Berry	1973	Dutch Clark*	1963
Charles Bidwill*	1967	George Connor	1975
Fred Biletnikoff	1988	Jim Conzelman*	1964
George Blanda	1981	Lou Creekmur	1996
Mel Blount	1989	Larry Csonka	1987
Terry Bradshaw	1989	Al Davis	1992
Jim Brown	1971	Willie Davis	1981

Member	Year Inducted	Member	Year Inducted
Len Dawson	1987	Franco Harris	1990
Dan Dierdorf	1996	Michael Haynes	1997
Mike Ditka	1988	Ed Healy*	1964
Art Donovan	1968	Mel Hein*	1963
Tony Dorsett	1994	Ted Hendricks	1990
Paddy Driscoll*	1965	Pete Henry*	1963
Bill Dudley	1966	Arnie Herber*	1966
Turk Edwards*	1969	Bill Hewitt*	1971
Weeb Ewbank	1978	Clark Hinkle*	1964
Tom Fears	1970	Elroy Hirsch	1968
Jim Finks*	1995	Paul Hornung	1986
Ray Flaherty*	1976	Ken Houston	1986
Len Ford*	1976	Cal Hubbard*	1963
Dan Fortmann*	1965	Sam Huff	1982
Dan Fouts	1993	Lamar Hunt	1972
Frank Gatski	1985	Don Hutson*	1963
Bill George*	1974	Jimmy Johnson	1994
Joe Gibbs	1996	John Henry Johnson	1987
Frank Gifford	1985	Charlie Joiner	1996
Sid Gillman	1983	Deacon Jones	1980
Otto Graham	1965	Stan Jones	1991
Red Grange*	1963	Henry Jordan*	1995
Bud Grant	1994	Sonny Jurgensen	1983
Joe Greene	1987	Leroy Kelly	1994
Forrest Gregg	1977	Walt Kiesling*	1966
Bob Griese	1990	Frank Kinard*	1971
Lou Groza	1974	Paul Krause	1998
Joe Guyon*	1966	Curly Lambeau*	1963
George Halas*	1963	Jack Lambert	1990
Jack Ham	1988	Tom Landry	1990
John Hannah	1991	Dick Lane	1974

Member	Year Inducted	Member	Year Inducted
Jim Langer	1987	George Musso	1982
Willie Lanier	1986	Bronko Nagurski*	1963
Steve Largent	1995	Joe Namath	1985
Yale Lary	1979	Greasy Neale*	1969
Dante Lavelli	1975	Ernie Nevers*	1963
Bobby Layne*	1967	Ray Nitschke*	1978
Tuffy Leemans*	1978	Chuck Noll	1993
Bob Lily	1980	Leo Nomellini	1969
Larry Little	1993	Merlin Olsen	1982
Vince Lombardi*	1971	Jim Otto	1980
Sid Luckman*	1965	Steve Owen*	1966
Link Lyman*	1964	Alan Page	1988
John Mackey	1992	Ace Parker	1972
Tim Mara*	1963	Jim Parker	1973
Wellington Mara	1997	Walter Payton	1993
Gino Marchetti	1972	Joe Perry	1969
George P. Marshall*	1963	Pete Pihos	1970
Ollie Matson	1972	Hugh Ray*	1966
Don Maynard	1987	Dan Reeves*	1967
George McAfee	1966	Mel Renfro	1996
Mike McCormack	1984	John Riggins	1992
Tommy McDonald	1998	Jim Ringo	1981
Hugh McElhenny	1970	Andy Robustelli	1971
Johnny McNally*	1963	Art Rooney*	1964
Mike Michalske*	1964	Pete Rozelle*	1985
Wayne Millner*	1968	Bob St. Clair	1990
Bobby Mitchell	1983	Gale Sayers	1977
Ron Mix	1979	Joe Schmidt	1973
Lenny Moore	1975	Tex Schramm	1991
Marion Motley	1968	Lee Roy Selmon	1995
Anthony Munoz	1998	Art Shell	1989

Member	Year Inducted	Member	Year Inducted
Don Shula	1997	Bulldog Turner	1966
O. J. Simpson	1985	Johnny Unitas	1979
Mike Singletary	1998	Gene Upshaw	1987
Jackie Smith	1994	Norm Van Brocklin*	1971
Bart Starr	1977	Steve Van Buren	1965
Roger Staubauch	1985	Doak Walker	1986
Ernie Stautner	1969	Bill Walsh	1993
Jan Stenerud	1991	Paul Warfield	1983
Dwight Stephenson	1998	Bob Waterfield*	1965
Ken Strong*	1967	Mike Webster	1997
Joe Stydahar*	1967	Arnie Weinmeister	1984
Fran Tarkenton	1986	Randy White	1994
Charley Taylor	1984	Bill Willis	1977
Jim Taylor	1976	Larry Wilson	1978
Jim Thorpe*	1963	Kellen Winslow	1995
Y. A. Tittle	1971	Alex Wojciechowicz*	1968
George Trafton*	1964	Willie Wood	1989
Charley Trippi	1968		
Emlen Tunell*	1967		

Appendix D

Card Companies, Card Show Promoters, and Auction Houses

• •

*T*his appendix lists some of the major sports card companies, card show promoters, and sports memorabilia auction houses. There are far too many card shops to possibly list here. You can find plenty of shops listed in the Yellow Pages of your local telephone directory.

Card Companies

Best
7115 Oak Ridge Parkway, Suite 180
Austell, GA 30168-5862

Collector's Edge
2485 W. Second Ave. #14
Denver, CO 80209

Donruss/Leaf
907 Avenue R
Grand Prairie, TX 75050

Fleer/SkyBox International
Executive Plaza
1120 Route 73, Suite 300
Mt. Laurel, NJ 08054

Pacific Trading Cards
18424 Highway 99
Lynnwood, WA 98037

Pinnacle Brands/Action Packed
1845 Woodall Rodgers Freeway
Suite 1300
Dallas, TX 75201

Playoff Corp.
2505 N. Highway 360, 7th Floor
Grand Prairie, TX 75050

Score Board
P.O. Box 1250
Cherry Hill, NJ 08034

Topps/Bowman
One Whitehall St.
New York, NY 10004-2109

Upper Deck
5909 Sea Otter Place
Carlsbad, CA 92008

Card Show Promoters

J. Paul Sports Promotions
P.O. Box 279
Holmes, NY 12531

Pastime Productions
P.O. Box 240
Hawthorne, NY 10532

Bob Schmierer
Eastern Pennsylvania Sports Collectors Club (EPSCC)
P.O. Box 3037
Maple Glen, PA 19002

Tri-Star Productions
4615 SW Freeway, Suite 555
Houston, TX 77027

Auction Houses

Leland's
36 East 22nd St. 7th Floor
New York, NY 10010

Mastro & Steinbach
1515 W. 22nd St. Suite 125
Oak Brook, IL 60523

Index

• *N* •

• *O* •

(continued)

Notes

Notes

Notes

Notes

Notes

Notes

IDG BOOKS WORLDWIDE
BOOK REGISTRATION

Register This Book and Win!

We want to hear from you!

Visit **http://my2cents.dummies.com** to register this book and tell us how you liked it!

- ✔ Get entered in our monthly prize giveaway.

- ✔ Give us feedback about this book — tell us what you like best, what you like least, or maybe what you'd like to ask the author and us to change!

- ✔ Let us know any other ...*For Dummies*® topics that interest you.

Your feedback helps us determine what books to publish, tells us what coverage to add as we revise our books, and lets us know whether we're meeting your needs as a ...*For Dummies* reader. You're our most valuable resource, and what you have to say is important to us!

Not on the Web yet? It's easy to get started with *Dummies 101*®: *The Internet For Windows*® *98* or *The Internet For Dummies*®, 5th Edition, at local retailers everywhere.

Or let us know what you think by sending us a letter at the following address:

...*For Dummies* Book Registration
Dummies Press
7260 Shadeland Station, Suite 100
Indianapolis, IN 46256-3945
Fax 317-596-5498

™

**BESTSELLING
BOOK SERIES
FROM IDG**